Bring on the Bard

NCTE Editorial Board

Steven Bickmore
Catherine Compton-Lilly
Antero Garcia
Jennifer Ochoa
Staci M. Perryman-Clark
Vivian Yenika-Agbaw
Kurt Austin, chair, ex officio
Emily Kirkpatrick, ex officio

Bring on the Bard

Active Drama Approaches for Shakespeare's Diverse Student Readers

Kevin Long
Harper College
Palatine, Illinois

Mary T. Christel
Adlai E. Stevenson High School
Lincolnshire, Illinois

National Council of Teachers of English
1111 W. Kenyon Road, Urbana, Illinois 61801-1096
www.ncte.org

Staff Editor: Bonny Graham
Production Editor: The Charlesworth Group
Interior Design: Jenny Jensen Greenleaf
Cover Design: Pat Mayer

Cover Images: iStock.com/shironosov; iStock.com/duncan 1890; Wikimedia Commons/Andreas Praefcke/Gallery 2011e

NCTE Stock Number: 03821; eStock Number: 03838
ISBN 978-0-8141-0382-1; eISBN 978-0-8141-0383-8

©2019 by the National Council of Teachers of English.

All rights reserved. No part of this publication may be reproduced or transmitted in any form or by any means, electronic or mechanical, including photocopy, or any information storage and retrieval system, without permission from the copyright holder. Printed in the United States of America.

It is the policy of NCTE in its journals and other publications to provide a forum for the open discussion of ideas concerning the content and the teaching of English and the language arts. Publicity accorded to any particular point of view does not imply endorsement by the Executive Committee, the Board of Directors, or the membership at large, except in announcements of policy, where such endorsement is clearly specified.

NCTE provides equal employment opportunity to all staff members and applicants for employment without regard to race, color, religion, sex, national origin, age, physical, mental or perceived handicap/disability, sexual orientation including gender identity or expression, ancestry, genetic information, marital status, military status, unfavorable discharge from military service, pregnancy, citizenship status, personal appearance, matriculation or political affiliation, or any other protected status under applicable federal, state, and local laws.

Every effort has been made to provide current URLs and email addresses, but, because of the rapidly changing nature of the web, some sites and addresses may no longer be accessible.

Library of Congress Cataloging-in-Publication Data

Names: Long, Kevin, 1967- author. | Christel, Mary T., author. | National Council of Teachers of English.
Title: Bring on the Bard : active drama approaches for Shakespeare's diverse student readers / Kevin Long, Mary T. Christel.
Description: Urbana : National Council of Teachers of English, 2019. | Includes bibliographical references and index. | Summary: "Offers active drama approaches that position students to engage with Shakespeare's rich plays through low-risk speaking and improvisation activities as part of any English language arts classroom, with a focus on the Folio Technique, which gets readers closer to Shakespeare's intentions"—Provided by publisher.
Identifiers: LCCN 2019025743 (print) | LCCN 2019025744 (ebook) | ISBN 9780814103821 (Trade Paperback) | ISBN 9780814103838 (Adobe PDF)
Subjects: LCSH: Shakespeare, William, 1564-1616—Study and teaching—United States. | Shakespeare, William, 1564-1616—Study and teaching—(Higher) | Shakespeare, William, 1564-1616—Study and teaching—(Secondary) | Performing arts—Study and teaching—United States. Drama—Study and teaching—United States. Drama in education—United States.
Classification: LCC PR2987 .L76 2019 (print) | LCC PR2987 (ebook) | DDC 822.3/3—dc23
LC record available at https://lccn.loc.gov/2019025743
LC ebook record available at https://lccn.loc.gov/2019025744

The First Folio remains, as a matter of fact, the text nearest to Shakespeare's stage, to Shakespeare's ownership, to Shakespeare's authority.
> —Charlotte Porter and Helen Clarke, Preface, *Complete Works of Shakespeare* (Pembroke ed., 1903)

Shakespeare *is* his text. So, if you want to do him justice, you have to look for and follow the clues he offers. If [a student reader and player] does that then [they'll] find that Shakespeare himself starts to direct [them].
> —John Barton, *Playing Shakespeare*

Contents

ACKNOWLEDGMENTS ix

PROLOGUE xi
        Mary T. Christel

CHAPTER 1   Tailor an Experience for Diverse Student Learners 1

CHAPTER 2   Pair the First Folio of 1623 with Print, Graphic, or Digital Editions 20

CHAPTER 3   Use Active Drama Approaches as Bell Ringers to Warm Up a Text 43

CHAPTER 4   Sort Out Language Clues Using the Folio Technique 65

CHAPTER 5   Understand Verse Clues Using the Folio Technique 90

CHAPTER 6   Explore Rhetorical Clues Using the Folio Technique 113

CHAPTER 7   Create Abridgements and Cue Scripts 151

CHAPTER 8   Connect Shakespeare to YA Fiction, Contemporary Literature, and Media Texts 175

EPILOGUE 197
        Kevin Long

APPENDIX A: SPEECHES FOR FURTHER STUDY ... 199

APPENDIX B: CUE SCRIPTS FOR *A MIDSUMMER NIGHT'S DREAM* ... 202

APPENDIX C: CAPSTONE ANALYSIS ACTIVITY ... 213

APPENDIX D: THE CLASH OF THE FILM CLIPS: IS IT SHAKESPEARE? ... 218

APPENDIX E: BUILDING YOUR "BARD BOOKSHELF" ... 221

REFERENCES ... 223

INDEX ... 231

AUTHORS ... 243

Acknowledgments

From Kevin: I did not make the journey to where I am today alone. I am the product of the village of people who have supported me all along the way. I received, and continue to receive, a rich education, nurtured by passionate teachers who deeply care about their students. Thank you Kate Buckley, Jeffrey Carlson, Angela D'Ambrosia, Susan Hart, Bob Mason, Alison Vesely, and Larry Yando. I also want to thank Marilyn Halperin, Molly Truglia, and the education department at Chicago Shakespeare Theater (CST) where I teach. It is thanks to the supportive guidance of Marilyn and Molly, helping to shape and focus my work at CST, along with their keen insights and educational expertise, that I am the effective teacher and workshop leader I am today.

I strongly believe that students are the reason we teach—not only because we as educators have important knowledge and information regarding a specific discipline to present, but also because we learn from our students as well. Thank you to all of my students—past, present, and future—who have effectively participated in this work with me. I want to thank Harper College, CST, the Ten Chimneys Foundation, Actors Training Center, and many other institutions for giving me the highest honor—the opportunity to teach.

Finally, I would like to thank my fiancée, Lulia Sarmiento; my son, Adam; my mother, Carol; my father, Stephen (supporting from the stars); and my entire family for their constant love and support.

From Mary: I would like to dedicate my work on this book to Anne Thurman, a creative dramatics pioneer in Evanston–Skokie School District 65, Illinois, and at Northwestern University, who brought active approaches into English language arts classrooms and taught several generations of teachers to bring all types of literature, including that of the Bard, alive for grammar, middle, and high school students, through theater games, improvisation, and readers theater. Anne was a constant source of inspiration and support throughout my teaching career.

My work with Shakespeare has been constantly informed and enriched by all the opportunities NCTE has afforded me to learn from educators and theater practitioners who are experts in all things Shakespeare from across the country and around the world. Much appreciation to the inspiration from the work of Peggy O'Brien, Michael LoMonico, Patti Slagle, Mary Ellen Dakin, and to the enduring legacies of Janet Field-Pickering and Rex Gibson.

Curriculum development has always been an important component of my professional life. I want to thank the Shakespeare Theater in Washington, DC, for providing me with a rich experience developing lesson plans for their Theater History Initiative during several blisteringly hot summers there. Like Kevin, I want to express my appreciation to Marilyn Halperin, Molly Truglia, and their team for allowing me to contribute to their teacher handbooks. Many thanks to Juliet Hart and the Living History Education team at TimeLine Theatre who provide me with rich challenges to develop curricula for contemporary and canonical plays that complement their interdisciplinary approach to interacting with dramatic texts in their school residencies.

Kevin and I particularly appreciate the time our teacher and student partners dedicated to our project. Thank you all for checking your emails faithfully and meeting our deadlines. Our CST Bard Core team members include Jennifer Bertacchi, Ron Chavetz, Theresa Dixon, Rita Göndöcs, Kate McDuffie, Renee Russo, Susan Schinleger, and Claire Walter. My Adlai E. Stevenson High School colleagues include Jennifer Arias, Laura L. Brown, Cynthia Burrows, Jacquie Cullen, Miriam Fisch, Stephen Heller, Noel Johnston, and Mark Onuscheck. And, someone who defies simple categorization, my former Stevenson High School colleague David Noskin, who currently teaches at New Trier Township High School. In addition, the most intriguing insights were provided by Cynthia Burrows's students: Dziyana Balakir, Hailey Keenan, Abby Sokol, and Laura Thornburg. Thanks also to Christine Heckel-Oliver, who provided valuable proofreading skills and an excellent image with text activity.

As always, thanks to my family, and especially my mother, who observed "quiet time" as I worked on the manuscript far too many times when I visited her. And I must add a special remembrance of my father, who encouraged my love of theater with so many small and powerful gestures of support, from taking me to my first children's theater performance to helping build a set or putting a finishing touch on a costume.

Finally, Kevin and I want to thank Bonny Graham for her unflagging support helping us bring this project to fruition.

Prologue

MARY T. CHRISTEL

William Shakespeare: the Bard of Avon, the Soul of an Age, a prodigious contributor to the English language, an acclaimed author of, at the very least, thirty-seven plays—truly a cultural icon. That elevated status can be intimidating for many students and teachers alike. For Kevin and for me, though, he is just "Bill." For our teaching colleagues and their students, "Bill" provides a unique opportunity to explore the richness of language, narrative, characterization, and theme. He demands much of us since his language is intricate and elevated, yet the plays' complexities provide worthy and satisfying challenges for performers, audiences, and readers. For the carefully trained eye and ear, Shakespeare reveals so many accessible clues that he placed in his texts to unlock their meaning for modern student readers, viewers, and performers.

Kevin and I have worked with students and teachers in many settings, both separately and together, at high school and college levels. I taught high school for thirty-three years, which included courses on theater arts, speech, world literature, creative writing, and cinema studies. Kevin has taught theater arts at the high school level and for most of his career at Harper College. Notably, we were brought together at teacher workshops sponsored by Chicago Shakespeare Theater, where Kevin introduces participants to the *Folio technique*, a lively method of identifying the clues that Shakespeare left in the plays for his actors to deliver their speeches "trippingly on the tongue" when they only had their lines or *cue scripts*, and not the entire play, with which to learn their roles in a very brief rehearsal process. Those clues, though initially intended for actors, effectively unlock the mystery of Shakespeare's language, syntax, and subtext, which often overwhelm or deter modern readers. We will pull back the curtain to reveal how Shakespeare virtually whispers into our ears and provides powerful clues to unlock the mystery and meaning of the poetry and prose in order to bring his characters to life.

One year, my teaching assignment included three twelfth-grade electives: Classic World Literature (College Prep), World Masterpieces (Honors), and

Themes in World Literature (Advanced Placement). That schedule offered me an opportunity to teach three different plays at the same time to three different ability levels—and I noticed three very distinct responses from those student groups about reading Shakespeare. As one would expect, the Advanced Placement (AP) students exuded the confidence of "I know I can do it!," having read Shakespeare as ninth and eleventh graders, and probably in middle school. The honors students expressed a bit of hesitation, more along the lines of "I think I can do this." Many of them hadn't read Shakespeare since the ninth grade, and only some had done so during the eleventh grade. The college prep students, who also last encountered Shakespeare in ninth grade, rolled their eyes and sighed, "Why am I doing this at all? It's sooo hard." That range of responses pretty much sums up how students view reading Shakespeare, or any text that, in their minds, presents formidable obstacles to comprehension, interpretation, and enjoyment. Many times, those three attitudes populate a single class. And, if a teacher has a fair number of students who ask, "Why am I doing this at all?" or "How will I survive this?," that teacher might fall into the trap of becoming the head translator and interpreter of the text. Many teachers—myself included—certainly have done this with struggling readers who "read it but didn't get it," to paraphrase Cris Tovani. Teachers who are lovers of the Bard have great hopes for their students to become collaborators in understanding and enjoying Shakespeare's work, but it takes a good deal of trial, error, and action research to assemble a toolkit of strategies to set the stage for success no matter the play or the students' experience with Shakespeare, reading ability, and motivation level for tackling a challenging text.

For me, the most satisfying dimension of planning to teach Shakespeare involves assembling the tools and strategies to open up the text and to allow the play's meaning to unspool depending on where students land on that "I can–might–can't do it" spectrum of readers. When I assemble a targeted pedagogical toolkit, I first consider how I might *choose and shape a text* to fit my curriculum's aims and my students' needs. When *choosing a text*, I try to consider which edition of a Shakespeare play I will use and why that selection is crucial to my students' success in becoming fluent readers of that text. Here are some questions I have in mind when I consider adopting a particular edition:

- Which edition(s) do I have in stock currently? Why was that edition initially acquired? What are its special features? What makes it "student friendly"?
- What are the advantages of other editions available in print and digital forms? What kind of support material do they provide?

- How closely are they based on the *First Folio edition* of Shakespeare's work? Why does a closer connection to the First Folio than a *quarto edition* matter?

As far as *shaping a text*, I try to keep in mind the following considerations as well:

- Should I act as editor of the version my students will read?
- How and why might I create an abridgement of a play?
- Is it "cheating" to have students study a thoughtfully *customized edition* of a play?
- How could that reading experience be combined with *active viewing* to create a comprehensive understanding of the play?

And, finally, I always consider which *films* best complement the published or customized edition of the play my students will read. Those films can range from documentaries to animated shorts to feature-length films, which I can share in excerpts or extended viewing before, during, and after reading the play. For me, these are crucial decisions to make before a unit begins.

Once the play is chosen by the teacher or designated by an established curriculum, what is the next step to prime students with strategies guided by the clues Shakespeare has provided in the Folio edition? Kevin and I believe that the careful, intensive analysis of several key speeches or excerpts from representative scenes using the Folio technique works toward building more fluent and engaged readers of the entire text, even if students are reading the play in a mass-market edition that regularizes the variant spelling and punctuation of the First Folio. This approach encourages students to play with language in order to explore its meaning, rhythm, emphasis, and syntax. Actually, many of our students already expertly decode the intricate language and syntax of rap and hip-hop, so learning to decode Shakespeare's language should not be so alien—if they understand the clues the Bard left behind. The Folio technique teaches students a method of annotation or *scoring the text* that, in its initial stages, diligently requires applying pen to text. This approach eventually becomes second nature, as the words, phrases, and patterns jump off the page and the reading process moves through an entire work. The Folio technique is best applied with baseline public speaking and creative drama activities that we refer to as *active drama approaches*. These strategies place Shakespeare's language in students' mouths and on their bodies using large- and small-group activities as well as low-risk individual performance that engages students. Mark Powell, associate director of the Salisbury Playhouse and education outreach advocate, believes that "[Shakespeare's] words were chosen to be spoken or heard, not to be read and deadened behind a desk—they wither when performance is removed." In this vein, we should keep in mind that studying a "play" could, and should, include the *purposeful "play"fulness* of active drama approaches, to encourage close reading, critical thinking, and empathy, as well as to maximize student engagement in a standard English language arts (ELA) classroom.

Even though the Folio technique—what it is and how it works—sits at the heart of this book, we also offer a series of activities that span a unit on Shakespeare and tap into developing a variety of skills. Those activities involve student performance, close reading, and focused viewing. Our approach heavily emphasizes prereading activities, since we believe that "readiness is all" and students can be empowered to make meaning of a complex text if they initially collaborate with their peers before taking on a more independent position as reader and interpreter. And those activities do not have to be used in total. You know what your students need and you should feel free to mix and match experiences that fit your students' abilities, your curriculum's objectives, and the time available. We do stress, however, that expanding the preparation time before reading the first scene of any play will pay dividends in student understanding, engagement, and enjoyment.

To make this approach as useful as possible, and to encourage you to give our activities a try in your classroom, we offer examples for *Romeo and Juliet*, *Hamlet*, *Macbeth*, and the sonnets, which we know from our experience are taught most often in secondary classrooms. We also include examples from *Henry V*, *The Tempest*, *A Midsummer Night's Dream*, and *Twelfth Night* in the hope you might consider teaching a play that is something other than a tragedy. We provide a smattering of examples from other works as well. Even if we don't apply a strategy or an activity to a play you teach, you can apply our approaches to any play and in almost any combination. In the final chapter, we offer suggestions for pairing a play with contemporary print and media texts so your students can directly experience the continuing impact that Shakespeare's work has on modern-day culture. Rebutting the argument that Shakespeare's plays, considering the difficulties they present, should not have a place in today's ELA curricula, J. Holtham reminds us:

> Shakespeare teaches us about love, honor, duty. About parents and children. About ambition and greed. These are things that all of us face, the things that make us human. There are other writers, of course, who write about these things, but most of them are in conversation with Shakespeare in one way or another.

Shakespeare's works indeed live in the present tense and deserve a place in ELA curricula, not as an intimidating monolithic literary figure but as an equal partner among a variety of challenging and accessible voices speaking to the human condition across time periods and cultures. We often say, "Thank you, Bill," when we consider all the ways his work enriches our partner teachers' curricula and expands their students' ability truly to enjoy rich, complex texts.

This book offers four chapters of performance-based activities. You don't have to be a trained drama or speech teacher to integrate active drama approaches into your classroom. Most of the teachers who join us at Folio technique workshops have no background or training in drama. They just have a desire to improve student engagement and foster understanding. To help you understand how these methods will work in your classroom, we feature the advice from classroom teachers who regularly teach Shakespeare's works as a part of ELA, AP, English language learner (ELL), and drama curricula using both traditional and active approaches in a variety of schools: urban and suburban, public and charter. We also share experiences from several high school students who will reveal which close reading and active drama activities have worked for them. Insights from those teachers and students are featured in "Teacher of the Bard" and "Student of the Bard" boxes throughout the book.

You don't have to incorporate every activity and strategy we present into your teaching. The first time out, choose a few. You will discover these active approaches can be introduced prior to reading Shakespeare to build cooperation and concentration as well as to ease performance anxiety: "All things are ready, if our minds be so," as wise King Henry says (*H5* 4.3). And, remember, even if you cannot choose the play you share with students or the edition they will read, you effectively can supplement and enrich your students' experiences in so many powerful ways, selecting approaches and resources presented in this book to expand your toolkit in order to "bring on the Bard."

Tailor an Experience for Diverse Student Learners

Who Gets to Read Shakespeare?

Within any single class, students will approach reading in general or any author in particular with a range of positive, negative, or ambivalent attitudes. Sometimes we shy away from selecting Shakespeare as a featured author because students have a negative attitude toward any text they deem "too old" or "too hard." Young adult (YA) fiction author John Green "hate[s] that, when it comes to books and learning, hard is often seen as the opposite of fun." Creating academic excitement and personal engagement are crucial to any unit's success, especially when we sense students pushing back on reading a challenging text. Students not only have varied opinions of what they can and cannot do in a classroom setting, but they also have varied and unique learning styles. We need to embrace a pedagogical approach that can tap into our students' natural cognitive strengths as well as encourage them to test out underdeveloped or unrecognized skills through carefully orchestrated activities that encourage experimentation, exploration, and playfulness.

To promote an academically sound sense of fun in tackling Shakespeare, integrating *active drama approaches* into a lesson plan adds improvisation to encourage experimentation and exploration, which place students at the center of making discoveries. These techniques introduce a *purposeful playfulness* to help students buy into a challenging academic experience as well as to sustain their interest with careful positioning of active drama approaches to preview a text, to check for understanding, and to deepen analysis throughout the course of a unit.

The challenge is to carefully link those experiences to more conventional reading, critical thinking, and writing activities, while recognizing that students learn and succeed differently by tapping into a spectrum of intelligences and learning styles to get them "Bard ready." In this chapter, we apply Howard Gardner's *multiple intelligences theory* as a framework to create anticipatory, formative, and summative activities that address the varied learning styles present in any classroom and lay the foundation for integration of the Folio technique.

Effective Engagement Strategies Using Gardner's Multiple Intelligences Spectrum

In *Frames of Mind*, which was first published in 1983, Howard Gardner presents his multiple intelligences theory. This theory offers an effective way of thinking about how we structure activities within a unit and use various approaches and activities that recognize students' cognitive differences and strengths, as well as promote meaningful differentiated instruction. Building on Gardner's theory, other researchers have published studies on multimodal learning preferences to examine how students express multiple preferences or intelligences and the levels of adaptability in receiving and transmitting information. Usually such studies classify learning preferences into three categories: visual, aural, and kinesthetic. Gardner differentiates forms of "intelligence" with seven classifications. Here's a thumbnail breakdown of the spectrum:

1. visual—thinks in terms of physical space
2. kinesthetic—uses body effectively
3. musical—responds to rhythm and sound
4. interpersonal—interacts well with others
5. intrapersonal—understands their own goals and can pursue them on their own
6. linguistic—understands and uses words effectively
7. logical—thinks conceptually and relies on reasoning and calculating

In Gardner's subsequent editions of *Frames of Mind* (1993, 2011), he expands the intelligence spectrum, but the original set of seven best serves our purpose here. To discover students' intelligence strengths or preferences, you can use one of the following tools to identify where they fall on the spectrum:

- the "Connell Multiple Intelligence Questionnaire"—available to download from teachables.scholastic.com/teachables/books/teachable-product-detail-9780439590204_001.html (Connell)

- the "Student Multiple Intelligence Survey"—available as a Word document from edprodevelopment.com/wp-content/uploads/Student-MI-Survey.doc (EdPro Development)
- the "Multiple Intelligences Survey"—available as a pdf file from surfaquarium.com/MI/inventory.pdf (McKenzie)

The Virginia Department of Education's CTE Resource Center website offers a comprehensive list of other sites, resources, and tools with which to differentiate instruction based on students' multiple intelligences: www.cteresource.org/featured/differentiated_instruction.html.

The results of any assessment can yield valuable information to plan preview activities as well as build out the entire unit on Shakespeare, though you can rely on the spectrum of intelligence preferences populating any given classroom based on your own interactions and observations of students.

Building Anticipation, Getting Students "Bard Ready"

For the most part, studying Shakespeare caters to those students who skew toward linguistic intelligence and who obviously enjoy reading and wordplay. Not all our students have that predisposition. Obviously, language is vitally important when engaging with a Shakespearean text. For students who are not naturally "linguistically minded," you will need to build anticipation by tapping into other intelligences. Appealing to visual, kinesthetic, musical, and interpersonal intelligences effectively supports integrating active drama approaches into the ELA classroom. The National Council of Teachers of English (NCTE) published a guideline titled "Informal Classroom Drama" in 1982 to encourage the organic and purposeful integration of creative drama into ELA curricula to "develop improved skills in reading, listening, speaking, and writing." Thinking in those terms will help anyone who fears they might be turning their ELA class into a drama class. Informal classroom drama or active drama approaches represent just one tool, albeit a highly effective one, among other strategies in a comprehensive classroom toolkit.

Teacher of the Bard Talk

Shakespeare's works [originally] were written to be heard and seen... by people who didn't read. So, focusing on the "literary-ness" of the work rather than the genius of the storytelling... keeps students at arm's length from the material. So, oddly, by *not* getting too caught up on the linguistics but encouraging students to experience the text as a *play*, as *their* words for *their* character, students discover the linguistics.

—Cynthia Burrows, Adlai E. Stevenson High School; drama and ELA teacher

Let's put Gardner's theory into practice by exploring five ways to preview a play tapping into four of the intelligences—visual, linguistic, musical, and kinesthetic—that combine with interpersonal, intrapersonal, and logical intelligences in order to build purposefully playful anticipation prior to reading a specific text.

Appealing to Visual Intelligence

At a first rehearsal or "table reading" of a play at a theater company, most productions employ a *dramaturg* or research assistant for the director, actors, and designers. At that first rehearsal, the dramaturg provides a packet or booklet of information to help the production team understand the play, its historical or social context, and the author, along with a glossary of terms from the text that need definition or clarification. Often the packet will include drawings, paintings, and photographs. In the same way, we can use the visual content found in a dramaturgical packet to activate the interest of students with a high visual intelligence preference.

Students can preview a play's content through images created by visual artists to represent its characters and events. For instance, sample images for *Romeo and Juliet* can be found using the following website searches:

- Wikimedia Commons—fine art images (e.g., commons.wikimedia.org/wiki/Category:Romeo_and_Juliet_in_art)
- Google Images—images with and without text (e.g., www.google.com/search?q=romeo+and+juliet+images)
- Getty Images—8,202 images from films, stage productions, ballet performances, paintings, modern day Verona (e.g., www.gettyimages.com/photos/romeo-and-juliet?excludenudity)

These images then can be tied to a variety of activities integrated throughout a unit.

Anticipatory Activity: The World of the Play in Images

A dramaturg selects a variety of images to provide actors with a visual context for the world of the play. You can select images that evoke the play's mood and setting as well as character relationships and conflicts. Images then can be loaded into a PowerPoint slideshow or a Prezi presentation. You also can create a gallery display on the classroom walls for students to walk through. As students browse the images, they should have a purpose for their viewing, which might take the form of jotting down their impressions of each image (or the most striking images of the set) as well as questions that the images pose.

Formative Activity: Getting Graphic

Since there are many comic book and graphic novel versions of *Romeo and Juliet*, you could select a single panel from various points in the plot or several related panels for students to examine, with the language either included or removed from the speech bubbles. It is helpful to reproduce the pages in full color, since Capulets and Montagues are usually grouped together visually by a distinctive color palette for each. If the text is removed, students must rely on the nonverbal details of each panel. Once they decode the images based on the visual cues, they could add their own dialogue, which creates a natural transition to other text-based activities. In Chapter 2, we will provide a set of questions to examine the use of words and images in an opening scene of a graphic treatment.

Summative Activity: Words of the Play and Pictures

One of our teaching partners, Christine Heckel-Oliver, culminates the study of a Shakespeare play with students matching images they gather from various pieces of artwork, professional photos, and visual elements from advertising with lines from the play. The images are mounted on a piece of paper with the lines copied below, including a citation of act, scene, and line numbers. The combination of text and image can illustrate the quotation in a serious, literal manner. The image also can provide a comedic or ironic commentary on the language. For example, students studying *Julius Caesar* couldn't help but pair "Friends, Romans, lend me your ears" with an image from a plastic wrap ad featuring two ears of corn. When they presented that example to the class, their teacher had the perfect opportunity to address how they turned the line into a pun. This activity certainly energizes students' attention to a line's meaning, both intended and reinterpreted.

Variation as Anticipatory Strategy: Words of the Play and Pictures

As a previewing activity, students could receive a series of famous lines from the play they are about to read and then be instructed to find an image that illustrates what they believe the line to mean without much context. Using this strategy before reading the play familiarizes students with some of the text's language, which later provides them the comfort of something familiar when they encounter a line in context. Students would then get the chance to assess how they illustrated a line they had earlier received without its proper context.

Appealing to Linguistic Intelligence

When creating activities to support or activate Gardner's multiple intelligences for studying Shakespeare, language comes into play one way or the other. The complexity of the Bard's language requires close attention before, during, and after reading a play. These activities offered to support linguistic intelligence can also support interpersonal intelligence when they are framed as collaborative small-group activities.

Anticipatory Activity: A Play in Pieces

Before students read the play, select a range of quotations from the text that represent the major characters and the language that turn themes into action. Scatter the individual quotations on the floor or on a table. Have students in small groups sift through the quotations and create "categories" or "themes" that link related quotations together. In this set from *Romeo and Juliet* (Figure 1.1), there are lines that focus on the nature of romantic love, civil unrest, and fate and free will, among other themes. A variation of this activity involves sequencing the lines to trace the development of a doomed love affair. Allow students to eliminate several lines that they feel do not fit. Have each group read aloud their version, with each member reading a line until all are shared.

Teachers who use this activity find it is helpful to suggest that students organize the lines around the three major narrative stages: (1) how things get started, then (2) get complicated, and finally (3) get resolved. Students can return to the results of this activity as they read the play and modify their initial sequence.

Anticipatory Activity: Shakespeare's Sonnet Scrambled

Another activity substitutes a sonnet snipped up into fourteen separate lines. Sonnets work well when introducing a comedy, since those plays focus thematically on love won and lost. This activity encourages students to look for patterns in language (diction, imagery, metaphor) as well as the rhyming pattern. When you prepare to snip apart the sonnet, scramble the lines on the template. Clever students might piece together their sonnet in no time flat by matching up the scissor strokes.

The previewing activity in Figure 1.2 is especially attractive for beginning *Romeo and Juliet,* as it contains three embedded sonnets that introduce key themes and conflicts. Some students will discover the rhyme pattern, which makes putting the speech in the "correct" order relatively easy. The end-of-line punctuation can provide helpful clues as well when grouping individual lines together to create a complete thought. Once students share their versions of the speech, it opens up discussion of which lines are difficult to "translate" or fully

> **Preparation for activity: Snip apart these lines and provide a set to each group of students.***
>
> - What, drawn, and talk of peace? I hate the word / As I hate hell, all Montagues, and thee.
> - Is love a tender thing? it is too rough, / Too rude, too boist'rous, and it pricks like thorn.
> - If love be rough with you, be rough with love; / Prick love for pricking, and you beat love down.
> - Here's much to do with hate, but more with love: / Why then, O brawling love, O loving hate, / O anything of nothing first create!
> - I fear too early, for my mind misgives / Some consequence, yet hanging in the stars / Shall bitterly begin his fearful date / With this night's revels …
> - Did my heart love till now? forswear it, sight! / For I ne'er saw true beauty till this night.
> - A plague a'both your houses! / They have made worms' meat of me.
> - Good night, good night! Parting is such sweet sorrow, / That I shall say good night till it be morrow.
> - What's in a name? That which we call a rose / By any other name would smell as sweet.
> - Wisely and slow, they stumble that run fast.
> - O! I am Fortune's fool!
> - Tempt not a desperate man.
> - O! She doth teach the torches to burn bright.
> - See, how she leans her cheek upon her hand! / O that I were a glove upon that hand, / That I might touch that cheek!
> - Hang thee, young baggage, disobedient wretch!
> - These violent delights have violent ends.
> - Talk not to me, for I'll not speak a word. / Do as thou wilt, for I have done with thee.
> - We will have vengeance for it, fear thou not: / Then weep no more.
> - This bud of love, by summer's ripening breath, / May prove a beauteous flower when next we meet.
> - And when I shall die, / Take him and cut him out in little stars, / And he will make the face of heaven so fine / That all the world will be in love with night, / And pay no worship to the garish sun.
>
> (* The presentation of these lines follows that of the Cambridge School Shakespeare edition of *Romeo and Juliet*; specific act, scene, and line numbers are omitted here as the point of the activity is not to know or have the context for each "piece" of the play.)

FIGURE 1.1. A Play in Pieces activity: Representative lines from *Romeo and Juliet*.

> **Instructions for Shakespeare's Sonnet Scrambled Activity**
>
> You will receive fourteen lines of text (from 1.0.1–14, 1.5.92–104, or 2.0.1–14) that you will need to assemble to make sense of a speech spoken by one of the characters in *Romeo and Juliet*. There are some helpful clues in those individual lines, so play close attention and become a text detective!
>
> Once you have agreed on a way to order these lines, answer the following questions:
> - How did you know that you were working with lines of poetry rather than lines of prose?
> - What made it difficult to decide on logical order for the lines in order for the speech to make sense?
> - What clues did you find in the individual lines that helped you piece the speech together?
> - What were some other strategies you used to organize the lines?
> - Which line stands out from the rest? Why?
>
> Now, provide a summary of what information is conveyed by these fourteen lines. What do we learn about what is happening or will happen?

FIGURE 1.2. Shakespeare's Sonnet Scrambled activity.

Tailor an Experience for Diverse Student Learners

understand and how the speech reveals information about the central conflict or a particular character's circumstances.

Edmund Spenser's sonnets are especially effective for this activity since his rhyme scheme is more intricate than Shakespeare's approach and his poems mine many themes found in the Bard's comedies and tragedies. Spenser's Sonnet 30 "My Love Is Like to Ice" is a student favorite.

Anticipatory Activity: Blackout Poetry from Blank Verse

Another way for students to experiment with text and play with language involves *blackout poetry* to isolate key words and ideas in a text nugget, whether it be a sonnet or a speech. Usually a blackout poem is crafted from a piece of prose: a page or two of a novel or work of nonfiction. Supposedly, a form of blackout poetry was created in the 1700s from early print newspapers by Caleb Whiteford and recently popularized by Austin Kleon, author of *Steal Like an Artist* (Hudson). When students apply this technique to a Shakespearean text, their goal is to isolate words and phrases that strike them as interesting or compelling. The selected words ultimately should reveal a theme, conflict, or character's train of thought. You can find a variety of print guidelines and video tutorials online that provide blackout poem instructions. One typical suggestion encourages students not to read the passage very deeply to begin the process, to see which words or phrases naturally are emphasized. If needed, provide a focus and direct students to look for certain types of words, such as parts of speech (nouns, verbs, adjectives) or words that express emotion. You are encouraging students to play with words and their individual meanings as well as to consider how a string of words creates impact even when plucked out of the original context. Since the vocabulary in any Shakespeare excerpt can prove challenging, have Early Modern English dictionaries and glossaries available that students can access in print format or online. Let's work with the prologue from *Romeo and Juliet* (1.0) (see Figure 1.3) to test this strategy, since it is pretty "newsy" to draw on this form's origins.

Here is a sample response with the words blacked out:

Student Handout: The Bard's Blackout Poetry

Romeo and Juliet* (1.0)

Two households, both alike in dignity,
In fair Verona (where we lay our scene)
From ancient grudge break to new mutiny,
Where civil blood makes civil hands unclean.
From forth the fatal loins of these two foes
A pair of star-crossed lovers take their life;
Whose misadventured piteous overthrows
Doth with their death bury their parents' strife.
The fearful passage of their death-mark'd love,
And the continuance of their parents' rage,
Which, but their children's end, nought could remove,
Is now the two hours' traffic of our stage;
The which if you with patient ears attend,
What here shall miss, our toil shall strive to mend.

(* Presentation corresponds to the Cambridge School Shakespeare edition of *Romeo and Juliet*.)

Instructions

We will be using this text to create a *blackout poem*. You will create it by eliminating most of the words in the text and by emphasizing certain words to craft a new piece of writing.

1. Skim the text and lightly underline the words you find interesting, dramatic, or emphasized through repetition. If you find a word you don't know, go ahead and look it up or figure out its meaning based on context clues. In any case, you can choose a word without knowing completely what it means.
2. Pull out the words that you have underlined, write them in order on a piece of paper, and see if they "fit together" to create some level of meaning.
3. Go back and read the passage more carefully, paying attention to what the author's purpose was in writing this speech. Compare what you think is the author's meaning with the words you underlined. Consider if you want to complement the author's meaning or go in a totally different direction. You are not looking for a "correct answer" in creating your poem.
4. Decide if the words you underlined are enough to create a blackout poem, or if you need to add or eliminate a few words. You don't necessarily have to form complete or grammatically correct sentences.
5. Now take a marker and *black out* the words you have eliminated, keeping only the underlined words visible.
6. Once you have your blackout poem completed, share it with the class (by reading it aloud or creating a gallery of blackout poems).

FIGURE 1.3. Blackout Poetry exercise.

Notice all the underlined words carry negative connotations. The students chose to emphasize the most tragic details in the speech. Since this speech is short and sums up the overarching plot of the play, it doesn't yield the variety of blackout responses that one of Hamlet's soliloquies or a piece of dialogue between the Macbeths would. Students easily can transfer this strategy to their personal-reading strategies toolkit to activate when they feel overwhelmed by a piece of text.

Formative Follow-Up: Sonnet Completion Challenge

This activity truly invites students to play with a sonnet's language; it's inspired by the word game Mad Libs, but without any helpful hints provided beneath the blank spaces. These sonnets help students understand how Shakespeare crafts extended metaphors in his poems and plays. Any of Shakespeare's sonnets can be transformed into a Mad Libs phrasal template, but those that develop an extended metaphor or conceit do work best. Students then can pick up on contextual clues that the provided words and details provide, as well as structural clues involving meter and rhyme. Figures 1.4 and 1.5 present two sonnets that work particularly well for this activity. Students naturally will *not* receive the words listed on the right-hand side; that list of words to complete the lines should be scrambled into a word bank, with a few more options added to the mix to increase the task's level of difficulty.

Sonnet 130

My mistress' _____ are nothing like the sun;	eyes
_____ is far more red than her lips' red;	Coral
If snow be white, why then her _____ are _____ ;	breasts, dun
If hairs be wires, black _____ grow on her head.	wires
I have seen roses damasked, _____ and white,	red
But no such _____ see I in her cheeks;	roses
And in some perfumes is there more _____	delight
Than in the breath that from my mistress _____	reeks
I love to hear her _____ , yet well I know	speak
That _____ hath a far more pleasing sound;	music
I grant I never saw a _____ go;	goddess
My mistress when she _____ treads on the _____ .	walks, ground
And yet, by _____ , I think my love as rare	heaven
As any she belied with _____ compare.	false

FIGURE 1.4. Sonnet Completion Challenge activity with answer key.

Sonnet 18

Shall I compare thee to a _____ day?	summer's
Thou art more _____ and more temperate:	lovely
Rough _____ do shake the darling _____ of May,	winds, buds
And _____ lease hath all too _____ a date.	summer's, short
Sometime too hot the eye of _____ shines,	heaven
And often is his _____ complexion dimmed;	gold
And every fair from _____ sometime declines,	fair
By chance, or _____ changing course, untrimmed:	nature's
But thy eternal summer shall not _____,	fade
Nor lose possession of that fair thou ow'st,	
Nor shall death _____ thou wander'st in his shade,	brag
When in eternal lines to _____ thou grow'st:	time
So long as men can breathe, or _____ can see,	eyes
So long lives this, and this gives life to _____.	thee

FIGURE 1.5. Sonnet Completion Challenge activity with answer key.

If students have completed the Shakespeare's Sonnet Scrambled activity (see Figure 1.2), they will be acquainted with the conventions of the sonnet form. If students don't have any prior experience with sonnet form, introduce the conventions with some direct instruction. Some teachers encourage students to work with the text for a bit and then take a "time out" to discuss and identify the patterns that define the sonnet form (iambic pentameter, rhyme scheme). Keep students away from their phones, tablets, or computers so they are not tempted to search for the sonnet online.

No matter which sonnet or speech you select for any of these "language play" activities, make sure it connects thematically with the play students will be reading so this experience can provide a touchstone text to revisit later in the unit.

Appealing to Musical Intelligence

To appeal to students who favor musical intelligence, teaching artists who work with high school students at Chicago's TimeLine Theatre preview conflicts, character relationships, and themes with playlists of songs. In some of those classroom residencies, students work with non-Shakespeare plays that depend heavily on music. The team creates an initial playlist and posts it to the audio-streaming platform Spotify. Students then add to the playlist, including any type of music that illuminates characters, conflicts, and themes.

Anticipatory Activity: Creating a Play's Playlist

Applying this strategy to Shakespeare makes sense, to create a link to current popular culture. As a previewing strategy, you can start by sharing a teacher-created playlist online and invite students to post comments regarding what the songs reveal about potential themes and conflicts in the play. The playlist can be introduced by playing one song each day at the beginning of class, which makes an effective musical *bell ringer*. Here is a sample playlist for *Romeo and Juliet*:

- "Check Yes Juliet"—We the Kings
- "Lovefool"—The Cardigans
- "Love Story"—Taylor Swift
- "Angel"—Leona Lewis
- "My Heart Will Go On"—Celine Dion
- "Beat It"—Michael Jackson

No matter how you reveal the playlist, students will discover several songs directly reference the play. Two of the six songs in the sample *Romeo and Juliet* playlist make fairly explicit references to the star-crossed lovers and their romantic predicament, which provides a natural means to discuss the presence of literary allusions in popular culture. "Lovefool" (which can be found on *William Shakespeare's Romeo + Juliet*, the soundtrack to Baz Luhrmann's 1996 film of the same name) and "My Heart Will Go On" (from the *Titanic* soundtrack) feature two different approaches to love: the first, impetuous infatuation; the second, never-ending devotion. The final song, "Beat It," introduces the idea of the danger on the streets of Verona between the quarreling Montagues and Capulets.

Teacher of the Bard Talk

I believe we can include "classics" such as Shakespeare and continue to make them accessible. In my opinion, *Romeo and Juliet, Hamlet,* and *King Lear* address a variety of themes that continue to be relevant. For example, I find contemporary nonfiction about forbidden love to make connections to *Romeo and Juliet*....I feel that students need some scholarly study of the canon, such as Shakespeare, because [he treats important and enduring themes] related to power, privilege, race, and justice. Eliminating all canonical works, such as Shakespeare, would not only rob students of enriching experiences, but also further [distance] them from achieving equity and access to "the table" so to speak.

—JENNIFER ARIAS,
Adlai E. Stevenson High School; ELL and ELA teacher

Formative Follow-Up: Creating a Character's Playlist

When an established world literature curriculum goes as far back as the *Epic of Gilgamesh*, Greek tragedy, and Dante's *Inferno*, connecting those texts to popular culture helps students recognize the enduring influence of culture and literature that they might initially find remote and irrelevant. In later chapters, we will continue to offer strategies to connect the study of Shakespeare to film, new media, YA literature, and graphic texts, so creating the link between popular music and Renaissance drama will not be much of a stretch for students if other contemporary texts are included sooner or later in the unit too.

Appealing to Kinesthetic Intelligence

Hitting all of Gardner's intelligences in a suite of previewing activities may be unrealistic due to inevitable time constraints. You may have noticed that the activities catering to visual intelligence are combined with linguistic intelligence in several instances. The next activity provides a way to bring kinesthetic and linguistic intelligence strategies together and get students out of their seats and engaged in playing with physical action and language.

Anticipatory/Formative Activity: Picturing the Line

Divide the class into small groups of four to five members. Provide each group with one line from the play culled from the linguistic intelligence activity (Figure 1.1). Have students create a *tableau* to illustrate their line. A tableau amounts to a frozen image or three-dimensional snapshot that captures an action or event. For example, one group might illustrate the lines "We will have vengeance for it, fear thou not: Then weep no more" by having several tableau players miming mourning and grief while being consoled by others who pose in physically superior positions with facial expressions that project determination at an outside force or opponent. After a bit of planning and rehearsing, each group then would share their tableau with the class. A tableau can be "sculpted" by having one or two group members place and position the other players, one at a time, until the image is complete. For a second round, have each group interpret the same line (or lines) and share their results. In Chapter 3, we introduce *active approaches* bell ringers that draw on theater games and improvisation activities that get students moving and thinking with their bodies.

Setting Expectations for "Text Detective" and Interpersonal Intelligence

Taking a collaborative approach is recommended for struggling readers and ELL students when approaching difficult reading tasks. Collaborative groups can be designed to bring together students who skew toward different intelligence preferences on Gardner's spectrum, and working in a collaborative team cultivates interpersonal intelligence. If students know that they will not bear solely the brunt of making meaning of a rich and challenging text, their anxiety will be diminished. Once students are introduced to Folio technique activities, they will become "text detectives" or one of Patrick Tucker's "verse nurses" (39), so giving students a focus will help establish close reading expectations that complement and support the more performance-based text analysis strategies.

Anticipatory/Formative/Summative Activity Strand: Tracking Language Motifs

Establishing a reading focus at the beginning of a unit helps students gain control of a difficult text. Students can focus on tracking language patterns and motifs. For example, if AP students are reading *King Lear*, randomly assign one motif per student, such as "nothing," blindness, foolish wisdom, madness, disorder, loyalty, etc. Since several students will be assigned the same motif in a large class, collaborative groups naturally form around that common denominator. Students annotate their texts and note if the occurrence of a motif moves the plot, develops character, or expands a theme. Students then discuss the emergence and development of their motifs in small groups at various points in the reading process, with students who tracked the same motif or with students who tracked different ones. Eventually, tracking a motif becomes the focus of a summative analytical writing experience.

You might think this strategy is best used with advanced students, but most students will feel less overwhelmed about "knowing everything" all at once and appreciate having a narrower focus to begin their reading. Some students new to reading Shakespeare get stuck on the "Renaissance-specific" words or phrases unfamiliar to the modern reader, so, in addition to or instead of tracking motifs, have a few students track how pronouns work. For example, when does Shakespeare use *you* and *your* versus *thee* and *thine*? In that case, students would be "on call" to help classmates understand the occurrence and usage of unusual words and phrases. Chapter 4's focus on the basic skills of the Folio technique will provide more strategies to get students comfortable with Shakespearean pronouns.

Anticipatory/Formative/Summative Activity Strand: Text Detective Teams

Students who lack confidence or experience reading Shakespeare can form collaborative groups around characters, such as "Team Capulet" or "Team Montague" (see Figure 1.6). This strategy allows each student to become an "expert" on a specific supporting character who wittingly or unwittingly supported or

> **Student Handout: Character Focus**
>
> _____ is a member of Team _____ *(Montague or Capulet)*.
>
> Provide details directly quoted from the play as often as you can to support your responses to the following questions:
> - Describe this character's relationship in the family/faction (relative, friend, servant).
> - How does your character demonstrate family/faction loyalty through their words or actions?
> - What do you think is most important to this character? How do they make this clear?
> - How does this character behave in a rash manner due to their family/faction loyalty?
> - What consequences must this character face as a member of their family/faction?
> - What direct influence does this character have on bringing Romeo and Juliet together or keeping them apart?
> - What would be missing in the play if this character were not present?
>
> As you read the play, jot down questions that you will bring up in discussion with your team members. Additionally, jot down questions that you will share with the class as a whole.

FIGURE 1.6. *Romeo and Juliet*: Character focus.

thwarted Romeo and Juliet's meeting, marriage, and/or demise. As with tracking the motifs or "weird words," students will share their insights with other "team" members and with the class as a whole.

The team approach can lead to formative and summative activities such as Romeo and Juliet writing love letters, sonnets, or even texts to each other (or Romeo to Rosaline, Paris to Juliet), creating a Verona town tabloid newspaper with a variety of articles that feature supporting characters as subjects or authors, or putting the Nurse and Friar Laurence on trial for their participation in Romeo and Juliet's secret marriage. Individually, students can create journals for their character, reflecting on specific incidents that occurred in the play. As an engagement strategy, students have a greater chance of developing an affinity for a character, which can lead to their investment in the text as a whole. These activities also encourage close reading, use of textual evidence, and imaginative, critical thinking depending on the selected analytical and creative tasks.

Transforming Special Challenges into Boon Opportunities

Unfortunately, Shakespeare's plays many times do not find their way into curricula designed for students who are ELLs or reading below grade level. If a play is included in a syllabus, many of those students think Shakespeare is too hard for them to understand or to enjoy. At an NCTE conference on teaching Shakespeare in 2000, two educators from the United Kingdom focused on bringing the Bard to elementary school classrooms. For them, many of Shakespeare's plays read like fairy tales: "Once upon a time, there was a king who had three daughters and he wanted to leave his kingdom to the one who professed her love and loyalty the best." They described how they introduce a chunk of Cordelia's speech from *King Lear* to first-grade students by relating the basic plot of the tragedy in the form of a fairy tale. What first grader doesn't enjoy a good fairy tale as an engagement strategy? Over the course of their elementary school years, those students each year would be introduced to a different play and a larger segment of text, and would engage with the text using active drama approaches. By the time those first graders were in secondary school, they would have developed the skills and desire to read, understand, and enjoy an entire play, based on interacting with Shakespeare in playful ways over the course of their elementary years.

Those UK educators worked in a variety of schools with diverse student populations, including ELLs. They asserted that students who are being immersed in a new language already feel its strangeness and are more open-minded about trying out Shakespeare's way with words. With older students, carefully sequenced experiences with Shakespeare might include a side-by-side translated version of the play. We address the use of parallel text editions in Chapter 2, since many Shakespeare purists shudder at the prospect of students using texts from a series like No Fear Shakespeare.

In our teaching experiences, we have encountered ELL students from Russia and other Eastern European countries in secondary-level world literature classes studying *The Tempest*. They were truly excited about reading Shakespeare in the "original language," because some had read or had seen a production of a play in a translated version. They might be accomplished readers of Shakespeare in a version translated into their first language, but reading Shakespeare in Early Modern English certainly presented new challenges. The oddness of Shakespeare's English wasn't in many ways any odder than the contemporary English they were learning. Their interest and enthusiasm raised the bar and piqued the curiosity of students in the class who spoke and read English as their first language but viewed Shakespearean English as too difficult and his plays too boring, whether they had read any Shakespeare or not. The interest of the ELL students created a teachable moment to discuss the influence and popularity of Shakespeare across cultures and over time. The class even watched a

> **Teacher of the Bard Talk**
>
> My goals in teaching Shakespeare to this age group are to develop an appreciation of Shakespeare's stories and the relevance to students' lives, to familiarize students with Shakespeare's unique text structures, to unlock certain text features that can provide clues to meaning, and, most of all, to allow students to have fun "playing" with challenging material.... I want students to have early experiences that give them specific strategies and the confidence to approach whatever plays they may encounter going forward.
>
> —JENNIFER BERTACCHI,
> *Carleton Washburne Middle School;*
> *ELA teacher*

short excerpt of a famous Russian film adaptation of *Hamlet* to get a sense of what Shakespeare "sounds like" in another language (bbbernardo). There was a marked difference in attitude and effort in other classes that didn't include ELL students.

Presenting the Bard as a Teller of Tales

Our aim is to make Shakespeare accessible to students who might not have all the reading and study skills to tackle a play without some level of struggle, and who are not necessarily first graders, but in relation to whom we can draw several important lessons from that presentation made by the teachers from the United Kingdom. Consider how those first graders—who are fledgling, not even novice, readers of the Bard—meet him in well-chosen nuggets that reveal him at his most basic level: as a teller of stories, and some of these resemble fairy tales. Most of his stories also are deeply rooted in archetypes and tropes that cut across so many genres, cultures, and time periods. Students will be more likely to engage in exploring an unfamiliar text by beginning with one that is more familiar and accessible. Beginning with an existing or teacher-created fairy tale that introduces the characters and central conflict is one approach to consider, even with older students. Charlotte Artese's *Shakespeare and the Folktale: An Anthology of Stories* presents folktales the Bard would have heard or read that might have inspired him, as well as forty folktales spanning other time periods and cultures that connect with eight of his plays. BBC *School Radio* has created a series, Shakespeare Retold, featuring short narratives from authors of children's books in the form of a simplified version of a play's plot or a parallel story to introduce a play's conflict or themes. There are YA novels and films that draw on Shakespeare as their source material and that would serve as a useful "anchor text." You might decide that reading an entire play is not the best choice for a group of ELL students or novice readers of the Bard who may struggle with Early Modern English and blank verse. Meeting students at various points on Gardner's multiple intelligence spectrum will help them find a path through which to engage a challenging text, as well as meeting them on a reading skills spectrum that moves from fledgling through to novice, developed, and accomplished readers of the Bard.

> **Teacher of the Bard Talk**
>
> I believe that there are some authors/texts that make us better teachers, and Shakespeare is certainly one of them. Reading Shakespeare with students provides a range of literary and rhetorical opportunities to help students become better readers and communicators; furthermore, the naturally visual and creative elements of plays can be quite appealing if incorporated into teaching strategies.
>
> —STEPHEN HELLER,
> *Adlai E. Stevenson High School; ELA teacher and AP language consultant*

Finding a Path into Shakespeare for All Students

As you consider how you currently make reading Shakespeare accessible for your students, regardless of their reading level or prior experience with the Bard, keep in mind what you want students to know or to learn based on the goals of your curriculum and the prevailing national and local standards. When Anna Wing-bo Tso outlined her approach to working with ELL students in Hong Kong, she framed her pedagogy with reference to Heron and Reason's "four kinds of knowing":

1. *propositional knowing*—the knowing of facts through ideas and facts (this is also the commonest kind that occurs in traditional learning processes)
2. *experiential knowing*—the knowing that takes place through the transformation of experience
3. *presentational knowing*—the knowing that encompasses intuition and reflection, imagination and conceptual thinking (and can move beyond linguistic expression and draw on other forms of expression and any of Gardner's multiple intelligences)
4. *practical knowing*—or "knowing how to do something" (based on an acquired skill or special talent)

> **Teacher of the Bard Talk**
>
> I have experienced some skepticism on the part of a small number of parents who were comfortable with a more traditional-looking classroom and formal study of text. When faced with questions about the appropriateness of "play" in the young adolescent classroom, I explain that "play" allows for creative expression, independence, physical activity, and, most importantly, joyful engagement with difficult material. I think that some may believe that "playing" is not rigorous, when in fact it is a highly effective way to wrestle with difficult material such as this. Experimenting with Shakespeare's words and stories provides opportunities to work in various learning modalities, and it is not uncommon to see kids who are more reserved in a more traditional learning environment really come alive. In my mind, there is no better way to bring a *play* to life!
>
> —Jennifer Bertacchi,
> *Carleton Washburne Middle School;
> ELA teacher*

In the past, ELA instruction tended to level off at the propositional knowing level and a demonstration of presentational knowing usually found its form in a literary analysis essay. The use of active drama approaches and the Folio technique combines experiential and presentational knowing to ultimately enhance propositional knowing, which hopefully will lead to practical knowing when students can demonstrate and showcase their abilities to speak and move in purposeful ways no matter the text or the occasion.

Throughout this book, we invite you to consider and integrate techniques that do encourage a sense of playfulness and stimulate academic engagement—and enjoyment. If you worry about the time it takes to try something new, allow yourself one new strategy linked to multiple intelligence theory for each unit in an academic year, not just when you focus on Shakespeare. Our partner teachers come out of workshops thinking, "I want to do them all!" Come Monday, they get overwhelmed and don't necessarily integrate any of these engagement strategies at all. We always recommend selecting strategies based on the multiple intelligences that you feel your natural pedagogical approach neglects or ignores. ELA activities are certainly heavy on their appeal to linguistic intelligence, and a classroom using collaborative approaches nurtures interpersonal intelligence. So, which students might feel overlooked or stymied? How can you support and validate other intelligences? How might studying "hard" texts be transformed into engaging, even "fun" experiences? YA author John Green certainly would approve.

2

Pair the First Folio of 1623 with Print, Graphic, or Digital Editions

Is the Play or the Edition of the Play "the Thing"?

When ELA curricula reading lists were dictated by the contents of a textbook, the Shakespeare play your students read was largely predicated on which title was included in that tome. Some publishers made sure to include a Shakespeare play in almost every survey textbook, with the obvious exception of an American literature survey. A ninth-grade textbook focusing on a genre approach probably would feature *Romeo and Juliet*. With British literature, students typically got either *Hamlet* or *Macbeth*. For world literature, *The Tempest* was a popular choice. Now most of us aren't saddled with decisions made by textbook editors. We might be able to choose not only the play we want to share with our students but also the edition and the format—print or digital—as well.

In this chapter, we begin with the First Folio of 1623 as a viable companion text in the ELA classroom. We present it as your "primary source" when teaching any play and as the foundation for implementing the Folio technique discussed in later chapters; the First Folio works *in combination* with a play's mass-market or digital edition. Then we examine the useful features of a variety of print and digital editions that may or may not be familiar to you as your primary teaching text. We want you to consider the benefits of making several of those editions available to your students as part of a classroom library so they can reap their rich and unique resources.

What *Is* All the Fuss over the First Folio?

In 2016 a copy of the First Folio of 1623 from the Folger Shakespeare Library traveled across the United States visiting each and every one of the fifty states along the way. In Illinois we expected it to stop at Chicago Shakespeare Theater, the Newberry Library, or even the Lincoln Library in Springfield. In February of that year, the First Folio found its temporary home at the modest Bess Bower

Dunn Museum, which was smack in the middle of one of Lake County Illinois's vast forest preserves. If it hadn't been winter, you could image that First Folio nestled in a Midwest version of the Forest of Arden. And 2016 indeed was a banner year for the First Folio, as the world observed the 400th anniversary of Shakespeare's death with all manner of celebration. With the First Folio as a centerpiece in that "Bardic revelry," it was a period to venerate and celebrate it as an important cultural artifact. For many, it is the most direct way modern readers and actors can access Shakespeare's work as he intended. Or, rather, as Ben Jonson intended. Or as John Heminges and Henry Condell intended. Or as the compositors in the print shop pieced together and intended it.

When we dive into the Folio technique, we privilege the "authority" of the First Folio of 1623 and the clues Shakespeare embedded therein for the benefit of the actor. When we do that, we regard the First Folio as a particular construct of intention and meaning. Since Shakespeare was not present to oversee the compiling, editing, and printing of the First Folio, we need to make a leap of faith that the text truly reflects Shakespeare's original intentions and literary production. For eighteen of the plays, it offers their only printed edition. We feel confident taking this position, since the men who spearheaded the project of collecting Shakespeare's works were colleagues of his, and the supposed proofreader of the collection was Edward Knight, the "book-keeper" for the King's Men who maintained the company's scripts (Greg).

The First Folio establishes Shakespeare as a major figure of Early Modern theater. The gathering of his works into one volume attests to his importance, greatness, and popularity. Printed volumes were expensive to produce and costly to own, but the fabricators of the First Folio were willing to take that risk to create 750 copies for the initial imprint. Business being business, they had to know there was a market. And, as the First Folio of 1623 was such a success, it spawned a reprinting through the fourth edition of 1685. Compilers and printers of "Team Folio" didn't produce those volumes with the hallowed halls of modern libraries and museums in mind. The existence of the First Folio and myriad quartos, authorized or not, turned Shakespeare into a literary figure. What was initially intended to be seen and heard transformed into something to be read, studied, and treasured. ELA curricula and textbooks would look very different from the nineteenth century to the present without the existence of Shakespeare in print dating back to the late sixteenth and early seventeenth century.

We will allow that a bit of tinkering occurred preparing the Folio's four editions, which may or may not have squared with Shakespeare's original manuscript or promptbook copies of his plays, but text tinkering also would have occurred under Shakespeare's watch in rehearsal as well. As a play goes from the page to the stage, what sounds right in the mind of the writer won't necessarily sound best on the lips of an actor. Accordingly, Shakespeare and the acting company's "book-keeper" or prompter would make adjustments to the text—both cuts and additions. Much of the controversy revolving around the production of the quartos and the folios actually focuses on the printing process of that time and the diligence or negligence of those "compositors." Modern scholarship has revealed five compositors worked on the First Folio of 1623, and this is evident by tracking spelling patterns as well as compositing virtuosity. As you and your students work with texts from the First Folio, consider that English became increasingly more standardized with the invention of the printing press in Germany and its introduction to England in 1476 by Henry Caxton. Many features of the English language, such as spelling, pronoun usage, and vocabulary expansion, became standard once they were memorialized on the printed page and not through academic or bureaucratic consensus. Shakespeare wrote at a time when the English language was far more elastic in its vocabulary and conventions, so it was easy for him to influence and shape the language as a whole.

Engaging Students in Learning about the First Folio, Its History, and Its Significance

Engaging students to explore the importance of the First Folio might take more than a lecture gleaned from your own research and interest. The Folger Library's *Shakespeare Unlimited* podcast series covers all things Shakespeare, including the history and importance of the First Folio. Each episode runs for between twenty-five and twenty-nine minutes and is easily excerpted to tailor the information to your students' needs and interests. You can find the archive of episodes at www.folger.edu/shakespeare-unlimited. Meanwhile, here are four episodes that work well to introduce the First Folio and the process of editing modern editions based on the available folio and quartos of a play:

- Episode 56, "How Shakespeare's First Folio Became a Star"—www.folger.edu/shakespeare-unlimited/how-first-folio-became-a-star
- Episode 47, "Creating Shakespeare's First Folio"—www.folger.edu/shakespeare-unlimited/creating-first-folio
- Episode 31, "Editing Shakespeare"—www.folger.edu/shakespeare-unlimited/editing-shakespeare
- Episode 17, "A New Folio Discovery"—www.folger.edu/shakespeare-unlimited/first-folio-discovery-france

For the visual learners, some video options available online include:

- *The Secret Life of Books: "Shakespeare's First Folio"* (29:40)—originally available from BBC Scotland
- *Dialogue: "Shakespeare's First Folio"* (28:50)—from Idaho Public Television (see www.youtube.com/watch?v=VjeD_kdwLYY)

For a "hands-on" activity, go to the Folger Shakespeare Library website for a "DIY First Folio" activity (www.folger.edu/publishing-shakespeare/first-folio/diy-first-folio). Building on the Folger's DIY project, Illinois State University has initiated its own Shakespeare in Sheets scheme, which allows students to download, print, and assemble pages to create a facsimile quarto version of *Romeo and Juliet*, among other plays. Instructions are available at about.illinoisstate.edu/shakespeareinsheets/Pages/How-to-Make-the-Books.aspx.

If you require more comprehensive information on the creation of the First Folio and its impact over time, we recommend *The Making of Shakespeare's First Folio* and *Shakespeare's First Folio: Four Centuries of an Iconic Book*, both written by Emma Smith. The first book takes you through the process of gathering the plays and securing the necessary financial backing by "Team Shakespeare" (as Smith affectionately calls them) as well as a frank and surprising discussion of Shakespeare's reputation and legacy by 1623. The second book, a "biography" of the First Folio, is organized around the following topics: owning, reading, decoding, performing, perfecting. That last chapter focuses on the assessment of the condition and legitimacy of "original" copies, the production of print facsimiles, and, more recently, the digitization of the First Folio. Both of these books provide useful information that you can share through anecdotes.

Graham Watts's book *Shakespeare's Authentic Performance Texts: The Case for Staging from the First Folio* could be retitled *The Case for Reading from the First Folio* for our purposes in writing this book. His introduction, "How Did This Argument Begin?," provides a relatively concise and thoughtful overview of the process that editors—or, as he calls some of them, "adapters"—use to reconcile the text variations in the available folio and quarto editions of individual plays. Watts offers valuable examples of how changes, great and small, take great liberties with language, character, stage directions, and the order of speeches and scenes. In subsequent chapters, he dives deeply into how the First Folio is our best chance to get as close as possible to Shakespeare's intent and original language. This book is brimming with examples from so many of the plays we teach in secondary classrooms that would nicely supplement the examples we offer in our Folio technique chapters.

So, are you ready to pair the First Folio with your classroom edition of a play? Now, your school might not have the funds to possess one of the 235 surviving copies of the First Folio of 1623, but, never fear, since access to facsimile versions and modern typeset editions abound in print or online. Many of the apps we recommend also include a link to the First Folio. Here are two of your best online options:

- The Bodleian First Folio (firstfolio.bodleian.ox.ac.uk/text/166)—virtually leaf through a copy of the First Folio held at the Bodleian Library; read a play page by page with the Folio text accompanied by modern printed text.
- Folger Shakespeare Library (www.folger.edu/publishing-shakespeare/first-folio)—here is a great "one-stop shopping" website for the Folio and classroom-friendly supporting material. The introductory page provides links to a digital version of Folio #68 as well as to information about the text's importance, the printing process, called "DIY First Folio," and links to the Shakespeare Unlimited podcasts previously mentioned.

If you are interested in using a quarto version of a play, they are available at:

- Internet Shakespeare Editions (internetshakespeare.uvic.ca/Library/facsimile/overview/book.html)—this site also includes all four Folio editions along with all the quartos for plays published in that format.
- The Shakespeare Quartos Archive (accessible with Firefox browser; www.quartos.org)—this site relies on the resources of the Bodleian Library of the University of Oxford, the Folger Shakespeare Library, the British Library, and the Huntington Library, among others. It features teacher resources for *Hamlet*, the play that fell victim to a particularly "bad quarto."

If you desire a "print" facsimile copy of the First Folio of 1623 in your classroom, Norton can provide one edited by Charlton Hinman. This edition draws on the best versions of each page found in the folios from the Folger Library collection. Applause Theater and Cinema Books have published the complete First Folio of 1623 set in modern type as well as editions of individual plays billed as "folio texts."

Understanding the Impact of Textual Variants in Early Modern Print Editions

King Lear provides a perfect example of how Shakespeare's plays must have been shaped and revised over time and different productions. In the First Folio version, Lear's final speech allows him to test the actuality of Cordelia's death, thinking her lips might still bear a sign of life. The most striking difference between the quarto of 1608 and the First Folio edition of 1623 is the rendering of the last twenty-one or twenty-three lines of the tragedy's ending. No, it's not Nahum Tate's "happy ending," but it provides a provocative look at which character literally gets the last word(s). In the quarto, Goneril's husband, the Duke of Albany, speaks the final lines. In the First Folio, that speech is given to Edgar, the horribly wronged legitimate son of the Earl of Gloucester.

Text Detective Activity: Examining Differences between Quarto and Folio Versions of *King Lear*

In Figures 2.1 and 2.2, excerpts from the two versions, which retain the Early Modern spelling (termed *old-spelling transcription*) from the Internet Shakespeare Editions website, allow students to examine the impact of textual variants—and

Student Handout: A Tale of Two Endings Text Comparison			
Quarto 1, 1608 (*Lr.* 24)		**Folio 1, 1623 (*Lr.* 5.3)**	
LEAR.	And my poore foole is hangd, no, no life, why should a dog, a horse, a rat of life and thou no breath at all, O thou wilt come no more, neuer, neuer, neuer, pray you vndo this button, thanke you sir, O, o, o, o.	LEAR.	And my poore Foole is hang'd: no, no, no life? Why should a Dog, a Horse, a Rat haue life, And thou no breath at all? Thou'lt come no more, Neuer, neuer, neuer, neuer, neuer. Pray you vndo this Button. Thanke you Sir, Do you see this? Looke on her? Looke her lips, Looke there, looke there. *He dies.*
EDG.	He faints my Lord, my Lord.	EDG.	He faints, my Lord, my Lord.
LEAR.	Breake hart, I prethe breake.	KENT.	Breake heart, I prythee breake.
EDG.	Look vp my Lord.	EDG.	Looke vp my Lord.
KENT.	Vex not his ghost, O let him passe, He hates him that would vpon the wracke, Of this tough world stretch him out longer.	KENT.	Vex not his ghost, O let him passe, he hates him, That would vpon the wracke of this tough world Stretch him out longer.
EDG.	O he is gone indeed.	EDG.	He is gon indeed.
KENT.	The wonder is, he hath endured so long, He but vsurpt his life.	KENT.	The wonder is, he hath endur'd so long, He but vsurpt his life.
DUKE.	Beare them from hence, our present busines Is to generall woe, friends of my soule, you twaine Rule in this kingdome, and the goard state sustaine.	ALB.	Beare them from hence, our present businesse Is generall woe: Friends of my soule, you twaine, Rule in this Realme, and the gor'd state sustaine.
KENT.	I haue a iourney sir, shortly to go, My maister cals, and I must not say no.	KENT.	I haue a iourney Sir, shortly to go, My Master calls me, I must not say no.
DUKE.	The waight of this sad time we must obey, Speake what we feele, not what we ought to say, The oldest haue borne most, we that are yong, Shall neuer see so much, nor liue so long.	EDG.	The waight of this sad time we must obey, Speake what we feele, not what we ought to say: The oldest hath borne most, we that are yong, Shall neuer see so much, nor liue so long.

FIGURE 2.1. *King Lear*: First quarto (1608) versus First Folio (1623).

> **A Tale of Two Endings: Discussion Prompts**
>
> Begin this activity reviewing the basic plotline and the roles that the Duke of Albany and Edgar play in the tragedy. You can find a plot summary of *King Lear* as well as character descriptions in *Shakespeare A to Z*.
>
> 1. Let your students experience what it is like to "edit" the Bard. Have half the class go through one of the speeches to "correct" or regularize the Early Modern spelling of the quarto version. Have the rest of the class do the same for the Folio edition. Refer to Chapter 4 for tips on how to address variants in the spellings Shakespeare used.
> 2. Have students annotate the entire text nugget, noting the differences: that is, added, deleted, and reassigned lines, with special attention to Lear's speech that begins the interaction as well as the speech that ends the play.
> 3. Discuss Lear's speech by activating the *folio clues* presented in Chapters 4 to 6, in order to focus on how internal capitalization, repetition, and punctuation add to the pathos of his final moments in the Folio version.
> 4. Based on what students have learned from reading the plot summary as well as the character descriptions for (the Duke of) Albany and Edgar, what do they think might have been the reasons for reassigning the final speech? To what extent does Edgar's story arc in the subplot mirror Lear's?

FIGURE 2.2. A tale of two endings: *King Lear* of 1608 and of 1623.

beg the question of how modern editors reconcile these differences. In fact, this exercise can complement any play students will be reading to demonstrate the challenges many editors face.

Selecting and Evaluating Modern Editions of Shakespeare's Plays

Since it is unrealistic to anticipate teachers will use the entirety of the First Folio edition of any play, it is important to consider which mass-market classroom edition pairs well with First Folio excerpts. For most teachers, the choice of edition when teaching *Romeo and Juliet*, *Hamlet*, or *Macbeth* is usually based on what is available in the bookroom. A Folger Shakespeare edition is probably most often available, and that series is expertly informed by the Folio scholarship applied by its editors. Some teachers have a broader choice of print or digital versions of plays they can use, so we will provide a survey of the best available options.

Print Option: Full Text

American publishers have developed and maintained a series of Shakespeare's works in classroom-friendly single editions. When these mass-market editions first appeared, the series editors became a major selling point. For example,

David Bevington helmed the Bantam Classic series for its initial 1988 iteration, which allowed for a single authoritative voice in the series' scholarship. The Signet Classic series (1972) has featured a "general editor," Sylvan Barnet, along with essays provided by notable Shakespeare scholars and cultural critics. The Folger Shakespeare series has been edited by Barbara A. Mowat and Paul Werstine and draws on the immense holdings from the Folger Library that Henry Clay Folger and Emily Jordan Folger amassed, the world's largest collection devoted to Shakespeare.

All of these popular Shakespeare series feature the text of the play on the right-hand page and the scene summaries and footnotes on the left-hand page or as footnotes at the bottom of each page. These editions also provide introductory material about the play, Shakespeare's life, the Elizabethan theater scene, and a variety of critical essays. Illustrations are presented in black and white and are usually drawn from woodcuts, drawings, and photographs of sculpture from the play's period as well as from Shakespeare's time. The text is clearly the "thing" in these editions and they sometimes skew a little more toward college students in their approach to the explanatory and enriching scholarship. Over time, publishers have created study guides suitable for high school curricula, available in print and later online, to offer teachers reading strategies and lesson planning guidance. For some students, the sea of gray print on a standard-sized paperback page doesn't offer much visual appeal, let alone leave space for their own annotations. As you consider the merits of the content of an edition, remember that presentation is also a key component for students who are more visual than the other, language-based learners in your classroom.

British publishers offer a number of classroom-friendly series as well. Many teachers across the pond favor the Pelican Shakespeare series, which first appeared in the late 1950s, edited by Alfred Harbage from Penguin Books. These volumes tend to be "slimmer" in their format, and feature a brief introduction to the specific play, an essay on Shakespeare's theater, and detailed notes to illuminate the play. Both the Cambridge and the Oxford university presses publish their own Shakespeare series aimed at college students, and those editions are certainly useful and accessible for International Baccalaureate and AP students too. Recently, the Royal Shakespeare Company (RSC) has partnered with the Modern Library publishing company to create a series that adds elements gleaned from the RSC's productions of the plays. And the Arden Shakespeare series provides comprehensive scholarship and voluminous footnotes, which might overwhelm high school readers but prove to be a helpful "resource text" in the classroom. Arden Shakespeare supplements its full-text play editions with several other series, including its Early Modern Drama Guides for single plays, which include chapters entitled "Critical Backstory," "Performance History," and "New Directions"; its State of Play texts, also featuring single plays, gather "new perspectives" essays from contemporary scholars; and its *Teaching Shakespeare with Purpose: A Student-Centered Approach* by Ayanna Thompson and Laura Turchi, two US-based educators, offers suggestions for collaborative approaches to studying the plays in secondary and college classrooms.

Of all the American and British publishing options, the Cambridge School Shakespeare series offers an affordable alternative that combines the complete text of a play in a larger-format book. If you shop at brick-and-mortar bookstores, you may have found copies of *Romeo and Juliet*, *Macbeth*, *A Midsummer Night's Dream*, or *Hamlet* on their shelves from this series. Cambridge School Shakespeare editions continue the tradition of the play's text being on the right-hand page and the footnotes on the left-hand page, but it adds a page-by-page summary of what is happening at the top of that left page as well as activity suggestions along with the usual footnotes and photographs from a variety of stage productions throughout the volume (but not necessarily on every page). In this instance, Shakespeare, in print, becomes visually livelier—and, we would argue, more appealing and accessible—for both high school and middle school students.

The series is now in its third edition, and the physical format of each book is larger with ample space for annotation. Each play begins with a series of photographs drawn from a variety of productions to illustrate main characters as well as key moments of action. Each photograph bears a caption that takes students through the plot. The text's back matter features brief essays focusing on themes, characters, language, and the play in performance (on stage and in popular culture). Those essays include student-directed questions or make suggestions for activities to stimulate further critical analysis. Students are not just taking in scholarly opinion; they are gently pressed to continue to make meaning from well-selected scholarly insights. The final section makes suggestions for more formal writing experiences. Teachers can take advantage of online resources as well. Overall the Cambridge School Shakespeare approach meshes well with the Folio technique that we introduce in Chapters 4 to 6 of the present book, since so many of the activities suggested on the left-hand pages of the former get students up on their feet speaking the text, using theater games to physicalize the language, and improvising onstage and offstage action to clarify language.

Teachers at Adlai E. Stevenson High School in suburban Chicago first tested the effectiveness of the Cambridge School Shakespeare series with AP students who were reading *Richard II* to prepare for attending a performance at Chicago Shakespeare Theater. The use of the text was going to be a "one and done" affair, since *King Lear* was a standard part of the curriculum in the Bantam edition, so it was easy to try out a new text series. When presented with the production photographs in the Cambridge School edition, some students found them welcome and helpful. A few students found the format a bit juvenile or that the edition was not as enriched with the scholarship as they had found in the Folger or Bantam series. Actually, the AP curriculum team recommended the Cambridge University Press edition of *King Lear* and then later *Richard III* instead of the Cambridge School editions, to provide students with a more scholarly approach that suited their needs and interests. Using the Cambridge School Shakespeare edition of *The Tempest* with more reluctant and struggling readers in a standard level (or college prep) class was far more successful. Ninth-grade teachers of *Romeo and Juliet* or *Julius Caesar* and tenth-grade teachers of *Macbeth* found the activities in the series extremely helpful in sparking their creativity and boosting their students' overall engagement in reading the text.

Teacher of the Bard Talk

Generally, I liked the Cambridge editions better [than others] because of the layout. Students seem to be able to annotate the text more easily, and the editions appear more like scripts than "books."

—MARK ONUSCHECK,
Adlai E. Stevenson High School; director of curriculum, instruction, and assessment

Print Option: Parallel or Side-by-Side Texts

When we have approached partner teachers about their use of editions featuring the Bard's language on one page and a translated text on the other, some have been absolutely opposed to the notion of providing students editions from the No Fear Shakespeare series published by Spark Publishing. When we asked teachers about using a translated text, we were not thinking of it as a broadly used edition for all, or even most, students. We frankly worry about teachers who must cover a play with students who are just not ready for blank verse and Early Modern vocabulary—let alone the "weird" Renaissance pronouns and inverted syntax. It may be an entire class of students or it might be a select few who would benefit from the support of a parallel text edition.

ELL specialist Jennifer Arias has used a parallel text when she teaches *Romeo and Juliet* to her Advanced ELL students. She recommends Barron's Shakespeare Made Easy series, as the "translated" text "maintains figurative language but is accessible (similes, metaphors, oxymorons) so students have the benefit of

Teacher of the Bard Talk

The modern text can be a really useful tool in helping students identify language and comprehend what they are reading. Moreover, the modern language versions often employ a more direct grammatical construction (vs. the Shakespearean English). Students often have trouble processing or comprehending this, so the leap straight to Shakespeare can make it prohibitive to constructing any meaning. The modern text allows them to have a framework and schema to attach meaning to and a building block to begin tackling the Shakespearean language.

—CLAIRE WALTER,
Wolcott School; ELA/lead teacher

analyzing that language." She has the students read the translated text, but, for certain key scenes, they will read and discuss the "original" text. When making the transition to more difficult language, Arias's students "study the content and meaning in the modern version, which gives them the tools to build an analysis of the original [text] that requires more sophistication." That analysis includes examining the sonnet structure of Romeo and Juliet's first meeting and explaining why using that poetic form is appropriate, or the use of inversion in particular lines and how certain words and ideas are emphasized through caesura or enjambment.

Text Activity Tip: To Conceal or to Reveal?
Should you decide to use a parallel text, consider distributing a colorful index card about the size of the book's page. Weaning students away from complete dependence on the translated text is a concern of many teachers who have used or would like to use the parallel text edition of a play. Students will obviously be the most dependent on the translated text early in the reading process, but they should be encouraged to cut themselves off from the modern language to give Early Modern English a try. The index card provides a complete physical barrier, covering the entire page while they read the entire untranslated page—or, they can allow the index card to slip down and reveal the translation side line by line. If you have students read a short scene in class and give them the option of the "cover-up" or the "line-by-line reveal," you can observe which option they select in order to gauge your students' levels of confidence negotiating the Shakespearean side of the text. Save that index card, because we use it again in the "Magic Index Card" exercise introduced in a later chapter.

If you use the introductory Folio techniques presented in Chapter 5 with students reading a parallel text edition, you will be providing the support they need to make the transition to reading more of the play in Early Modern English over the modern version. And you may decide to wait to introduce the Folio technique activities until after students have read Act 1, so they don't have to tackle the challenges of Shakespeare's language until they have acquainted themselves with the setting, characters, and inciting incidents that create the conflict.

Print Option: Graphic Texts

The ELL teachers who have shared their experiences teaching Shakespeare with us have openly expressed a wish to have access to a graphic novel version of a text, especially for students who have never read Shakespeare in English. Some teachers have faced barriers "selling" this option to curriculum directors or department chairs, though. Shakespeare equals words, not pictures supplemented with words. Having copies of a graphic novel version of a play, however, is a boon to differentiated instruction for struggling readers.

There are definitely pros and cons to using graphic texts. The first "pro" is that struggling readers will welcome the opportunity to have difficult language actually visualized for them. If they have experience reading graphic novels or manga panels, they will understand how the images and text flow across and down the page. A second "pro" is that the original play is edited for length, space, and clarity. Now, here comes the first "con": many of the suggested graphic series translate the Early Modern English into contemporary speech. For some teachers, reading Shakespeare in a translated form with pictures is an absolute nonstarter, even though some of these adaptations retain key images, figures of speech, and rhetorical devices like some of the parallel text editions. Weaning students away from the visual support of the graphic texts and moving on to visualizing the language themselves constitutes another "con." In a visually saturated culture, who wouldn't prefer Shakespeare with a side of expert illustrations? After we review your options in this category, we suggest some strategies with which to wean students from the graphic novel as their primary source for reading and understanding Shakespeare.

At the time we are writing this book, here are the most promising series among the graphic novel adaptations of Shakespeare:

Teacher of the Bard Talk

Students with dyslexia often have very strong visual reading skills that can act in a compensatory way for their struggle with printed text. Sometimes, if a student is really struggling with the text, I will supplement their reading of the text with a graphic novel. The key is developing a reading plan with the student so they understand how this can be used as a reading tool to aid in comprehension and allow them to access the same skills and challenges as their typically developing peers rather than a straight "substitute."

—CLAIRE WALTER,
Wolcott School; ELA/lead teacher

No Fear Shakespeare: Graphic Novels

Spark Publishing is extending its brand from the No Fear parallel text editions to graphic novels that marry the "translated" version of a play to graphic novel black-and-white illustrations. The text does pare down the original plot a bit, but it really doesn't read as if much plot or character is missing. The translation once again preserves the crucial images, figures of speech, and rhetorical devices. In reviewing their edition of *Hamlet*, turn to pages 81 and 82 for Hamlet's most famous soliloquy. The language is altered but not in a jarring or dumbed-down manner. The rendering of the soliloquy in panels and images gives students a lot to discuss, as the speech is broken down into illustrations of what Hamlet fears as he contemplates his mortality. You might find yourself looking for some assistance to discuss the "grammar and syntax" of the visual content of graphic novels. We make a few suggestions at the end of this section.

Gareth Hinds's Graphic Novels of Classic Works

Gareth Hinds has been adapting classic literature from the *Odyssey* and *Beowulf* to the works of Shakespeare as well as those of the Brothers Grimm and Edgar Allan Poe as graphic novelizations featuring adapted text and full-color illustrations. His graphic novel treatment of *Romeo and Juliet* is set in Renaissance Italy but it features a multiracial cast. The color panels of *Macbeth* bring the Scottish play to bloody, vibrant life. If your students struggle with *The Merchant of Venice*, Hinds streamlines the plot effectively without sacrificing characterization and the overall arc of the narrative.

Hinds has exhibited his work at NCTE and clearly is attuned to the needs of ELA teachers of students of all reading abilities. You can access a variety of resources online in which he talks about his interests, process, and their results (e.g., Manno and Kallenborn) as well as a review of his adaptation of *Macbeth* (M. Russo).

Classical Comics

This series offers *Romeo and Juliet, Macbeth, The Tempest, Much Ado about Nothing,* and *Richard III* in full-color comic book editions in three different text versions: original, plain, and quick. The "original text" version features an edited version of Shakespeare's text, the "plain text" offers the original language translated into modern speech, and the "quick text" relies on highly simplified language to provide an overview of the plot, characterization, and themes. The publisher recommends their "quick text" edition to introduce the play's plot structure and characters to struggling or reluctant readers, and not necessarily to replace either the "original" or the "plain" versions.

The website stresses using the various editions in concert with one another, which can be an expensive proposition for most classrooms. Interactive Motion Comics is their latest product line, and it brings the comic books to life panel by panel with animation and audio. It is designed to be loaded on a classroom computer for a single reader, or projected on a whiteboard for full class analysis. This format allows toggling between Shakespeare's original text and the translated versions, which is probably the most cost effective approach and is available for purchase through a site license.

Other teacher resources are available with the purchase of the paperback editions and have many tools that are "whiteboard ready." "No text" panels are part of free resources downloadable at the publisher's website (www.classical

comics.com/education/free-resources/). These panels allow students to complete speech bubbles for a short scene, based on a brief prose synopsis. You can download scene panels from the three published text versions, so students then can compare the three Classical Comics versions with their own versions, which provides an opportunity for students to examine and discuss the pros and cons of reading one of Shakespeare's plays in his own words (though edited), in more familiar English, or in its most bare-bones form. This is a great anticipatory activity, whether you use a Classical Comic edition or not.

Manga Shakespeare

This series is the most robust and comprehensive of the three we suggest. As of the publication date of our book, Manga Shakespeare has fourteen titles in print, with more on the way. This series obviously draws on the conventions of Japanese manga. Now, you might dismiss manga as too rooted in popular culture, but its origins reach back to twelfth-century Japanese scrolls and innovated reading of a visual text from left to right. In the twentieth century, "manga" became synonymous with "comics" in Japan, with series designed for young readers (mostly male) and adult readers (featuring very "mature" content). Manga's reach extended to the West in the form of comics and anime. And, since Japanese readers have long admired Shakespeare, the marriage of manga and the Bard comes as no surprise.

Manga Shakespeare is designed for manga enthusiasts as leisure reading and for secondary students as a text for study. This graphic treatment offers an abridgement of Shakespeare's original text, which makes it a cut above the translated texts in the other series. The British publisher's promotional material cites the input from a leading Shakespeare scholar in developing the series, which offers not only access to teaching materials but advertises online workshops.

Many of the Manga Shakespeare treatments reposition a play in another setting or context; for example, *King Lear* is set in a Native American context, while *Hamlet* is set in 2017 when climate change and warfare waged in the cyber world have seriously impacted Denmark. The ethnic diversity of the series' artists is evident in the visual style from play to play. If you are a Renaissance purist in terms of the "look" of Shakespeare's work on stage, on screen, or in graphic novel form, you will have to recalibrate your expectations. While graphic novels have their own visual "grammar and syntax," manga layers in another set of conventions. You can bring yourself up to speed through the resources available at the Manga Shakespeare Learning website (mangashakespeare.com) as well as by reviewing:

- manga iconography on, for example, en.wikipedia.org/wiki/Manga_iconography
- "manga Effects" on the TVTropes website, tvtropes.org/pmwiki/pmwiki.php/Main/MangaEffects

Graphic Novel Reporter, part of the Book Report Network, summarizes the conventions in two brief reference lists:

- visual references—admin.graphicnovelreporter.com/manga-visual-references
- a glossary of terms pertaining to manga genre conventions—admin.graphicnovelreporter.com/manga-glossary

If you decide to use a graphic novel version of a play, what will that experience look like in your classroom? Our partner teachers who work with ELL and struggling readers have shared that graphic editions work very well for students who have had no experience with reading Shakespeare. Many of those students have experience reading comic and graphic novels for pleasure, so you may or may not need to provide an extensive *reading readiness* mini-lesson. Even if students have experience reading graphic texts, it is important to make sure everyone has a consistent working vocabulary with which to analyze the texts effectively. Kym Francis's *Getting Graphic: Using Graphic Novels in the Language Arts Classroom* (gettinggraphic.weebly.com/vocabulary.html) offers a list of vocabulary to introduce the conventions of the form with a few visual examples that will help you apply and illustrate (pun intended) the concepts.

Some teachers worry that students might be tempted to skim the language and focus primarily on the visuals to convey the general meaning of the plot. Since much of Shakespeare isn't always about physical action, the psychological conflicts facing characters will only be telegraphed through facial expressions. Students need to regard the text and the visuals as the "peanut butter and jelly" of graphic novel reading. As with a "language-only" version of a text, students need a basic set of questions to guide their reading. Also, don't have them read too quickly: allow students to pace themselves for reflection and analysis.

> **Teacher of the Bard Talk**
>
> If they are going straight graphic novel, I would recommend doing a unit on visual analysis with ideas of closure, juxtaposition, negative space, etc., so that students can work on analyzing the images. I would also recommend bringing in the actual text to complement the graphic novel reading depending on their goals.
>
> —CLAIRE WALTER,
> *Wolcott School; ELA/lead teacher*

Anticipatory Activity: Learning the Conventions of a Graphic Text

The Getting Graphic website suggests that you preview any graphic adaptation with a "picture walk," even with high school students. Figure 2.3 presents an adaptation of this anticipatory strategy. If you find that students lack the vocabulary to analyze a graphic text, have them take a "quizlet" that introduces the key terminology in an interactive way. You can find that tool at quizlet.com/14100364/graphic-novel-panel-gutter-balloons-vocabulary-flash-cards/, or have your students access a list of terms and an application activity at the InThinking subject site www.thinkib.net/englishalanglit/page/13891/graphic-novel.

Instructions for Picture Walk

Distribute copies of the play to the class. Use the following set of questions to walk your students through key images in order to preview the play's plot and characters.

1. Begin with the cover illustration.
    - How does the cover present the main character(s)?
    - How does the cover preview the conflict the main character(s) will face?
    - How does the artwork—especially the design of the background—set the mood of the play?
2. Flip to the back cover.
    - Does the back cover include any illustrations? If it does, what information is conveyed by those images? How understandable are they out of context? What questions do those images raise for you?
    - How does the text on the back cover provide some details about the play's content? And how does that information work to pique the reader's curiosity to read more?
3. Examine the opening pages, which may introduce the characters.
    - What do the images of each character reveal about the personality and the role they will play in the drama?
    - What text is added to the presentation of each character? What information does it provide?
4. Slowly go through the first scene page by page, having students focus solely on the images.
    - Does a single image ever dominate a single page? What is presented in that single frame?
    - When a page features multiple panels, which image jumps out from the rest? How are the multiple panels on a single page linked together?
    - What are key facial expressions, gestures, clothing, and objects that help to tell the story?
    - How does color (and this includes black-and-white artwork) play a role in drawing your attention to certain features on a page or within a single frame?
5. Once students have gone through the first scene focusing only on the images, ask them to determine what the visual content lacks in establishing the characters, their relationship to one another, and their circumstances in the exposition piece of the plot.
6. Ask students to select a page or a single panel in the first scene where language is crucial to understanding the visual elements. Have them explain how the image(s) supports the text.

FIGURE 2.3. Previewing a picture walk: Graphic Shakespeare.

For all the visual pleasure a graphic version of a play provides, the actual text found in those versions are "plot driven and lack nuance" (Walter). As students gain control over the basics of plot, characterization, and theme as developed in the graphic text, select a short piece from the original text and have students compare the standard (Shakespeare's) version and the adapted or translated form. Claire Walter's students undertake that comparison to note what general changes are made, what in particular is eliminated, how that eliminated text helps understanding, and what is lost in the editing process. For Walter's students, who attend an independent urban school that caters to pupils with learning differences, "transitioning to the standard also works best with very structured and carefully sequenced assignments to give students specific questions for what to look for in the [original] Shakespeare and then build into the larger ideas in the text." For a scene like Friar Laurence's speech in 2.3 of *Romeo and Juliet*, students can take small steps toward language analysis by looking at strong patterns of oppositional words (*light* and *dark*) and examining how they take on certain connotations in the "standard version." Then they can compare how that pattern is treated (cut or retained) in the adapted version. If students toggle reading the graphic version to gain a general understanding of the play and then take a closer look at key scenes and speeches from Shakespeare's original text, they can be weaned away from an adapted or translated version. It's all a matter of preparation, pacing, and focus for the analysis of gradually longer and more complex passages of unedited Early Modern English.

Digital Option: Full Text

If your school has adopted the use of Chromebooks, iPads, or any other tablets, going digital with Shakespeare is a natural progression. We offer options that are free, as well as those available for under $10 or around $15 per download. Obviously, once you pay for an app, your access to support material expands, but the no-cost options are nonetheless fairly robust, user-friendly, and, occasionally, the source platform for a paid app.

The Complete Works Online

The following online sites and app provide access to all the plays, sonnets, and narrative poems. Even though your students will get everything, the sites are reasonably easy to navigate to reach an individual play and the resources supporting it.

OpenSource Shakespeare
Free. This site provides all the plays, sonnets, and narrative poems; concordance; and search features for text and characters. No frills, but you can easily print full scenes and acts from the site.

PlayShakespeare.com
Free. This site provides users with each play in the First Folio and a modern edition, along with a synopsis, character description, scene breakdown, and documents related to the play.

Shakespeare, ShakespearePro
Shakespeare, free; ShakespearePro, fee based. This app provides all the features of PlayShakespeare.com, but with a variety of content enhancements, especially the "power concordance search" that is only available as a "basic" feature on the free app, Shakespeare. You will notice, in a later chapter, the glossary embedded in this app helps navigate defining Early Modern vocabulary.

Individual Play Apps for Tablet Computers

The following apps allow students to download individual plays (for a fee). We anticipate that the supply of single play apps will expand as publishers digitize their paperback versions to meet the demand for access on tablets.

Folger Luminary Shakespeare
Fee based, under $10. This series of apps connects the reader with the complete Folger Shakespeare edition of a play along with footnotes, expert commentary, a full audio performance, and images. All these features are easily accessed on an iPad or other tablet as needed. Students can share insights and queries on a social platform, connecting with their classmates to form reading groups.

Heuristic Shakespeare
Fee based, under $10. This app series launched in 2016 with *The Tempest* (featuring Sir Ian McKellen), using notes from the Arden edition of the play. As the student opens the app, they will be able to identify their level of experience reading Shakespeare and experience an audiovisual tour of the app and its features. This identification process sets the sophistication level of the Arden footnotes linked to the text. The reader level (1–3) can be easily reset. Students also can download enrichment essays on various aspects of the play and videos featuring Shakespeare scholars. They can view the complete play as it appears in the First Folio too.

As students read the text, they can download a video featuring actors speaking the text when they hold their tablet in portrait view and remove the video when they orient to the landscape view. "Footnoted" words and phrases are underlined and just a tap brings up the definition or explanation. And, if there is too much audio to process, students can mute the sound effects that accompany some of the scenes.

Shakespeare in Bits

Fee based, over $10. The Shakespeare in Bits, or "SIB," series initially reached the marketplace on CD-ROMs. Though more than twice the price of the other single play apps listed above, the enriched format of the SIB versions makes it worth the cost for struggling or reluctant readers to more fully engage with the text. Each scene is accompanied by an animated performance of the text. Holding the tablet in landscape orientation, the video appears on the left and the full text on the right. Students can turn on the "subtitles" feature to activate the text appearing on the screen. Like the other apps, students can access the play act by act, scene by scene, along with character information, supplemental information, and literary analysis, among other features.

The tenth-grade curriculum team at Adlai E. Stevenson High School decided to adopt the SIB app edition as their text for teaching *Macbeth*. Students use school-issued iPads loaded with the app. Purchasing the app for four hundred tenth graders drove down the cost per pupil to almost half. Members of the team, Jacquie Cullen and Noel Johnston, here share with us their experiences of using digital Shakespeare with students of varying reading skills and enthusiasm for the Bard.

At the beginning of the unit, Cullen takes students through the app to explain and demonstrate the features. Figure 2.4 shows how she gets her students started with SIB. Cullen expects her students to bring a fully charged tablet computer to class for large- and small-group work; otherwise, students will have to use a paperback copy of the play for that class period, which might put them at a disadvantage, based on the day's activity. Setting ground rules for which aspects of the app will be used in class and at home is also important. Cullen prefers that students access the animation and vocal performances at home, when she assigns short scenes to be read outside of class. Cullen has found that the features of the SIB app helps her students conduct a series of *table reads* of key scenes in small groups in class. Students will read shorter scenes for homework to prepare them for the in-class readings in either large or small groups. To take the pressure off students when assigning reading roles, Cullen has them draw slips of paper that will indicate a role or give them a pass, so a student who isn't assigned a role can take a role already drawn when a student who gets

> **Getting Started with Shakespeare in Bits**
>
> Once students have the app loaded on their tablet, go through the basic features using the following instructions.
>
> **Instructions**
>
> 1. Open the app and click on "The Play."
> 2. Click on the first scene of Act 1.
> 3. When it opens, you will see the video on the left and the text on the right. Across the top, there are four tabs: Text, Notes, Synopsis, and My Notes.
> 4. When you are ready to read, click on the "Synopsis" tab to familiarize yourself with what will happen in that scene.
> 5. The "My Notes" feature will allow you to create notes and questions and to skim those notes as you read more of the play.
>
> **Understanding the Highlighted Words and Purple Bubbles Features**
>
> Have students click on "Text" and change the yellow-highlighted words to orange with a tap. In this way, students are immediately drawn to words and phrases that they might not know or would be able to define without doubt today. That simple tap substitutes a word that is easier to understand; for example, *broil* changes to *battle*.
>
> Point out the purple bubbles on the left-hand side of the text. Those bubbles are labeled "L" for language, "M" for miscellaneous, and "T" for theme. They are the app's variation on footnotes. Coach students to stop and read the bubbles as close to the related line(s) as possible so that it is helpful information. When students are reading on their own, they might click more frequently on one bubble category than another.
>
> **Accessing the "Notes" Feature Early On**
>
> Show students that the "Notes" tab on the upper-right bar provides additional staging information or historical context. You might want to direct students to read those notes during the early scenes, and then rely on the students eventually to read them on their own when they need that support.
>
> **Using the Video Feature**
>
> Point out that your students can not only watch the scenes play out in an animated form, but they can also run the video with or without the text appearing in the video box to the left of the play's full text.
>
> **Balancing the Need to Know and Avoiding Spoilers**
>
> Finally, go through an overview of what else is on the app. Across the bottom of the screen, there are additional tabs: the "Scenes" tab takes students to a table of contents for the play; "Cast" provides character information and a relationship map of how the characters are connected; "Analysis" provides more depth to the play, including a plot summary. There are some spoiler alerts, so caution students not to read too much if they don't want to ruin the play. They can also make use of other tabs labeled "Themes," "Imagery," and "Symbols."

FIGURE 2.4. Introducing the Shakespeare in Bits app series.

a "pass" slip lobbies to read a role. Cullen says that students will advertise the availability of a role poised to be passed off. Students usually draw their roles at the beginning of an act and redraw roles for subsequent acts. To keep students engaged whether they are reading a part or not, Cullen organizes the tasks as described in Figure 2.5. The responsibilities of the text support roles can be combined if a smaller number of students in a single group would function better.

When Noel Johnston was first presented with the opportunity to use the SIB series of apps, he was concerned that having the video and audio features might make for a passive experience for some students. For him, "part of the learning and appreciation is [the] deliberate unpacking of Shakespeare," and it is impor-

> **Table Read Instructions**
>
> As a small group, you are going to conduct a table read of *Macbeth* (1.2). The following *characters* have *speaking parts* in this scene: Duncan, Lennox, Ross, Malcolm, and Sergeant. In addition, there are *text support roles* as follows:
>
> - The *synopsis reader* will begin the scene by reading the Synopsis and Notes sections, and then they will evaluate how the Synopsis effectively previewed the scene and review how the Notes helped explain or clarify difficult aspects of the scene.
> - The *stage manager* will read the stage directions, plus keep the table focused and on task; they could also develop questions with the group to explore the scene and lead a post-scene discussion.
> - The *bubble reader* draws attention to the purple bubbles as the scene unfolds and can stop the reading to reveal the information in a bubble as well as pause to reveal the substitution for a word highlighted in the text.
> - The *scribe* keeps track of the notes that the group wants to add to My Notes, including the most important lines of the scene that develop character, advance the plot, or reveal a theme.

FIGURE 2.5. Table read of *Macbeth*.

tant to check that students are using the tools in the app for that unpacking process. Abbas Pourhosein Gilakjani, who has studied the impact of multimedia instruction on ELL students, views the effectiveness of audiovisual components more positively:

> When used effectively, animated content can improve learning. Animation appears to be most effective when presenting concepts or information that students may have difficulty envisioning. Animation is more effective when students have the ability to start and stop the animation and view it at their own pace or are able to manipulate various facets of the animation. (60)

Stevenson High School student Dziyana Balakir here shares her experience moving from reading *Romeo and Juliet* in an ELL class using a parallel text to using the SIB *Macbeth* app in a standard college prep class:

> I have been using an app which has a synopsis of each scene and vocabulary [substitution] for the confusing words. That made the experience easier, but for some students in my class [it made them more] careless because they had all the notes written for them.

Dziyana certainly confirms Johnston's concern, so he regularly checks for understanding in a variety of ways when students begin to read more of the play on their own. To assess how well students are reading carefully and understanding what they read, Johnston provides students with a text excerpt without footnotes, asking them either to paraphrase or to answer a set of questions. He uses an excerpt from the homework assignment or from an upcoming scene. His goal is to help students read and understand more of a play while relying less and less on the interpretive support, since many students probably will move on to reading Shakespeare in a paperback edition as eleventh and twelfth graders.

Ebook Option

It might not be an app but it's a great ebook option. The Arden Shakespeare Third Series of their scholarly editions are available for download, as well as a new series, the Arden Performance Editions, which is "designed to meet actors' needs." Surprisingly, this new performance series meets the needs of students who have not had success with Shakespeare. In its paperback version, the pages have room for lots of personal annotation, and, married with an annotation app or tool, the ebook format offers similar space.

> **Teacher of the Bard Talk**
>
> I work to find the right "reading recipe" for each student. Some students can come to Shakespeare and just "pick it right up." For students that have difficulty as a result of their learning challenges, I use summaries, parallel texts, audio texts, film versions, [and] talk through with a partner/adult as prep for them reading the "standard text." I meet with each student and experiment on what the right "order" to read in is. Some students require multiple supplements before they are ready and able to tackle the "standard." It is an ongoing process, and I often work to encourage students with the idea into "building" to read Shakespeare, and then, if it is a struggle at the beginning, the hope is that, by the end, we will have found a system that works for them.
>
> —CLAIRE WALTER,
> *Wolcott School; ELA/lead teacher*

A Note about the Editions We Use throughout the Book

We use extracts and examples primarily drawn from the First Folio of 1623 sourced from the Internet Shakespeare Editions (University of Victoria) website—internetshakespeare.uvic.ca/—throughout the text, since it is an open access source. In most instances, we identify the play and the character but not the website. If we use an example from any other edition, Folger or Cambridge Shakespeare, those excerpts are cited by publisher or series in addition to the play and character. In many instances, we don't use line numbers, as they can vary from edition to edition based on modern editors' interventions.

Going beyond the Mass-Market Paperback Edition

For most of us, the edition of Shakespeare we use is based on what sits in the bookroom. And, for many students, a mass-market paperback might work just fine, but, as Claire Walter points out, some students just don't "pick it right up" when it comes to reading and understanding Shakespeare. If students have access to a tablet or classroom computers, we can make available editions of Shakespeare enriched with multimedia features, not to mention links to supplemental information. Many paperback editions of parallel text and graphic novel versions are available in paperback and digital forms. We have potential resources to create appropriate "reading recipes," as Walter does for her students to maximize their experience with Shakespeare, but we may lack the budget to add those resources to our classroom toolkit. If budget is a stumbling block, consider exploring DonorsChoose, a nonprofit organization that allows teachers to pitch a project that needs funding, such as providing a set of graphic novels or a site license for SIB series titles. Your search for funding need not stop there. Seek out other local or national organizations that work to support various education initiatives. A robust range of resources at your disposal will allow you to create the best learning environment for your students. And you don't need to raise money to afford your own original copy of the First Folio of 1623. You've got a computer or tablet that can help you access that—at least in an open-source facsimile form.

Use Active Drama Approaches as Bell Ringers to Warm Up a Text

How Can Passive Students Transform into Active Participants?

This chapter offers practical activities with which to transform your students into active and engaged participants—*players*—in an ensemble, in a safe classroom performance space. The goal is not to transform students into actors but to help them develop a more expressive voice and a poised physical presence. As teachers, we need to create an environment in which students feel comfortable taking risks in order to grow in their understanding and appreciation of Shakespeare's plays. As you and your students work together, you are creating and building a strong collaborative team or ensemble. An NCTE Guideline recommends integration of *informal classroom drama* into ELA curricula, and defines these activities as "unrehearsed drama . . . a process of guided discovery led by the teacher for the benefits of the participants and not intended necessarily for an audience." The application of informal drama activities or theater games must be organic to the overall objectives of a unit or curricula. We want to stress the notion of *students as players*, since that approach fosters active engagement and leads to both the experiential and presentational types of knowing we examined in Chapter 2 (Heron and Reason).

A Rationale for Active Approaches in Your ELA Classroom

The continuing emphasis on active learning in the ELA classroom invites us to rethink how students develop a variety of skills to help them make meaning of rich texts. We also want to keep in mind Gardner's multiple intelligences theory in curriculum and unit planning, to tap into a variety of intelligences—including visual, musical, kinesthetic, and interpersonal—over the course of a class period, and not just to privilege linguistic intelligence. This approach to bell ringer activities promotes speaking, listening, and moving as crucial elements of the engagement process to bring a piece of literature to life by getting it into students' mouths and ears as well as onto their bodies. The transformation of a classroom into a playing space also suggests that something will happen. The act of performance, or *playing*, requires that something will be accomplished, something that is observable. When we invite all students to perform simultaneously, everyone is on a level playing field, and a teacher has the opportunity to observe the level of skill or understanding each student possesses at any given moment.

Teacher of the Bard Talk

In order to make this work, teachers must be willing to be vulnerable and to take the same risks we ask of our students. It took me a long time to develop the confidence to put myself out there and really model play for them. These types of interactions cannot be rehearsed, but rather are a spontaneous response to the text and to the students.

—JENNIFER BERTACCHI,
*Carleton Washburne Middle School;
ELA teacher*

If you have prior training or a natural affinity for these creative drama activities, feel free to go directly to the next chapter and dive right into the Folio technique. However, we strongly encourage you to examine the exercises provided in this chapter as they may enhance your own engagement toolbox and provide you with some fresh ideas promoting student focus, concentration, and directed energy in preparation for more sophisticated activities.

If you don't have any experience with theater games or improvisation techniques, don't feel intimidated. We encounter many teachers, in our classroom residencies and workshop experiences, who approach this work with trepidation, since they are not performers themselves and may not feel comfortable leading performance-based activities initially. You also may be slightly out of your comfort zone, but please do not let that stop you from trying. You can do this! You already motivate and inspire your students to tackle reading, writing, and critical thinking tasks that they would feel reticent to pursue on their own.

Student of the Bard Talk

One piece of advice I have is to make sure students are comfortable with the exercises you're doing. Theater games often require a lot of energy and the will to step out from the crowd. For some kids, this is so far out of their comfort zone it isn't even funny. So, encourage them to get involved, but these games don't really work unless everyone is willing to give themselves up to it.... Make learning fun and engaging.... Be flexible with every student.

—HAILEY KEENAN,
Adlai E. Stevenson High School

When your students first participate in this approach, they may feel reluctant as well. This is a vulnerable time for them. We are all familiar with students who are more comfortable hanging back, sometimes even hiding out, in the hopes of not participating. However, if you introduce the concept of *ensemble* to them gradually and acknowledge that everyone will be working on this new challenge together as one team with a common goal, you will achieve success. Many of our teacher partners find it helpful to share with their students that they also are taking a risk trying these active approaches with them. This should encourage students to begin to take some small risks and try some new things along with you. Activities that have students speak or move simultaneously can reduce natural performance anxiety. If you approach this work in a positive and energized way, your students will follow your lead and some will gradually take the lead themselves.

As we share these activities, we acknowledge our debt to our acting teachers, many workshop leaders, and the pioneering work of Viola Spolin and Augusto Boal, whose books provide a compendium of theater games and improvisation scenarios that form the basis of active drama approaches. Many of those activities have been adapted in Folger's Shakespeare Set Free series and Katherine S. McKnight's improvisation strategies to teach ELA content, so they may be familiar to you.

A New Approach to Bell Ringers: If "Readiness Is All," How and Where to Begin?

You might be wondering how you will carve out time to integrate these activities. We encourage you to use these activities as bell ringers to help students gather their focus and energy at the beginning of a class period. This would not be unlike using an entrance slip exercise. If you teach on a block schedule, these activities work very well to energize students and redirect their focus at any point in a longer class period. Our partner teachers have found success introducing these activities gradually to complement traditional bell ringers well before they begin a unit on Shakespeare that features more sustained speaking and performing activities. Students then will find the expectations to speak, move, and improvise part of their normal classroom routine. Now, you might be thinking, "I am teaching English, not drama," but the exercises presented here essentially foster public speaking skills and improved poise in front of an audience—skills that apply to a wide variety of situations students encounter both in and out of your ELA classroom.

Primed for Conversation, Ready for Recitation: "Speak the Speech . . . Trippingly on the Tongue"

This first set of exercises focus on students' speaking voices. In a time of texting over talking, some students literally have lost a speaking voice suitable for more than face-to-face interpersonal conversation. When have you asked students to speak up or to speak more distinctly during a large-class discussion? How often do students get a case of the giggles when they have to speak in front of their peers? And, since speaking and listening go hand in hand, these activities require students to listen actively as well.

The objectives for this set of activities are to help students to:

- limber up articulation for more precise pronunciation
- experiment with variations in pitch, pace, and volume
- gain confidence speaking aloud in a group and as a solo performer
- strive to be understood when they are speaking in class discussion or other performance activities

Vocal Exercise #1: Loosen Up Those Lips!

Preliminary Side Coaching
Asking students to close their eyes during this part of the exercise will lessen their temptation to laugh and not take this warm-up seriously.

Instructions
Introduce the exercise with the following instructions:

1. Let's wake up your mouth so you will be able to speak clearly and with precise articulation.

Continue with the following instructions:

2. Close your eyes. This will make you feel less self-conscious.
3. Let's wake up your tongue! First, stick it out as far as you can.
4. Then bring it back into your mouth. Repeat this action five to six times.
5. Move your tongue in a circular motion around your closed mouth and teeth for at least one full minute.
6. Let's wake up your mouth! Open your mouth as widely as you can—really stretch it out.
7. Now, pucker your mouth—make it as small as possible.

8. Do this open wide–pucker combination five to six more times, adding the following vocal sounds: when your mouth is open, say "AAHH"; when your mouth is puckered closed, say "OOOO."
9. Now imagine that you are chewing the biggest piece of gum in the world. For one minute, really chew to wake your mouth up.
10. Blow through your lips like you are imitating the sound of a motorcycle. You should feel your lips tingling as you do this.
11. Open your eyes, and let's get to work on adding some phrases.

Once your students have limbered up their lips, move directly into practicing a few simple tongue twisters, such as those listed below. Have students repeat the phrases with specific instructions from you to speak faster or slower, louder or softer, etc.:

- moonshine at noon time
- moaning and groaning in mellow tones
- many mighty mountains
- ringing things
- dumb dodos

Initially, you might introduce students to warming up their voices prior to class discussions and any other speaking activities. It is important to stick to a routine so students see this as a natural part of the speaking skills they are building in your class. Many teachers turn over leading these vocal warm-ups to their students.

Vocal Exercise #2: Tackling Tougher Tongue Twisters

Eventually you can add longer tongue twisters after students are comfortable with the first set of vocal warm-ups. Tongue twisters help to improve strong articulation and diction. Have students repeat each of the phrases listed below five times. And, since accuracy is more important than speed, have students begin by repeating a phrase slowly or even in vocal "slow motion" so they can practice clearly articulating each sound in the phrase. Then gradually increase the pace of their recitation.

Shorter Phrases for Practice

- kinky cookie
- eleven benevolent elephants
- red leather yellow leather
- unique New York
- toy boat
- abominable abdominals
- sushi chef

Sentences for Practice

- A big black bug bit a big black bean, which made the big black bean bleed.
- Susie sells seashells at the seashore.
- A skunk stood on a stump. The stump thunk the skunk stunk, but the skunk thunk the stump stunk.
- Moses supposes his toeses are roses, / But Moses supposes amiss. / For Moses, he knowses his toeses aren't roses / As Moses supposes his toeses is.

SIDE COACHING

Students will find these phrases funny and fun to recite. This, of course, is fine; however, this may mean that the point of doing these tongue twisters may get lost. Really focus on diction and articulation. For example, participants may get lazy saying "unique New York" five times. They should really stress and punch up those "k" sounds. You also will find that students know a few classroom-appropriate tongue twisters to contribute to the exercise.

Many of the well-known tongue twisters we offer here are found in Edith Skinner's *Speak with Distinction*, which might prove a useful resource to vary your vocal warm-up options. Lists of tongue twisters also are available online, and short passages from Dr. Seuss's books work well.

Vocal Exercise #3: Warming Up the Voice, Warming Up for the Bard

You can link vocal warm-ups to reciting lines from a specific work of literature, such as "It was the best of times, it was the worst of times" from *A Tale of Two Cities*. This strategy could be introduced well before your students study Shakespeare so that they are accustomed to playing with language in this manner by focusing carefully on an iconic line. This example quickly and memorably establishes the time period and makes powerful use of parallel structure at the beginning of Dickens's novel. In the following exercise, students are divided into groups depending on the number of words in the chosen "phrase of the day."

INSTRUCTIONS

1. After you divide students into groups, each student will be assigned one word of that phrase.
2. In small groups, students will practice reciting the phrase one word at a time, focusing on making the several voices blend into a seamless recitation of the line.
3. Once students have mastered speaking the phrase, instruct them to vary the speed, pitch, and tone: fast then slow, high then low, seriously then comically.

Initially have the groups recite their line simultaneously and then have each group "showcase" their approach individually to give students a taste of taking "center stage." You also could have all the groups work on the same line. Or you could have students take one line or sentence from a speech or passage, work on them individually, and then put those lines together to create a group recitation, one word at a time. Eventually introduce lines from Shakespeare that are fairly easy to understand, feature parallel structure that make them easy to remember, and rely on strong, regular iambic pentameter that makes the phrase more rhythmic (see Figure 3.1 for some suggestions). After students have mastered the word-by-word recitation, you can have them recite lines syllable by syllable for an added challenge. If you adopt the "phrase of the day" recitation, you can use the phrase as a discussion starter or journal entry allowing students to explore the phrase's meanings and implications, and this can be tied to whatever they are currently studying.

> **Teacher of the Bard Talk**
>
> Keeping students focused on the skills of these games is key—again, so the warm-ups do not turn into a performance or a "one-upping"...activity. Frankly, when that happens, the whole point of such warm-ups is lost. Students have to feel safe to get [or to] do something wrong in order to risk getting something more than just right, but something inspired.
>
> —CYNTHIA BURROWS,
> *Adlai E. Stevenson High School; drama and ELA teacher*

- Love all, trust a few, do wrong to none. (*All's Well That Ends Well* 1.1)
- Praising what is lost makes the remembrance dear. (*AWW* 5.3)
- Pity is the virtue of the law, and none but tyrants use it cruelly. (*Timon of Athens* 3.5)
- Like as the waves make towards the pebbled shore, / So do our minutes hasten to their end. (Sonnet 60)
- Mine honour is my life; both grow in one. Take honour from me, and my life is done. (*Richard II* 1.1)
- By the pricking of my thumbs / Something wicked this way comes. (*Mac.* 4.1)
- If it were done when 'tis done, then 'twere well / It were done quickly. (*Mac.* 1.7)

FIGURE 3.1. Options for Shakespeare's "phrase of the day."

Moving with Purpose and Poise: "Do Not Saw the Air Too Much"

Once students become comfortable performing the vocal warm-ups, you should begin to shift their attention to the expressiveness of their body. Some of these activities require a defined playing space, but don't let a cramped classroom prevent you from adapting these activities to your spatial limitations.

The objectives for this set of activities will help students to become aware of the body—how it works, how it feels, and how to prepare it for work—and to become alert to how the body and mind work together, and discover techniques that will provide the necessary energy with which to speak any text—improvised, contemporary, or Shakespearean.

Movement Exercise #1: Shake Out by Eight

This exercise helps foster body awareness as well as releasing any tension students might hold in their arms and legs. For many teachers, this is a great exercise to repeat if students lose momentum or focus in more complicated physical warm-ups. And this is an exercise that doesn't require students to push back their desks.

PREPARATION

Begin this exercise by having students stand up straight with their hands at their sides. Then have them reach their hands up to the ceiling and stretch out gently and return their hands back to their sides. Have students repeat the stretch several times, even encouraging them to get on their tippy toes. They can also imagine grasping on a rope overhead to vary their movements. You can bring students back to this stretch if you need them to refocus at any time.

Instructions

Tell students that you will be "counting loudly to eight." And add, "While I am counting, you will be moving either your hand or your leg." Demonstrate how this will work using these verbal cues:

- Say "1, 2, 3, 4, 5, 6, 7, 8" (shaking right hand).
- Say "1, 2, 3, 4, 5, 6, 7, 8" (shaking left hand).
- Say "1, 2, 3, 4, 5, 6, 7, 8" (shaking right leg).
- Say "1, 2, 3, 4, 5, 6, 7, 8" (shaking left leg).

After this, perform the same exercise, but count only to seven:

- Say "1, 2, 3, 4, 5, 6, 7" (shaking right hand).
- Say "1, 2, 3, 4, 5, 6, 7" (shaking left hand).
- Say "1, 2, 3, 4, 5, 6, 7" (shaking right leg).
- Say "1, 2, 3, 4, 5, 6, 7" (shaking left leg).

After this, perform the same exercise, but count only to six. Continue in this manner until you get down to counting only to the number one. When this happens, use the following verbal cues:

- Say "1" and shake your right hand.
- Say "2" and shake your left hand.
- Say "3" and shake your right leg.
- Say "4" and shake your left leg.
- Say "5" and shake your right hand.
- Say "6" and shake your left hand.
- Say "7" and shake your right leg.
- Say "8" and shake your left leg.
- Shout "Woo!" and jump.

After you demonstrate, repeat the counts and the movements with the students following along. Vary the tempo as you repeat for several rounds.

Side Coaching

Initially, keep the pace slow enough so students can maintain easy control of these movements.

Movement Exercise #2: Mirror Me

This is a common exercise found in many theater game books. It continues warming up the body as well as fostering concentration.

INSTRUCTIONS

You can begin having students mirror your movements as they did in the "Shake Out by Eight" exercise. This time, students don't need a count and movements aren't confined to just shaking hands and legs.

1. Begin with small gestures or movements that students can follow easily.
2. Once they are comfortable and proficient following your lead with small movements, begin to scale up those gestures and motions.
3. After trying this a few times, tell students they need to not only mirror your gestures and movements, but your facial expressions as well. Provide them with both subtle and exaggerated expressions to mirror.

If at any time students lose focus and get the giggles, return to "Shake Out by Eight" to reset the exercise.

VARIATIONS

Students should eventually mirror a partner, and eventually mirror in a group of three. When they get to this level, establish an "A" and "B" (and eventually "C") student for each group. This will allow you to determine who "leads" the movement. Eventually, students can be instructed to take and relinquish control spontaneously without your command. The pace of the mirroring can also be dictated by tapping out a rhythm or by using music that changes tempo.

This is a particularly good exercise to use at the midpoint of a class period if students need to regain focus or to switch gears.

Movement Exercise #3: "Marking" Up the Body

This exercise requires students to combine large movements with vocalization. Be prepared for them to feel particularly silly initially. "Shake Out by Eight" is a good way to energize them. If students have trouble, bring them back to focus by using the mirroring exercise as a fallback and then return to this exercise.

INSTRUCTIONS

1. First, imagine you have a permanent marker pen attached to one hand.
2. Draw numbers 1 to 10 with that hand while speaking these numbers aloud.
3. Speak at a normal volume and at a rate that matches your movements.
4. Next, imagine that you have a marker pen on your chest.
5. Draw numbers 1 to 10 with your chest while speaking these numbers aloud.
6. These actions should be performed slowly and with full voice.
7. Now, imagine that the marker pen is on your head.

Repeat the instructions, focusing their imagination on using the marker pen with their head.

8. This time, imagine that you have two marker pens, one on each elbow.
9. Repeat the exercise as described above; however, for this round, draw the letters of the alphabet from A to J.

Repeat the exercise as described above, focusing their imagination on using the marker pens with their elbows.

SIDE COACHING

Encourage the students to really use their whole body and their full voice. Encourage them to be specific with their "marker" pen and remind them that their voice "draws" along with their body. So, if they begin at the top and "draw" down for number one, their voice should start at the top of their range and work down to its lower range as they "draw" the number 1, and so forth. The same should be done when "drawing" letters of the alphabet. Students may need to be coached to keep breathing through their movements.

The next three activities require students to push back the desks to create a playing space.

Movement Exercise #4: My Name, My Action

In this activity, students begin to take center stage speaking and performing by responding to a simple set of directions: "speak your name," "identify something you like to do" (this can be serious, silly), and "perform that action." Taking center stage in this exercise is very brief and hopefully therefore nonthreatening.

INSTRUCTIONS

Have students stand in a circle. Then start the exercise by issuing the following instructions.

1. Begin by saying your name and what you like to do. For example: "My name is *Juan* and I like to *eat pasta*."
2. When you say what you like to do, combine it with an appropriate action to act out the phrase. Here, it would be twirling and slurping pasta.

Go around the circle: each person says their name, states what they like to do, and performs that action. Then go around the circle a second time: each person repeats the sequence again, but this time the whole group will say, "That is *Juan* and he likes to *eat pasta*" and pantomime the related action for each classmate.

If you have students who respond well to vocal bell ringers early in the year, this is obviously a great icebreaker and a way for students to learn their classmates' names.

> **Student of the Bard Talk**
>
> In "Wait for the 'Yes,'" one person starts and says someone in the circle's name. The person called out then responds with "yes." As soon as the person who initially called the name hears the "yes," they walk to the other person's spot, and the second person repeats the process, calling someone else's name. This game builds patience and listening. More steps can be added to enhance other important qualities, like enhancing eye contact by taking out the names and only using eye contact. There are so many more [warm-ups] that have taught me so many skills that helped me engage in classwork ... because I have enhanced my skills, such as eye contact, energy, listening, teamwork, collaboration, physicality, and more.
>
> —ABBY SOKOL,
> *Adlai E. Stevenson High School*

Movement Exercise #5: Walk the Space

This exercise can be accomplished with or without pushing back the desks and chairs.

INSTRUCTIONS

1. Tell the group to walk the classroom space slowly to explore it.
   - They must not walk in circles, but walk with purpose as if they are walking to get to class or meet a classmate.

- They also should walk with their heads up looking carefully at the details of the room. Ask them to pick a focal point and walk toward it rather than toward a classmate.
2. As students are walking, tell them to vary their pattern within the space.
3. Instruct the group to walk according to the number that you call out, with 10 being the fastest and 1 the slowest. Instruct students that they cannot run at 8–9–10.

Variations

- Walk the space shaking hands with other players in your path, not letting go of a grasped hand until the player finds another.
- Walk the space and make eye contact with another player.
- If you are in a very large classroom, walk the space and shake hands with players you meet and verbally greet them.

Of all the variations suggested for this exercise, the one that requires students to make contact is particularly important. Students can have difficulty making and maintaining eye contact in discussion, public speaking, and drama activities. If you sequence this exercise with "Mirror Me," they have had experience sustaining eye contact with one or two partners.

Movement Exercise #6: Making Machines

This physical warm-up encourages creativity and requires both cooperation and collaboration. It works best if students combine vocalization—sounds or words—to accompany their movements. The exercise also requires students to make judgments about how a gesture adds to the existing "machine," which anticipates more complex on-the-spot decisions in other activities.

Instructions

1. Ask your students to stand in a circle. Or you have them stand at their desks and establish the playing space at the front of the classroom.
2. Select one member of the group (Player A) to move to the established playing space. Ask Player A to make a simple repeatable gesture.

Player A could add a sound to their movement. Sounds could be made vocally (whistles, groans) or physically (clapping, stomping, slapping).

3. Select another student (Player B) to come into the playing space. Instruct Player B to create a different repetitive gesture (and sound). They should "attach" in some way to Player A's movement.
4. Continue this process to use everyone in the class or to fill up the playing space.
5. Players must maintain their original gesture and sound throughout the exercise. The entire group is thereby making one large "Rube Goldberg machine."

SIDE COACHING

You might want to "freeze" the machine and reactivate it if students fall out of synchronization or lose concentration. Feel free to instruct students to slow down or speed up their movement.

VARIATION WITH A DASH OF SHAKESPEAREAN INSULTS

Provide students with a word to accompany the movement they add to the machine. You can suggest onomatopoeic words like *hiss, bang, plop,* etc. This approach can be combined with the study of any type of poetry. For future rounds, provide students with words that are commonly used by Shakespeare. Use a list of words he used to create insults, which is easily found online or, for example, in Folger's Shakespeare Set Free: Sourcebooks for Classroom Teachers series (see www.folger.edu/shakespeare-set-free). Debrief this variation of the "Making Machines" exercise by asking students how the word they were given informed the action they chose to perform.

Beyond the Bell Ringer: "Suit the Action to the Word, the Word to the Action"

These exercises will go beyond the time limit of a typical bell ringer and will introduce more sustained improvisation skills, building on the previous physical warm-ups. The first activity asks students to match an action to a specific adverb. This exercise might seem fairly natural for ELA teachers new to this bell ringer approach since it focuses on an often-neglected part of speech. The second and third activities introduce language and pieces of action from Shakespeare's work that fit nicely into prereading activities to build curiosity around learning about the Bard in general and anticipation for reading a specific play.

These activities require students to take "center stage" individually, in pairs, or in groups. Some students will still find those circumstances uncomfortable or even threatening. We feel it is critical that all students experience being center stage. Mixing volunteers with students who tend to hang back and do not get involved offers the best scenario for success. Often, the longer a reluctant student waits, the more intimidatingly that performance experience looms. Certainly you will need to step in from time to time to support anxious students. It helps to suggest they close their eyes and focus on their breathing to regain composure as best they can.

The objectives for this set of activities will help students to:

- use appropriate vocal and physical strategies to express an idea or to follow a set of performance instructions
- take center stage to complete a performance task with increasingly better focus and poise
- improvise appropriate actions and/or dialogue to match a set of verbal instructions
- understand the importance of "give and take" behavior when performing an improvised exercise with a partner

Diving into the Fishbowl of Life

You can use an engagement strategy called "The Fishbowl of Life" to maximize active participation and minimize passive observation. Set a plastic fishbowl containing numbered slips of paper at the classroom door. Each time the students come into the room, they choose a number from "The Fishbowl of Life." When it is time for students to "volunteer," call out a number. The student with that number then participates. This takes out the awkwardness of the dreaded question, "Can I have a volunteer?" Then simply call out, "Number 7, you are up." Students then will expect to participate during that class period.

Establishing audience approval norms is critical as well. Instead of clapping at the end of a performance, let students know they can snap their fingers at any time to show their approval. You should model this behavior so it catches on with your students. It is also great for expressing affirmation during class discussions and is less intrusive than clapping. Students have remarked that snapping instead of clapping is "kinda cool."

Improv Exercise #1: "Adverbly" Done (Basic-Level Improv Skills)

PREPARATION

On slips of paper, create a pool of adverbs (e.g., *confidently, reluctantly, angrily, slowly*) and a pool of simple actions (e.g., dance, sing, eat, work out with weights, read a book, make a sandwich) that can be easily pantomimed. Place the slips with adverbs in one box, bag, or fishbowl, and put the slips with the simple actions in another container.

This is an exercise for which students can remain at their desks, with a performance space established at the front of the room.

INSTRUCTIONS

1. Player A leaves the room.
2. While Player A is not present, Player B draws an adverb from the pool and shares it with the class.
3. Player A returns to the group, draws an "action" from the pool, and asks Player B to perform that physical action in the manner of the adverb's meaning.
4. Player B performs the action to reflect the meaning of the adverb chosen by the group. Examples might be "Dance for me" (shyly), "Run for me" (anxiously), "Sing for me" (threateningly), etc.
5. After Player B performs the action, Player A tries to guess which adverb was applied to the action.
6. If Player A doesn't guess the correct adverb, Player C could perform the same action based on the same adverb to see if Player A can make a correct guess. Or Player A could select a different action that Player C would perform applying the same adverb.

Have students engage in one to three rounds of this activity over a week. You can place a time restriction on the student who performs the action as well as the time it takes to elicit responses from the rest of the class so that this activity sticks to the allotted bell ringer time. This exercise creates an engaging "teachable moment" to address the function of adverbs in sentence construction and in description specificity. Sometimes, it evolves into a vocabulary lesson too, depending on the adverbs included in the pool.

Improv Exercise #2: Shakespeare's Charades (Basic-Level Improv Skills)

The clues you use for charades can certainly come from whatever shared knowledge you want to highlight, but beginning a unit on Shakespeare, or any literary work, can preview what's ahead in addition to assessing what students already know. Since most students have played charades, this exercise is a less threatening way for them to take center stage. And, as with the "Adverbly Done" exercise, you can facilitate several short rounds as a bell ringer over the course of a week.

Preparation
On slips of paper, feature the titles of plays by Shakespeare, famous lines by Shakespeare, famous characters of Shakespeare, etc. Place the slips in any type of container.

Preparation Tip
Since it is difficult to fully understand the depth or breadth of students' knowledge of Shakespeare's plays and characters, you might want them to generate names of plays, characters, and famous lines well in advance of introducing this exercise.

Instructions

1. Have a student volunteer draw one of the slips from the pool of Shakespeare-focused charade options.
2. That student then has to act out the title, quote, or character listed on the slip of paper to the entire class or to their team. They are given two minutes to try to get their classmates to guess correctly. The player may not speak, sing, hum, or make any noises at all. They also may not mouth the words to their group or write out letters or numbers in the air.

Some common charades signals to review include:

- opening palms to signify a book
- pretending to use an old-fashioned movie camera to signify a film
- ear-tugging signifies "sounds like"

- holding a number of fingers up in the air to let the group know how many words are on the slip of paper
- holding a number of fingers against the forearm to signify the number of syllables in a word

Reframing popular party games or playground activities as performance-based bell ringers can draw even reluctant students into participating due to their familiarity, though it is critical that students are aware of how these reframed games serve a pedagogical purpose.

Teacher of the Bard Talk

I always begin by having my middle school students create Shakespearean insults by combining one word from each of three columns printed on a worksheet. Once completed, I get them on their feet and have them "hurl" them at one another in a round-robin format [as they deliver their newly created insults]. If I have a particularly shy group, I bring in the ball, have one student shout the insult, and then [I] throw the ball to another person, who, in turn, shouts [their] insult and throws the ball, and so on. This really wakes them up and lets them know that this is to be a playful experience.

—JENNIFER BERTACCHI,
Carleton Washburne Middle School; ELA teacher

Improv Exercise #3: Oh!, Why?, Sorry!— The Three-Word "Scene" (Advanced-Level Improv Skills)

This activity introduces students to improvising a scene based on a set of instructions that restricts the language they are able to use but does not restrict how they use their bodies and the available space to develop their scenarios. You can introduce this exercise by using simple, generic scenarios and then come back to it as part of the preparation for reading a specific play or introducing key actions before reading a specific act. This strategy encourages students to experience what characters face to promote greater empathy and to foster critical thinking.

SETUP

Students create a simple, very short scene using the three words *Oh!*, *Why?*, and *Sorry!* They will have to create the "Who," "What," "Why," "Where," and "When" for their characters based on a simple scenario. It will be up to the scene partners to determine where they will place the three words when they act out the scenario. When trying this exercise for the first time, start simply for best results. You also might have a sample scenario on video to play for students so they have a concrete example of how this improvisation works. So, for example:

- Player A—A parent is on their way home from work with groceries. They did not have the opportunity to get to the grocery store over the

weekend and now they need to rush to the store to get ingredients to make dinner for the family.
- Player B—A student is late for an evening class and is trying to make it on time. This is the night of the final exam, and, if they are late, they will not be able to take the exam.

Here is how that set of instructions played out in performance:

1. Both Player A and Player B are walking to their desired destinations from opposite directions.
2. Player B bangs into Player A, knocking the groceries to the ground: breaking eggs, spilling milk, etc.
3. Player A says, "Oh!" (as a result of being hit).
4. Both look at the groceries on the ground.
5. Player A then says, "Why?"
6. Player B says, "Sorry!" and continues to rush away to class.
7. Player A stands and thinks about the consequences of what has just transpired and cleans up the mess on the ground.

Preparation Tip

Create scenarios that pair up characters with conflicting objectives. What does each character need to accomplish and how does the other character get in their way?

Instructions

1. Students will need to pair up.
2. Distribute slips of paper with a scenario that assigns students their roles and scenario.
3. The students need to plot out the beginning, middle, and end of this very short scene; however, they can use only the words *Oh!*, *Why?*, and *Sorry!* They are allowed to speak those three words only once between the two of them. How they divide up the three words is up to them.
4. Give the students at least five to ten minutes to work on this very short "scene."

5. Have students showcase their scene, but they do not share their set of instructions with the class.

6. Debrief each scene by posing the following questions:
   - Where did this scene take place?
   - What activities occupied the characters?
   - What objective did each character want to achieve in this scene? How did the other character provide an obstacle for achieving the objective?
   - How did using the three words help to clarify the situation?
   - How did the placement of the three words build tension or conflict between the characters?
   - What could have been clearer in the way the situation was presented?

VARIATION

Base the scenarios on the piece of literature students will be reading. This is an effective way to preview the basic conflicts characters will face. Students are able to explore characters' motives and circumstances before they dive into the particulars of that short story, novel, or play. Here are a few scenarios based on *Romeo and Juliet*:

- Neighborhood rivals meet on the street and argue over their turf rights.
- A teenage boy is teased by his friend about the serious crush he has on a girl.
- A teenage boy and his friend decide to crash a party that might place them in an awkward, even dangerous, situation.
- Boy meets girl at the party he crashes, falls in love at first sight, but can't stay there with her because he wasn't invited in the first place.
- Boy tries to get to know girl better under the pressure of being discovered despite some physical distance between them.
- Mother tells her daughter that a recently offered marriage proposal must be accepted. The daughter reluctantly accepts knowing she can't go through with the wedding.
- A teenage girl asks an adult confidante to help her deceive her parents in the name of love.

- A teenage boy asks a priest to perform a secret marriage ceremony that might resolve the long-standing conflict between the two families—or make it worse.

You can break down any literary work into these short scenarios. As mentioned earlier, you can use dramatic moments drawn from a play (or a novel) as a means to investigate characters' motivations before students reach a certain point in that literary narrative. Students can be given the same scenarios, so they can showcase similar and different approaches to the same situation. In this way, they have been primed to analyze characters' reactions and responses in a given situation as presented by the author.

> **Teacher of the Bard Talk**
>
> [While] students can get a bit silly together [with improv activities],... they can relax [and focus] enough to risk the terrible truth of admitting they might not know or understand something, which opens up the community of the class to growth. Everyone in the space benefits from the comfort and safety of the ensemble by fully contributing to the ensemble.
>
> —Cynthia Burrows,
> *Adlai E. Stevenson High School; drama and ELA teacher*

Rethinking Bell Ringers to Activate Speaking, Listening, and Body Awareness Skills

Once again we want to affirm that the goal of integrating these activities in an ELA classroom is not to produce student actors in the way a drama class would. Instead, we see these activities as a means to help students gain poise in using their voices and bodies in more purposeful ways. This approach cultivates skills found across the linguistic, interpersonal, kinesthetic, and musical intelligences spectrum. The exercises presented in this chapter can be combined easily with those described in Chapter 1 to expand the range of active approaches bell ringers.

In addition, you should consider adding these titles to your resource shelf for many more activity options: Augusto Boal's *Games for Actors and Non-Actors*, Katherine McKnight and Mary Scruggs's *The Second City Guide to Improv in the Classroom: Using Improvisation to Teach Skills and Improve Learning in Content Areas*, and Viola Spolin's *Improvisation for the Theater: A Handbook of Teaching and Directing Techniques*.

By reducing performance anxiety, a teacher's toolkit can then include a variety of improvisational and text-based activities to help students try on the behaviors of characters in one of Shakespeare's plays, which makes the language less remote and the play's central conflicts more accessible. Students can transfer these speaking, listening, and body awareness skills to a variety of situations in and out of the classroom that put them center stage in everyday large- and small-group settings. These activities also prepare students to fulfill the speaking and listening strands identified by Common Core State Standards for high school that focus on preparation for discussion, collaborative engagement, and adaptive use of language to fit their academic circumstances.

Sort Out Language Clues Using the Folio Technique

What Is the Folio Technique? How Does It Work?

Shakespeare developed what we call the *Folio technique* to aid his actors. With the rigorous performance schedule of the repertory system during his day, there simply was no time for these actors to rehearse as we do today. Therefore, Shakespeare created a system that quickly and efficiently provided an actor with the entirety of their character. We must remember that actors were not given a complete copy of the play. They were given *cue scripts* containing their lines and the three- or four-word cue that preceded the speaking of their line. An actor probably would have experienced the complete play for the first time during the first full performance in front of the Globe audience. How were actors able to perform these plays effectively? Shakespeare helped his actors by placing essential *clues* directly into the text. The actors would not be able to know the complete play or the true essence of the character they were playing using a cue script. Shakespeare left clues in the text to help an actor achieve the correct emotional state of their character and the high stakes of the character's conflict. Thus, if we apply this performance-based technique to your work with your students, they—just like Shakespeare's actors—will begin to experience the play on a physical and emotional level. Knowing how to recognize and understand these clues, your students' reading fluency, comprehension, and understanding also will increase dramatically.

Over the next three chapters, we present an approach to the Folio technique as it helps students to navigate the conventions of Early Modern English, to understand blank verse, and to analyze characters' use of rhetorical strategies. We address how basic, intermediate, and advanced Folio technique skills can be integrated into prereading, while reading, and in post-reading activities tailored to students' reading levels and prior experience with Shakespeare. Let's begin by examining the Folio technique's basic skills to support the prereading process in an ELA classroom and demystify troublesome aspects of Early Modern English.

Previewing "Weird Words" with Strange Spellings and Even Stranger Meanings

Basically, the Folio technique helps students to access a specific set of language decoding strategies to prepare them to read, understand, and enjoy any of Shakespeare's plays. Previewing a play with a single speech, part of a speech, or sonnet will familiarize students with conventions of Renaissance or Early Modern English spelling, pronouns, and vocabulary, which make the text distinct from contemporary speech. Instead of students feeling overwhelmed by the strangeness of Early Modern English conventions, this strategy will encourage them to become the "text detectives" we introduced in Chapter 1, unearthing and activating language clues left by Shakespeare. You can choose a speech from the play they will study or select one from another source that allows you to work through the Folio technique language clues. Using that text nugget from the First Folio presents Shakespeare, in a sense, at his most unusual and even "exotic." Even if students aren't reading a play in total from the First Folio, this experience helps them adjust to the decoding challenges present even in a modern, edited version. Remember that we recommended, in Chapter 2, that excerpts from the First Folio work effectively as a supplement to any mass-market edition of Shakespeare as well as with parallel text versions and graphic adaptations.

Early Modern Spelling and Pronunciation in the First Folio

When we start with a piece of text from the First Folio, we need to note that Shakespeare often used existing or created his own variant spellings. The English language was not standardized then in the way we understand that concept today. As he was writing with his actors in mind, it is helpful to remember that often he spelled words the way he wanted them to sound when spoken by an actor. Shakespeare many times uses *phonetic spelling* rather than strictly *variant spelling*. Once you speak the word as he spelled it, you may find a crucial acting choice or clue. In *Henry V* (3.2), for example, the original First Folio spellings reveal the pronunciation of the various regional dialects of the men fighting with Henry, so each soldier's land of origin is apparent in their speech:

> Scot.   I say gudday, Captaine *Fluellen*.
> Welch. Godden to your Worship, good Captaine *James*.

GOWER. How now Captain *Mackmorrice*, haue you
quit the Mynes? haue the Pioners giuen o're?

IRISH. By Chrish Law tish ill done: the Worke ish
giue ouer, the Trompet sound the Retreat. By my Hand
I sweare, and my fathers Soule, the Worke ish ill done:
it ish giue ouer: I would have blowed vp the Towne,
so Chrish saue me law, in an houre. O tish ill done, tish ill
done: by my Hand tish ill done.

WELCH. Captain *Mackmorrice*, I beseech you now,
will you voutsafe me, looke you, a few disputations with
you, as partly touching or concerning the disciplines of
the Warre, the Roman Warres, in the way of Argument,
looke you, and friendly communication: partly to satisfie
my Opinion, and partly for the satisfaction, looke you, of
my Mind: as touching the direction of the Militarie discipline, that is the Point.

SCOT. It sall be vary gud, gud feith, gud Captens bath,
and I sall quit you with gud leue, as I may pick occasion:
that sall I mary.

Standardizing the spelling to make this exchange more understandable for modern readers would miss the point that Henry's "band of brothers" boldly represents the breadth of Britain. Most modern editions will specify the desired accent for a character in the stage directions rather than through idiosyncratic spelling.

Spelling for Emphasis

In the next example, from *Richard II* (3.3), the various spellings of the word *we* (the Royal "we") are notable. In this case, spelling doesn't vary to indicate how to pronounce a word but changes the emphasis or meaning of the word in its application and context:

RICHARD. **Wee** are amaz'd, and thus long haue **we** stood
To watch the fearefull bending of thy knee,
Because **we** thought our selfe thy lawfull King:
And if **we** be, how dare thy ioynts forget
To pay their awfull dutie to our presence?
If **we** be not, shew vs the Hand of God,
That hath dismiss'd vs from our Stewardship,

> For well **wee** know, no Hand of Blood and Bone
> Can gripe the sacred Handle of our Scepter,
> Vnlesse he doe prophane, steale, or vsurpe.

Richard uses *Wee, we, we, we, we,* and *wee,* in that order. Modern editions will regularize and print all as *we.* However, when an actor uses the First Folio spellings, we see that Richard is stressing two of those *wes* in a much stronger way. The variations in spelling here help map out options for what the actor can play and provides the reader with a glimpse into Richard's understanding of his power and kingship.

Some of these words indeed could be actual misspellings, as Shakespeare was still experimenting with language; however, a pattern does emerge. Often, the printers shoulder much of the blame for hard-to-explain variant spelling, though Shakespeare interchanged certain letters from what we use today. Let's take a look at Prince Escalus's final speech of *Romeo and Juliet* (5.3), as it showcases these interchanged letter patterns:

> PRINCE.   A glooming peace this morning with it brings,
> The Sunne for forrow will not fhew his head;
> Go hence, to haue more talke of thefe fad things,
> Some fhall be pardon'd, and fome punifhed.
> For neuer was a Storie of more Wo,
> Then this of *Iuliet,* and her *Romeo.*

The first of these discoveries is that he used the symbol **f** for the letter *s.* This can be seen in the words *forrow* (sorrow), *fhew* (shew / show), *thefe* (these), *fad* (sad), *fhall* (shall), *fome* (some), and *punifhed* (punished).

The second of these discoveries is that he interchanged **u** for *v.* This can be seen in the word *vp* (up) in another example from *Romeo and Juliet* (1.1):

> BENVOLIO.   Part Fooles, put vp your Swords, you know not
>   what you do.

The third of these discoveries is that he interchanged **i** for *j.* This can be seen in the word *Iuliet* (Juliet), for example, in 1.3:

> CAPULET'S WIFE.   Marry that marry is the very theame
>   I came to talke of, tell me daughter *Iuliet,*
>   How stands your disposition to be Married?

When working with the First Folio or any Early Modern English document, your eye will become accustomed to these slight differences quickly. That said, some of our partner teachers feel these variant spellings present too great a difference between an excerpt from the First Folio and their classroom edition even to examine them in a brief prereading activity.

If you feel that it is not helpful for your students to sort through the variant spellings, you should "edit" a First Folio excerpt by regularizing the spelling before sharing the text with them. Please don't hesitate to be your own editor. Using the regularized spelling admittedly will help students speak lines and passages with less hesitation. Some partner teachers have students identify the variant spelling and "correct" it as a class. We offer an activity later in the chapter that links "correcting" Early Modern spelling with the analysis of other language features that reveal Shakespeare's characterization strategies.

To Voice or Not to Voice Ending Syllables

Even if you don't choose to use the First Folio version of a speech, students often do complain about the odd endings to some words in any edition of the Bard. For example, do we pronounce the extra syllable or not? Well, *that* is the question! Exploring the many modern editions of Shakespeare's work, you will find a variety of strategies to address Early Modern suffix patterns. Which is correct? If we look in the First Folio, Shakespeare makes this clear to us in a very simple way: if you are to sound the extra syllable, he wrote it in. If you are not to sound the extra syllable, he took it out.

Unvoiced Syllable

- -**'d** and -**'st**—for example, *banish'd, know'st, thron'd, see'st*

In these example four words, we would not pronounce the extra syllable because Shakespeare did not write it.

Voiced Syllable

- -**ed** and -**est**—for example, *banished, knowest, throned, seest*

Teacher of the Bard Talk

Kevin allowed me to see the teaching of Shakespeare as an activity akin to doing an excavation of an ancient Greco-Roman landmark in Alexandria. He reassured teachers like me who feel compelled to have all the answers to make Shakespeare a collective excavation in the classroom. His approach allowed me to relax more and focus on the purpose of reading Shakespeare in the first place, which is to understand and appreciate the beauty of language and the human condition.

—RITA GÖNDÖCS,
World Language Academy; ELA teacher

In these four words, though, we *would* pronounce the extra syllable, because Shakespeare spelled it out for us.

Shakespeare provided us with a clean, clear, simple, and concise way to understand those odd, "old-timey" suffixes. "Thank you, Bill" for clearing that up!

Sorting through Early Modern Pronoun Clues

Our teaching partners have shared that many students experience some stress and confusion when encountering the second-person pronouns used in Shakespeare. *Thee* and *thou* versus *you* and *your* cause many students to stumble and wonder what the difference is between them. However, once the students are introduced to the concept of the second-person pronoun and *why* it is used in a particular way, the moments become more meaningful and exciting as they discover that a character is *using* language to achieve a particular result from another character on stage. During the Elizabethan period, there was a difference between the use of the pronouns *thee/thou* and *you/your* and this difference revealed the intimacy that people shared. While this distinction no longer exists in modern English speech, this idea is reflected in the works of Shakespeare and provides important clues. The Elizabethans used *thee/thou* to represent an informal (more intimate) relationship to another person, while they used *you/your* to represent a formal relationship. Conversely, our students today feel that *thee/thou* is very formal or poetic—or too "old timey"—and thus it skews their reading of the text.

Let's look at the first time that Romeo and Juliet meet and speak at the Capulet ball (1.5), and examine the use of their pronouns:

ROMEO. If **I** prophane with **my** vnworthiest hand,
This holy shrine, the gentle sin is this,
My lips to blushing Pilgrims did ready stand,
To smooth that rough touch, with a tender kisse.

JULIET. Good Pilgrime,
You do wrong **your** hand too much.
Which mannerly devotion shewes in this,
For Saints haue hands, that Pilgrims hands do tuch,
And palme to palme, is holy Palmers kisse.

ROMEO. Haue not Saints lips, and holy Palmers too?

JULIET. I Pilgrim, lips that **they** must vse in prayer.

ROMEO. O then deare Saint, let lips do what hands do,
　　　　They pray (grant **thou**) least faith turne to dispaire.

JULIET. Saints do not moue,
　　　　Though grant for prayers sake.

ROMEO. Then moue not while **my** prayers effect **I** take:
　　　　Thus from **my** lips, by thine **my** sin is purg'd.

JULIET. Then haue **my** lips the sin that **they** haue tooke.

ROMEO. Sin from **my** lips? O trespasse sweetly vrg'd:
　　　　Giue me **my** sin againe.

JULIET. **You** kisse by'th'booke.

Notice how Juliet uses the formal *you* when addressing Romeo. Romeo then introduces the pronoun *thou* when he wishes to kiss Juliet. He is longing for a more intimate relationship with her. Even though they kiss, Juliet still insists on using the more formal pronoun *you*. She's not quite ready to move to a more intimate relationship with him at this time. However, once we get to the balcony scene (2.2), take a look at how many times both characters use the intimate pronouns *thee/thou*. Juliet desires a much more intimate relationship with Romeo by this point.

ROMEO. O wilt **thou** leaue **me** so vnsatisfied?

JULIET. What satisfaction can'st **thou** haue to night?

ROMEO. Th'exchange of **thy** Loues faithfull vow for mine.

JULIET. **I** gaue **thee mine** before **thou** did'st request it:
　　　　And yet **I** would it were to giue againe.

　　Students will quickly recognize the importance of this wonderful clue from Shakespeare and begin to look for it throughout the rest of their study of the text in order to gauge the familiarity or formality of characters' relationship to one another. And most modern editions retain the differentiation of second-person formal and informal pronouns.
　　These excerpts from *Romeo and Juliet* can be used as "stand-alone" examples to reduce student confusion about pronouns. If students are studying this play and they encounter these stumbling blocks, you can use these teachable moments to help students understand the various pronouns in context. You should not feel everything must be front-loaded in the prereading process when introducing Folio technique basics.

Pronouns Used Strategically

The use of pronouns becomes even more interesting when a character switches from formal to informal and then back to formal within the same speech, scene, etc. Barry Edelstein, in his book *Thinking Shakespeare*, suggests we ask the probing question, "Why is this character using these specific words right now?" (41). A great example can be found in *As You Like It* (1.3), when Duke Frederick enters to banish Rosalind from the court. This exchange between the Duke and his daughter Celia is an incredible barometer of their relationship, which is made clear through the deft use of pronouns.

> DUKE. **She** is too subtile for **thee**, and **her** smoothnes;
> **Her** verie silence, and **her** patience,
> Speake to the people, and **they** pittie **her**:
> **Thou** art a foole, **she** robs **thee** of **thy** name,
> And **thou** wilt show more bright, & seem more vertuous
> When **she** is gone: then open not **thy** lips
> Firme, and irreuocable is **my** doombe,
> Which **I** haue past vpon **her**, **she** is banish'd.
>
> CELIA. Pronounce that sentence then on me **my** Leige,
> **I** cannot liue out of **her** companie.
>
> DUKE. **You** are a foole: **you** Neice prouide **your** selfe,
> If **you** out-stay the time, vpon **mine** honor,
> And in the greatnesse of **my** word **you** die.
> *Exit Duke, &c.*

One can visualize the Duke pulling his daughter away from Rosalind to try to manipulate her to get her on his side. He is using the more intimate pronoun *thee*. This doesn't work, as Celia continues not only to defend Rosalind but then suggests that he banish her as well. So the Duke changes to the more formal pronoun *you*, thus shutting the door on the relationship with his daughter. Both women decide to flee the court. Once again, "Thank you, Bill!," this time for helping us understand that shift in allegiances through the use of the humble pronoun.

Early Modern Words and Their Definitions

All of the choices actors make playing a role arise out of a careful and specific analysis of the text. We should never assume we know what the words mean.

Characters *need* the words they speak in order to *effect change* in another character on stage. Otherwise, they would remain silent and thus unfulfilled in most of their objectives. Again, we continue to ask the probing question, "Why must this character use *these* words *now*?" It is estimated that Shakespeare added 1,500 words to our English language. Words spoken by the character are specifically chosen in order to get what they want. Words articulate intentions as well as the tactics to achieve those intended aims. If a specific word he needed did not exist, Shakespeare probably created it for a specific character in a particular moment to effect change in another specific character on stage. Therefore, we need to know exactly what we are saying at *all* times. Again, in the spirit of becoming text detectives, entertaining and investigating context clues lead students to defining an unfamiliar word, but, other times, they need an authoritative source—and that source might not always be your classroom edition's footnotes. When we need to discover what these words meant to the Elizabethans in a more comprehensive manner, there are several recommended sources we can use and many of them are online:

- Alexander Schmidt's *Shakespeare Lexicon: A Complete Dictionary of All the English Words, Phrases and Constructions in the Works of the Poet*—this source has been around for a long time (it was first published in 1874) and, now available online as part of Tufts University's Perseus Digital Library project, remains an excellent resource for discovering what each word meant during Shakespeare's day.
- The "Glossary" on David Crystal and Ben Crystal's Shakespeare's Words website—this is also an excellent resource for discovering the Elizabethan definitions of words, and is less intimidating on the eye.
- *Shakespeare's Bawdy: A Literary and Psychological Essay and a Comprehensive Glossary*—Shakespeare had a lively and curious interest in sex and there is a lot of sexual innuendo buried in his texts; Eric Partridge's book defines the sexual connotation of the words of Shakespeare.
- *Shakespeare A to Z*—Charles Boyce's book is like an encyclopedia; each play has an entry that provides an excellent scene-by-scene synopsis as well as scholarship about the play; each character in the canon also has an entry.
- Shakespeare Pro—this app from PlayShakespeare.com includes the complete works of Shakespeare (his plays, sonnets, and poems) as well as access to Shakespeare's Words.

Student of the Bard Talk

Students will always encounter language that they aren't comfortable with in academic texts, old[er] fiction, and foreign languages. Reading Shakespeare is an entertaining way to develop skills that can be applied in every kind of reading [challenge]....Many of the plays I've read ask to what extent an individual can pursue ambition morally. Shakespeare wrote plays that gave women status and ... minorities humanity in a time that many didn't.

—LAURA THORNBURG,
Adlai E. Stevenson High School

At various times in this book, we suggest print resources you might want to have on hand in your classroom so students can easily consult them to supplement information provided by the footnotes in their classroom editions. Allowing students to investigate various scholarly opinions helps them discriminate between authoritative sources. You will be surprised when they develop their own preferences, declaring, for example, "Let's go *Shakespeare A to Z* on this one!" Or assign a different student each day to be the "Shakespeare pro" and have them consult *Shakespeare's Words* on the app when word meaning questions arise.

Folio Language Clue: Key Words and Their Early Modern Meanings

Let's look at an example of a word commonly used today that takes on different meanings through Shakespeare's application in a single speech. In line 7 of our example from *Romeo and Juliet* (3.3, with cuts), we have the word *mean* repeated twice:

>
> ROMEO. 'Tis Torture and not mercy, heauen is here
> Where *Iuliet* liues, and euery Cat and Dog,
> And little Mouse, euery vnworthy thing
> Liue here in Heauen and may looke on her,
> . . . .
> But *Romeo* may not, hee is banished.   5
> Had'st thou no poyson mixt, no sharpe ground knife,
> No sudden **meane** of death, though nere so **meane**,
> But banished to kill me? Banished?
> O Frier, the damned vse that word in hell:
> Howlings attends it, how hast thou the hart   10
> Being a Diuine, a Ghostly Confessor,
> A Sin-Absoluer, and my Friend profest:
> To mangle me with that word, banished?

As mentioned, we should never assume the meaning of words. If we do, we risk losing the true intent and the deeper meaning within the text. If you look up the word *mean* in the *Shakespeare Lexicon and Quotation Dictionary*, you will discover both meanings of this word:

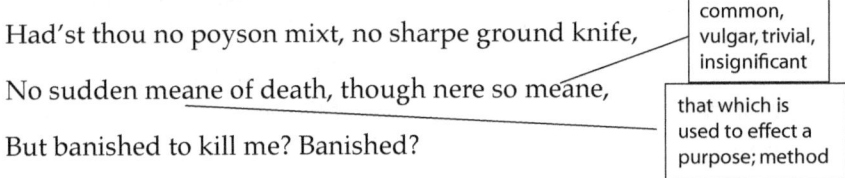

Had'st thou no poyson mixt, no sharpe ground knife,

No sudden meane of death, though nere so meane,

But banished to kill me? Banished?

Knowing what these words meant to the Elizabethans gives us a greater connection to Romeo's intent as to "why he is using these words now." We could paraphrase this section in the following manner, "Don't you have poison, a sharp knife, or any method of death to quickly kill me, nothing so common, except banishment?" Once we know what the words meant to the Elizabethans, we then can determine *why* we must use them in order to effect change in the other character. This should be done with the entire section of text.

Folio Language Clue: The Ecphonesis O

"O Romeo, Romeo . . . ," what is really meant by this weird syllable? The concept of the *Ecphonesis O* comes from the Greek theater and it is a cry of passion. If you are confronted with the spelling *Oh*, it is clear that Shakespeare wanted you to pronounce it as you normally would. However, if you encounter the spelling *O* in your text, then this is the Ecphonesis O and Shakespeare is looking for the actor to cry out in passion. Remember, Shakespeare's characters are living, breathing human beings who just happen to speak beautifully. Let's use a modern example. Say you have asked your significant other to take out the garbage three times and they still have not done so. If this were a moment written by Shakespeare, your line might look like this:

O why dost thou not do what I have ask'd?

Would you, in this very human situation, say this line in this manner: "Ooooooooo why dost thou not do what I have ask'd?" No, of course not. Human beings don't speak in this way and neither do Shakespeare's characters. If we used the Ecphonesis O in the way it is intended to be used, you might speak your line this way:

Ugh [a sound] why dost thou not do what I have ask'd?

This is much more in line with the correct emotion of a character at this time. Characters *need* the Ecphonesis O in order to effect change in the other person—to make them feel guilty for not doing what has been asked. It's more human, it's more alive, and it's more in line with the true intent of Shakespeare. Just this one clue will immediately open up a new world for your students. Try it!

We will start scoring the text by using a highlighter to draw attention to the Ecphonesis O:

Romeo and Juliet (2.2)
JULIET.   O *Romeo, Romeo,* wherefore art thou *Romeo*?

Twelfth Night (1.5)
OLIVIA.   O, I haue read it: it is heresie. Haue you no more to say?

Julius Caesar (3.1)
ANTONY.   O pardon me, thou bleeding peece of Earth:

Let's apply this clue to the text we are using from *Romeo and Juliet.* There is one Ecphonesis O in the piece:

O Frier, the damned vse that word in hell:
Howlings attends it, how hast thou the hart   10

Its use here underscores Romeo's need to persuade the Friar to share his anguish over his banishment. Have the students speak the text exploring this new clue. Your classroom will immediately light up with energy and excitement!

Folio Language Clue: Internal Capitalization

The first word of a line of verse, proper names, and titles are always capitalized; however, Shakespeare will often capitalize words within the verse lines that are grammatically "incorrect." Remember, Shakespeare is writing for the *actor*—not for the reader. He is signaling the actor to take note of these words. He's a guy who didn't have the benefit of a highlighting pen and there is something special about a particular word, and so he has capitalized it. Never ignore this wonderful clue. Always make a choice about what that word means to your character. Why *must* you use *this* word *now* in order to *effect change* in another character?

Capitalized words within the verse lines can indicate irony or contrast, or be used as a tool toward a deeper emotional connection. We will circle these words. They become the "stepping-stones" for our characters.

> Romeo. 'Tis (Torture) and not mercy, heauen is here
> Where *Iuliet* liues, and euery (Cat) and (Dog,)
> And little (Mouse) euery vnworthy thing
> Liue here in (Heauen) and may looke on her,
> But *Romeo* may not, hee is banished.   5

We have started "scoring" our sample texts with two different categories of words: Ecphonesis Os and internally capitalized words. We continue to add symbols to our scoring system in subsequent chapters with other verse and rhetorical strategy clues. Some of our partner teachers ask students to use colored pencils to score a passage to better track the clues and the patterns they form. Students notate each clue with a different color. In this way, their eyes will see the clues each time they read or speak the text. Some students, especially those skewing toward visual intelligence, love to "color."

Previewing Shakespeare's Language, Activating Folio Clues

At this point, we have addressed how to mitigate the challenges of Early Modern pronunciation, spelling, pronouns, internal capitalization, and vocabulary. Now we can turn our attention to how students can become more skilled readers of Shakespeare by activating strategies that identify and unlock the *Folio clues* as part of a prereading process.

Prereading Exercise: Working a "Text Nugget" to Understand Early Modern Spelling, Capitalization, and a Bit of Sentence Structure

The excerpt (3.3.1832–53; edited) from *Romeo and Juliet* presented in Figure 4.1 is a great "all-purpose" text nugget to introduce the First Folio and to explore language clues since students are generally familiar with the circumstances of the setting, conflict, and characters from popular culture, which makes it a great previewing speech no matter which play students study.

We find it valuable to show any First Folio text on a large interactive whiteboard to identify and discuss which clues the 1623 text provides compared to any modern classroom edition the Folio is supplementing. An online edition

First Folio (1623)	**Cambridge School Shakespeare edition**
ROMEO. 'Tis Torture and not mercy, heauen is here	ROMEO. 'Tis torture, and not mercy. Heaven is here
Where *Iuliet* liues, and euery Cat and Dog,	Where Juliet lives, and every cat and dog
And little Mouse, euery vnworthy thing	And little mouse, every unworthy thing,
Liue here in Heauen and may looke on her,	Live here in heaven, and may look on her,
But *Romeo* may not, hee is banished. 5	But Romeo may not, he is banished. 5
Had'st thou no poyson mixt, no sharpe ground knife,	Hadst thou no poison mixed, no sharp-ground knife,
No sudden meane of death, though nere so meane,	No sudden mean of death, though ne'er so mean
But banished to kill me? Banished?	But 'banished' to kill me? 'Banished'?
O Frier, the damned vse that word in hell:	O Frier, the damned use that word in hell;
Howlings attends it, how hast thou the hart 10	Howling attends it. How hast thou the heart, 10
Being a Diuine, a Ghostly Confessor,	Being a divine, a ghostly confessor,
A Sin-Absoluer, and my Friend profest:	A sin-absolver, and my friend professed,
To mangle me with that word, banished?	To mangle me with that word 'banished'?

FIGURE 4.1. *Romeo and Juliet*: Language clues.

of the First Folio is free to access through the Internet Shakespeare Editions website (for *Romeo and Juliet*, see internetshakespeare.uvic.ca/doc/Rom_F1/complete/), which is the source of the example we use here. The classroom version is the Cambridge School Shakespeare edition, and we regularly use this series alongside First Folio excerpts.

First Step: Correct the Variant Spelling

Since Shakespeare's spelling is an obstacle to reading and speaking text from the First Folio fluently, have students model how modern editors "update" variant spelling. This single-focus activity helps to build students' reading stamina, especially for struggling or reluctant readers. Begin the activity by sharing just the Folio version with your students. Have students first note the Folio's use of "weird spelling" and then ask them to make necessary "corrections" using modern spelling conventions. When just examining the text for the variant spelling, students are reading the passage for understanding in a playful yet purposeful manner. They are not under pressure to master the full meaning of the speech. They have one goal: make sense of one unusual text feature and make it understandable. That is a strategy they can apply to other unusual features of the text: identify an unusual feature, note its impact on understanding, and apply a strategy to make sense of that feature through substitution or translation.

Second Step: Compare Differences in Capitalization and Sentence Structure

Now students can move on to compare the First Folio version with a modern edition to explore differences in internal capitalization and sentence structure. These differences highlight the clues Shakespeare left for his *actors* to immediately access the intention of their character, while editors often eliminate or diminish important clues that would help *readers* understand characters' intentions and tactics. In this activity (see Figure 4.2), for example, students begin to examine punctuation differences that we treat more fully in Chapter 5 with respect to verse clues. "Messy" punctuation reveals a character's emotional

---

Before we explore the textual differences between the First Folio and the modern text setting from the Cambridge School Shakespeare series, let's review the situation at hand: Romeo is currently hiding with Friar Laurence, and becomes distraught when the news of his banishment is revealed.

As we are at the beginning of our work with the text, let's focus on two of the more obvious differences between the two versions, as follows:

1. Note how many sentences the Folio version and the modern text contain. Why is this important? What do you think this reveals about Romeo and his current emotional state? Why do you think modern editors made this change? Which version is more effective?
   - The Folio version contains four sentences, while the text is reset into six sentences in the modern edition.
   - Take special note of lines 1 to 5 in both versions. The Folio sets this as one sentence, whereas the modern text has reset this into two sentences. The same is true with lines 9 to 13.
   - Remember, Romeo is in a heightened state of mind. He is highly emotional in the moment, as opposed to highly grammatically correct. The ideas and images are rushing through his head one right after the next. The longer, less grammatically correct Folio version is more human. It's "messier." This is how we as people think "in the moment." When we are in highly emotional states, how many of us speak in perfectly crafted and grammatically correct sentences?
2. Note how many words are capitalized in the Folio setting as opposed to the Cambridge setting. Why do you think these words are set with capitalized letters? What does this reveal?
   - *Torture, Cat, Dog, Mouse, Heaven, Divine, Ghostly, Confessor, Sin-Absolver,* and *Friend*
   - Obviously, this is not conventional capitalization. Remember, Romeo is emotionally heightened and not thinking or expressing himself in a controlled manner.
   - Do you think he wants the Friar to convince him that banishment is a good thing—he will at least continue to live? Does Romeo want to exist without Juliet? Maybe, then, the capitalized word *Torture* is an extra stressed word to make the Friar realize there is no life without Juliet. It's **T**orture and not mercy.
   - Why do you think *cat, dog,* and *mouse* are capitalized? Perhaps Romeo is making the point that even these insignificant creatures have the joy of seeing or being with Juliet when he cannot have that same joy.
   - Why do you think all of the references to the Friar in lines 11 and 12 are capitalized? Again, in Romeo's current state of mind, he can't understand why the Friar would have the heart to "mangle" him (cut him into pieces) with the word *banishment*. So, perhaps the capitalized words are an attempt to make the Friar feel guilty. If he truly is a man of God, a spiritual confessor, and, most important, his **F**riend, the Friar should understand.

Remember, there is no right or wrong answer. We are just exploring possibilities revealed in the text based on the situation.

FIGURE 4.2. *Romeo and Juliet*: Textual differences—discussion prompts.

state as well as disrupting the regularity of the verse's rhythm. Recognizing the importance of these clues embedded in the Folio will, in turn, pull your students directly into the text in ways that are exciting and engaging. For more advanced readers, it can encourage discussion of how far an editor should correct the "messier" aspects of capitalization, punctuation, and grammatical structures to make modern readers more comfortable with the text.

In subsequent activities, the First Folio text is presented with regularized spelling to make the text more accessible to your students while still preserving authorial intention. Many of our teaching partners regularize the language for their classrooms before presenting the text to their students.

When presenting these smaller excerpts from whichever edition you prefer, provide students with the context of the excerpt before the class analyzes the text. A wonderful source to use is *Shakespeare A to Z: The Essential Reference to His Plays, His Poems, His Life and Times, and More* by Charles Boyce. It contains documented entries for every character and every play, including an incredible scene-by-scene synopsis. Providing the students with the character summary and the synopsis of the scene that contains the excerpted text will greatly aid the work you are about to undertake with your students.

"Speak the Speech, I Pray You!" Activating the Text Using Language Clues

"Trying on" Shakespeare's language is a crucial engagement tool. Speaking the text and feeling the words resonate in your body produces the exciting results that any dramatist aims to achieve. Speaking aloud enables us to connect with the text in a more visceral way. Doing so is active, engaging, and incredibly rewarding. Ah, but to get our students up on their feet, and then to get them to speak—ay, there's the rub! Students are reluctant to participate in an effective way for as many reasons as there are students. Not only do we receive the nonverbal feedback of the teenage "eye-roll," but we also hear mutterings along the lines of "I've already done this. Why do I have to do this again?" While we wish we could provide you with the "magic wand" that

Teacher of the Bard Talk

Choral reading and repetition are perhaps the most essential components in getting shy and reluctant students involved in the reading of Shakespeare. One of my favorite activities involved a large group reciting the refrain "Double, double toil and trouble …" (*Mac.* 4.1), in their *witchiest* voices, in response to a few brave souls who read the other sections of the spell. After a few run-throughs, the group knew the lines by heart, and were then encouraged to get on their feet, circle the spell-readers, begin to crouch and hunch a bit, and slowly increase volume and intensity. All were involved and having fun in the process.

—JENNIFER BERTACCHI,
Carleton Washburne Middle School; ELA teacher

will encourage your students to participate with total joy and enthusiasm, these *basic skill* activities can rely heavily on group recitation to minimize students feeling self-conscious. If you have implemented some of the bell ringer suggestions from Chapter 3, the transition to these speaking activities should not be so unusual or threatening to your students.

Now is the time to get Romeo's speech (or any other preview text) "into the mouths" of the students. The following exercise is a great way to get the students immediately engaged with language. This one is patterned after the "Paper Trick" from Barry Edelstein's excellent book *Thinking Shakespeare* (170–71).

Exercise #1: "Magic" Index Card

Purpose of the Exercise
To enhance the student's initial understanding, clarity, and sense of Shakespeare's text.

Setup
You'll need a blank index card and a copy of the speech (one per student).

Instructions
1. Students need to stand, either at their desks or in a circle.
2. Give each student an index card.
3. Have the students use the index card to cover the text.
4. The students will then all speak aloud, at their own pace, but speaking at one-fifth of their full volume. In this way, if students have trouble pronouncing a word during this first round, they will not be heard so strongly as to "expose a weakness."
5. Instruct the students to actively *listen to themselves* as they are speaking aloud.
6. Say: "When you get to the end of the first verse line, move the index card down so that the second line is now revealed."
7. Say: "Keep doing this until the full speech has been spoken."
8. Say: "Don't cheat. It's vital that only one line at a time is revealed and that you do not move the index card until you've reached the end of the line you are working on."
9. After this exercise is complete, ask the students if they need correct pronunciations of words or ask if they need any words defined.

10. After the text is clarified, repeat the exercise one more time.

> **Student of the Bard Talk**
>
> Because Shakespeare is speech, [his words] make more sense—even if the speaker doesn't understand the words—when she speaks them aloud in the sentences ...instead of as lines of verse. Adding in different intonation for different punctuation also changes the meaning (or gives the words meaning). For me, reading the words out loud is super helpful, but reading them just standing up is even more helpful, because I've found that, when I focus on the words, I move naturally in response to them.
>
> —LAURA THORNBURG,
> *Adlai E. Stevenson High School*

Because all of the students are speaking simultaneously at one-fifth of their full volume, this exercise enables each student to begin to speak Shakespeare's words aloud without having the added pressure of everyone focusing on one student. Therefore, if students mispronounce words or stumble through the text, it will not be revealed to the larger group. Reticent students will be more comfortable participating because they are not in the spotlight. This exercise also enables the students to speak the text aloud while taking in one line at a time. In doing so, what would have been a mystery is already significantly clearer. After speaking the text two times this way, students are ready for the next exercise.

Exercise #2: Getting Comfortable with Those "Weird" Pronouns

PURPOSE OF THE ACTIVITY
To differentiate between formal and informal pronouns and their application.

SETUP
Changing pronouns from formal to informal ones generally suggests a shift in a character's intentions by using a specific language tactic. Tactics are intentions translated into action: sometimes verbal, other times physical, most times both. Try this simple activity with your students and this chunk of text from *Romeo and Juliet* (2.5) (don't forget to apply the text clues we have learned: Ecphonesis O and capitalized words). Romeo has given the Nurse a message for Juliet that she should go to Friar Laurence this afternoon and there they shall be married. The Nurse returns to deliver this message to Juliet, who has been waiting quite impatiently for her return. The Nurse mercilessly teases Juliet by withholding Romeo's message as long as she can. Juliet does whatever she can to try to get information from the Nurse. Notice Shakespeare's brilliant use of *thee/thou* and *you/your* pronouns in this small exchange. The use of pronouns matches the desired intent of each character.

JULIET. O God she comes, O honey Nurse what news?
Hast **thou** met with him? Send **thy** man away.

NURSE. *Peter* stay at the gate.

JULIET. Now good sweet Nurse:
O Lord, why lookest **thou** sad?
Though news, be sad, yet tell them merrily.
If good **thou** sham'st the music of sweet news,
By playing it to me, with so sower a face.

NURSE. I am a weary, give me leave awhile,
Fie how my bones ache, what a jaunt have I had?

JULIET. I would **thou** had'st my bones, and I **thy** news:
Nay come I pray **thee** speak, good good Nurse speak.

NURSE. Jesu what haste? can **you** not stay awhile?
Do **you** not see that I am out of breath?

JULIET. How art **thou** out of breath, when **thou** hast breath
To say to me, that **thou** art out of breath?
The excuse that **thou** dost make in this delay,
Is longer then the tale **thou** dost excuse.
Is **thy** news good or bad? answer to that,
Say either, and I'll stay the circumstance:
Let me be satisfied, ist good or bad?

NURSE. Well, **you** have made a simple choice, **you** know
not how to choose a man: *Romeo*, no not he though his face
be better then any mans, yet his legs excels all mens, and
for a hand, and a foot, and a body, though they be not to
be talked on, yet they are past compare: he is not the flower
of curtesie, but I'll warrant him as gentle as a Lamb: go **thy**
ways wench, serve God. What have **you** dined at home?

JULIET. No no: but all this this did I know before
What says he of our marriage? what of that?

NURSE. Lord how my head aches, what a head have I?
It beats as it would fall in twenty pieces.
My back a' t'other side: O my back, my back:
Beshrew **your** heart for sending me about
To catch my death with jaunting up and down.

JULIET. I'faith: I am sorry that **thou** art so well.
Sweet sweet, sweet Nurse, tell me what says my Love?

NURSE. **Your** Love says like an honest Gentleman,
And a courteous, and a kind, and a handsome,
And I warrant a virtuous: where is **your** Mother?

JULIET. Where is my Mother?
Why she is within, where should she be?
How oddly **thou** repli'st:
Your Love says like an honest Gentleman:
Where is your Mother?

NURSE. O Gods Lady dear,
Are you so hot? marry come up I trow,
Is this the Poultis for my aching bones?
Henceforward do **your** messages yourself.

INSTRUCTIONS

1. Have students stand up, script in hand, and speak aloud.
2. When a character uses the intimate pronoun *thee/thou,* have the student playing that character move closer to the other student.
3. When a character uses the more formal pronoun, have the student playing that character move away from the other student.
4. Have students speak and move several times until their reading of the lines is fluent and their movement is intentional.

VARIATIONS

- If students aren't ready to speak lines on their own, have half the class line up and face the other half. Assign a character to each half (i.e., Team Juliet, Team Nurse) and have students read and move in unison. To get a good, meaningful read–move combination, you might have to try the exchange several times. After that, pair students up to read and move according to the original set of instructions.
- You can use a strategy based on a technique called "feeding in," which involves one student reading a character's lines while another performs the gestures and movements based on those lines. You can

Student of the Bard Talk

As a non-English native speaker, I had to adjust to Shakespeare more than most of the students. I will not lie. At first, I thought that Shakespeare will be the hardest unit. …Elizabethan language has a lot of "thee" and "thy" in it, which are not words I have been using in [the English I have learned]. I had to force myself to slow down and [enunciate] each word.…I catch myself up to this day unintentionally saying "thee, thy" in my normal speech.

—DZIYANA BALAKIR,
Adlai E. Stevenson High School

have students form groups of four for this exchange between the Nurse and Juliet to explore the "dance of the pronouns."

This simple physical exercise will clearly demonstrate how a character can achieve specific objectives with the aid of the humble pronoun. After this, your students will have less concern about the use of these "weird" pronouns. They will relish how characters use them as tactics.

Exercise #3: Breathing Life into Ecphonesis O with an Added "Oscar Moment"

PURPOSE OF THE ACTIVITY
To understand the way the Ecphonesis O is voiced in a line, and how proper vocalization reveals a character's emotional temperature.

SETUP
Here are various versions of the Ecphonesis O found throughout the works of Shakespeare. Cut them into slips of paper, fold them, and place them in a hat.

- Why then, O brawling love, O loving hate, / O anything, of nothing first created: (Romeo)
- It is my Lady, O it is my Love, O that she knew she were, (Romeo)
- O God she comes, O honey Nurse what news? (Juliet)
- O! I am Fortune's fool. (Romeo)
- *Tybolt*, my Cousin? O my Brother's Child, / O Prince, O Cousin, Husband, O the blood is spilled / Of my dear kinsman. (Capulet's Wife)
- O I have bought the Mansion of a Love, / But not possessed it, (Juliet)
- O pardon me, thou bleeding piece of Earth: (Antony)
- O God, O God! / How weary, stale, flat, and unprofitable / Seems to me all the uses of this world? (Hamlet)
- O what a Noble mind is here o're-thrown? (Ophelia)

Teacher of the Bard Talk

[The] Ecphonesis O is something all students have seen before in their studies of poetry.... Students are ...willing to play around with natural reactions and sounds they might utter in response to various situations. Some students growl, some moan, some sigh, and still others scream! They love it. They really get a kick out of it when I run a game of Simon Says to wake them up at the beginning of class and say, "Simon Says create an Ecphonesis O!"—and they all did, loudly and proudly!

—JENNIFER BERTACCHI,
Carleton Washburne Middle School; ELA teacher

- O when mine eyes did see *Olivia* first, / Me thought she purg'd the air of pestilence; (Orsino)
- O for a Muse of Fire, that would ascend / The brightest Heaven of Invention: (Chorus)
- O sweet-suggesting Love, if thou has sin'd, / Teach me (thy tempted subject) to excuse it. (Proteus)
- O Grace! O Heaven forgive me! / Are you a Man? Have you a Soul? Or Sense? (Iago)
- O monstrous! monstrous! (Othello)
- O perjur'd woman, thou do'st stone my heart, / And makes me call, what I intend to do, / A Murther, which I thought a Sacrifice. / I saw the Handkerchief. (Othello)
- If Heaven have any grievous plague in store, / Exceeding those that I can wish upon thee / O let them keep it till thy sins be ripe / And then hurl down their indignation / On thee, the troubler of the poor World's peace. (Margaret)
- O stay but till then. (Benedick)
- O, and I forsooth in love, / I that have been love's whip? (Berowne)
- O monstrous. O strange. We are haunted; pray / masters, fly masters, help. (Peter Quince)
- O teach me how you look, and with what art / you sway the motion of *Demetrius's* heart. (Helena)
- O these naughty times / Puts bars between the owners and their rights. (Portia)
- What my young Master, oh my gentle master, / Oh my sweet master, O you memory / Of old Sir Rowland; why, what make you here? (Adam)
- O time, thou must untangle this, not I, / It is too hard a knot for me t'untie. (Viola)
- O God of Battles, steel my Soldiers hearts, / Possess them not with fear: (Henry V)

INSTRUCTIONS

1. Have the students choose an Ecphonesis O line from the hat.
2. Instruct students to fully experiment vocally before presenting their lines individually. Give the students a few minutes to practice.

3. Bring class together and have students voice their lines in unison using the following directions:
    - Give that Ecphonesis O line a good Tarzan yell to start off the line.
    - You don't want anyone to hear you, but you have to get that line out.
    - You drift off to sleep and you yawn that Ecphonesis O line.
    - You are very, very frustrated. How does that Ecphonesis O line sound now?
    - You are excited, delighted, and need to share that O!
4. Once students have experimented in unison, have them rehearse their line reading to get at the heart of what they think the line (out of context) means—and not just automatically go for the melodramatic punch of the "O."
5. Have students form a circle and voice their line one by one, emphasizing what they think is the proper meaning of the line and how strongly or lightly they should hit the opening "O."

VARIATION

Have students come up individually for their "Oscar Moment" (their award-winning reading and physicalizing of the line).

This is a good activity to get students up and speaking a very brief piece of text, and invites playing around with inflection and emphasis. It also works well as a bell ringer or mid-class energizing activity to reset focus even before you start preparing to read a play.

Teacher of the Bard Talk

At the beginning of the term [we began] with a passage from 2.1 of *The Taming of the Shrew*, when Kate and Petruchio first meet. The conversation was chock full of great text clues, and it was a great way for the students to get used to looking for these devices.... Students will point out an Ecphonesis O—how many teenagers can identify those by name?—and will call out anyone who reads it as a straight "O."

—ROBIN RUSSO,
Steinmetz High School; ELA teacher

Activating Language Clues Later in the Reading Process: Mind the Internal Capitalization

Since classroom editions edit out much if not all of the internal capitalization, you might want to pull out key speeches and soliloquies from the First Folio that rely heavily on internal capitalization to compare to the mass-market edition your students are using at various points in their reading process. Students then can access this language clue to dig deeper into a character's intentions and tactics as one of Shakespeare's actors did. You might ask students to predict which words should be capitalized for emphasis within lines before taking a look at the First Folio. Appendix A offers a selection of speeches that work well as stand-alone analysis experiences to introduce the basic skills.

So that students will remember the Folio clues from the basic through the intermediate and advanced skills, you will find a *clue card* at the end of each of the Folio technique chapters. To maximize the effectiveness of the clue cards, Robin Russo shared with us that she laminates the clue cards so students can check off the clues in the texts they analyze with dry erase markers. The laminated clue cards are both available and durable. And, if you use the same passages frequently, you can laminate them as well to save on duplication.

Mining the Prereading Payoff

Many teachers already feel that they don't have adequate time to cover the extensive curriculum they are required to teach. Every teacher confronts this legitimate concern as they plan and assess their students' progress throughout the school year. However, if we can spend some of our valuable time learning, exploring, and applying these close-reading Folio technique strategies with a smaller section of text, not only will the reading fluency of your students increase, but their eye will also spot these clues as they continue to study the full play. Not only will they spot them, but, because you have spent structured time to learn, practice, and exercise these skills from the beginning of their study, they will also automatically begin to apply them, and you may find that you are moving through the play in a more expedient and meaningful way. Most students will become accustomed to the Early Modern vocabulary, pronouns, internal capitalization, and the Ecphonesis O by the end of reading Act 1. As they prepare for Act 2, it should be time to address how blank verse and iambic pentameter create the pulse of the play by exploring the Folio technique's verse clues.

Basic Folio Clue Card: Language Conventions

Folio Technique Clue	✓	Definition	Scoring the Text
Extra Syllable Pronunciation		-'d or -'st = no -ed or -est = yes If Bill wants you to pronounce the extra syllable, he will add it in the text.	If thou lov'st me = no If thou lovest me = yes

Informal versus Formal Pronouns		thee/thou = informal (intimate)
		you/your = formal
		
		If a character normally uses thee/thou and switches to you/your, something major has happened in terms of a relationship.
			QUEEN. Let not thy Mother lose her Prayers, *Hamlet*.
			        I pray **thee** stay with us, go not to Wittenberg.
			HAMLET. I shall in all my best
			        Obey **you**, Madam.
			(Ham. 1.2)

Defining Early Modern Words		Make it a strong practice to look up and define unfamiliar words. We must know what we are saying at all points. Use one of the sources listed in this chapter to define these words.	Write definitions in the right margin of the text.
Ecphonesis O		When Bill writes O in the text, this represents a cry of passion, emotion, etc.	O thou wilt speak again of banishment. *(Rom.* 3.3)
Internal Capitalization		A capitalized word within the verse line is a clue from Bill that this word is special for some reason. Choose it, highlight it, stress it, etc.	Have not (Saints) lips, and holy (Palmers) too? *(Rom.* 1.5)

5 Understand Verse Clues Using the Folio Technique

What's Worse Than Not Understanding the Verse?

Verse enabled writers well before Shakespeare to dramatize a character in the throes of heightened emotions through the equally heightened language of poetry. A well-placed Ecphonesis O might not be sufficient to express fully a character's passion, delight, or despair. Shakespeare's manipulation of verse helps us to gauge a character's emotional state through their deft control of iambic pentameter. We want students to embrace the poetic conventions of the plays by making that verse read and sound human and purposeful—not archaic and "Shakespearean." We want them to understand the pulse of the iambic pentameter and how it is the engine of a character's heartbeat, made manifest through their words. Language embedded in blank verse, once remote or mysterious, can become clearer on a first reading, hearing, or speaking when applying the *verse clues* that follow. In this chapter, the featured Folio technique strategies help students to achieve an understanding of how verse works in an immediate and visceral way through speaking the text and using physicalizing strategies to instantly grasp a character's emotional state.

Complex Characters and Their Complicated Emotions

Let's begin with a feature that you may not immediately classify as a verse clue but certainly controls the rhythm of a line. That verse clue is punctuation. One of the most amazing elements in Shakespeare's work emerges when his characters are in control of their emotions and the situation at hand, as this is reflected in their speech. However, when things are out of control, the structure and punctuation of their speech becomes highly irregular, erratic, and "messy." This "messiness" is sometimes attributed to compositor or printer errors in the attempt to reconcile irregularities in Shakespeare's original manuscripts. Modern editions at times dismiss the idea that this "messiness" could actually have been the *intent* of Shakespeare—giving the actor more clues that his character is indeed in crisis, and this state is reflected by how the language is presented on the page (punctuation, spelling, capitalization, etc.). This is "actor punctuation." It may not be perfect in terms of grammar, poetry, and logic, but it is human and actable. Modern editors tend to "clean up" the text and regularize it based on more modern rules of grammar and poetry. If we look in the First Folio and embrace the "messiness" Shakespeare intended, we gain a stronger and clearer sense of the character as Shakespeare originally intended.

We touched on this "messiness" in Chapter 4, when students compared Romeo's speech as rendered in the First Folio and in the Cambridge School Shakespeare edition. For a quick review, let's look at the opening speech of Antonio in *The Merchant of Venice* (1.1) (Figure 5.1). Here, we have a character who is quite wealthy, usually buying drinks, food, and most everything else for those in his company; however, he is now deeply sad and can't determine why. If we look at the First Folio version next to the Folger edition, we can see the difference between "messy" punctuation and "clean" punctuation.

The speech as it appears in the First Folio reveals some interesting clues. Most notably, we can see that lines 1 to 6 in the First Folio form one complete sentence broken up with "messy" punctuation. Where you find commas, colons, and semicolons in the First Folio, you find instead periods and complete sentences in the Folger edition. The Folio version reveals that Antonio is "in the moment," trying to figure out the source of his sadness. Thoughts and images are running through his head and he is trying to make sense of them. He is not settled. Periods, exclamation points, and question marks reveal the end of a character's thought. The fact that you have commas, colons, and semicolons throughout the six lines (one long run-on sentence) indicates that he is "working hard" to land the end of a thought—indicated by a period. It takes him six lines to do this in the First Folio. On the other hand, the Folger edition reveals lines 1 to 7 as four complete sentences. By taking the First Folio's one long run-on sentence and changing it into four individual sentences, the Folger's version of Antonio now appears more in control and less "troubled" by his sadness.

First Folio (*MV* 1.1.1–6)	Folger edition (*MV* 1.1.1–7)
Antonio. In sooth I know not why I am so sad, It wearies me: you say it wearies you; But how I caught it, found it, or came by it, What stuffe 'tis made of, whereof it is borne, I am to learne: and such a Want-wit sadnesse makes of mee, That I have much ado to know my selfe.	Antonio. In sooth I know not why I am so sad. It wearies me, you say it wearies you. But how I caught it, found it, or came by it, What stuff 'tis made of, whereof it is born, I am to learn. And such a want-wit sadness makes of me That I have much ado to know myself.

FIGURE 5.1. *The Merchant of Venice*: First Folio versus Folger edition.

He seems to have a *logical* approach to trying to figure this out, as opposed to a much more human, emotional, and *messy* approach. By "cleaning up" the text's punctuation, we lose a key aspect of the deeper internal turmoil that Antonio is experiencing.

Punctuation does shape a character's speaking rhythm and cadence as well as influence the regularity of the iambic pentameter and the musicality of the verse.

Punctuation, Breathing, and Meaning

It is helpful indeed to think of Shakespeare's punctuation as being equal to musical rests. Punctuation determines where to breathe, to pause, or to keep going, which either accelerates or decelerates the rhythm of a speech. Breathing and punctuation work together simultaneously when using the Folio technique. Through punctuation, Shakespeare indicates a place for a new idea. This informs the actor that there should also be a breath; however, the length and option to breathe are determined by the punctuation. Shakespeare uses breathing and punctuation quite naturally. When it is odd or does not feel natural to the actor, Shakespeare, once again, is providing us with clues. He will punctuate a piece to create a physical feeling as you speak the text. Through this physical feeling (being out of breath, taking many breaths, continuing to speak by picking up the pace, etc.), Shakespeare is giving you the emotional state of the character. Without the luxury of a modern rehearsal period, Shakespeare indicated the intended emotion and its intensity through how he punctuated the text.

Let's put this idea into practice using a piece of text from the First Folio version of *Macbeth* (1.7) (see Figure 5.2). In this scene, Macbeth is worried what will happen to him in the afterlife if he goes through with the murder of King Duncan. Lady Macbeth taunts him and passionately persuades him to stick to their plan, and Macbeth agrees to commit the murder.

Exercise #1: Don't Lose What You Learned: Applying Language Clues First!

PURPOSE OF THE EXERCISE
To review and apply the language clues discovered working through Romeo's speech in Chapter 4, continue to reinforce and refine linguistic skills.

> LADY.   Was the hope drunk,
>   Wherein you drest yourself? Hath it slept since?
>   And wakes it now to look so green, and pale,
>   At what it did so freely? From this time,
>   Such I account thy love. Art thou afear'd   5
>   To be the same in thine own Act, and Valour,
>   As thou art in desire? Would'st thou have that
>   Which thou esteem'st the Ornament of Life,
>   And live a Coward in thine own Esteeme?
>   Letting I dare not, wait upon I would,   10
>   Like the poor Cat i'th'Addage.
> MACBETH.   Prithee peace:

FIGURE 5.2. Text for analysis: Language and punctuation clues.

SETUP

You will also ask students to pull out that "magic" index card to go over the speech line by line.

INSTRUCTIONS

1. Begin by defining words and/or phrases that are unfamiliar to your students. This could even be the assigned homework the night before you begin work on this scene. Use the online source Shakespeare's Words (www.shakespeareswords.com) to complete this work. Some words and/or phrases to look up might include:

    - account thy love
    - Valour
    - desire
    - esteem [Lady Macbeth uses this word twice]
    - Ornament of Life
    - wait upon
    - Cat i'th'Addage

2. Use the "Magic" Index Card Exercise (Chapter 4), allowing the students to speak the text aloud.

3. *Say to students:* Look at the pronouns Lady Macbeth uses throughout the speech. She switches from **you/your** to **thy/thou** in this section. Why? What does this reveal about her relationship with her husband? Based on her use of pronouns, what different tactics might she be using to get her way?

Let's get the students physically engaged with this new piece of text with an exercise that we have found highly successful for building an awareness of and sensitivity to the impact of punctuation.

Exercise #2: Sharing the Text, Sharing the Dish Towel

Purpose of the Exercise
To help the students become physically engaged with the text. This will help activate kinesthetic intelligence while tapping into linguistic intelligence skills.

Setup
A dish towel is needed—or, for you Shakespeare purists, a tea towel!

Instructions
1. Have the students stand in a circle.
2. Have students speak the text (here, Lady Macbeth's speech) aloud all at the same time.
3. Ask if the students need anything clarified in terms of pronunciation, etc.
4. Have the students speak the text aloud again. This time, change speakers each time you come to a punctuation mark.
5. When finished, have the students speak the text aloud again in this same way but beginning with a new student so that everyone speaks a new section.
6. When finished, ask the following questions to debrief the experience:
    - What did speaking the text aloud in a group help to clarify?
    - Which words stood out when we shared the speaking of the text this way?
    - Was there a place in the speech when we were changing speakers often?

- Did anyone have a longer period of speaking?
- Did you notice any patterns in Lady Macbeth's speech?

7. Speak the text this way one more time, but this time in a whisper, as if Lady Macbeth is sharing a secret that no one should hear. Make sure the students whisper with energy and that there are no pauses between speakers. They should speak as if they are one voice.
    - What did reading the speech this way reveal to you?
    - What is Lady Macbeth's state of mind?
    - To what extent are her emotions being fully revealed or kept in check based on the pace at which she speaks?

8. Speak the text aloud one final time. You will need that dish towel now! The students will again speak the text aloud, switching at each punctuation mark. They will move in a counterclockwise direction. Have the student to the speaker's left hold one end of the dish towel and the speaker will hold the other. While the student is speaking, they should pull and try to take the dish towel from the student to their left. The student to the left should give resistance in order to make the speaker work to take it. When the speaker gets to the punctuation mark, they should fully take the dish towel. They now serve as resistance for the next speaker. Continue in this manner until the entire speech has been spoken. It might take a few rounds with the speech and the dish towel for the most effective results.

9. To debrief this experience, ask the students if working with the text this way helped them better understand how punctuation emphasizes or clarifies certain ideas expressed in the speech as well as how punctuation controlled the pace of how the speech should or could be read.

IMPLEMENTATION TIP

We have tried using water bottles or rolled up paper instead of the dish towel, but a filled water bottle can be "lethal" if players lose their grip, and the paper cylinder crushes too easily.

The pace or the melody of verse is regulated most broadly by the text's punctuation marks. These preliminary exercises combine Chapter 4's language clues with the impact of punctuation in organizing a character's thoughts and revealing their emotion. The music of blank

Teacher of the Bard Talk

The dish towel activity allowed students to get up on their feet and express a character's emotional state with the tug of a towel ...[and] made students better understand the meaning of Helena and Hermia's dialogue in *A Midsummer Night's Dream* (1.1) by connecting it with a series of emotions.

—RITA GÖNDÖCS,
World Language Academy; ELA teacher

verse can be "scored" with a series of annotations that foster close reading of the text and prepare students to experiment with speaking and physicalizing the language.

Folio Verse Clue: Full Thoughts

Student of the Bard Talk

[Shakespeare's words] begin to make more sense if you speak in the sentences that Shakespeare wrote instead [of stopping at the end] of the lines of verse. Adding in different intonation for different punctuation gives the words meaning or also changes the meaning. For me, reading the words out loud is super helpful, but reading them just standing up is even more helpful, because I've found that, when I focus on the words, I move naturally in response to them.

—LAURA THORNBURG,
Adlai E. Stevenson High School

Anywhere you find a period, question mark, or exclamation point in the text signifies the end of a thought—a full thought. To begin scoring the text's punctuation, we highlight the last three or four words before every period, question mark, and exclamation point. Not only does this show us where the full thoughts are, but we also discover the length of our character's thoughts. In addition, if you are confused as to what the full thought means, usually the last three or four words will "magically" clear it up for you. Let's apply the technique of underlining the last three or four words before every period, exclamation point, and question mark (as well as scoring the other intermediate clues introduced in this chapter) using the piece of text from *Macbeth* presented earlier in the chapter.

LADY.	Was the hope drunk,	
	Wherein <u>you drest yourself</u>? Hath <u>it slept since</u>?	
	And wakes it now to look so green, and pale,	
	At what it <u>did so freely</u>? From this time,	
	Such I <u>account thy love</u>. Art thou afear'd	5
	To be the same in thine own Act, and Valour,	
	As <u>thou art in desire</u>? Would'st thou have that	
	Which thou esteem'st the Ornament of Life,	
	And live a Coward in <u>thine own Esteeme</u>?	
	Letting I dare not, wait upon I would,	10
	Like the <u>poor Cat i'th' Addage</u>.	
MACBETH.	Prithee peace:	

Exercise #3: The "Ups and Downs" of Shakespeare: Full Thought Exercise

PURPOSE OF THE EXERCISE
To fully grasp in both an intellectual and physical way where the full thoughts of the character are and how long each thought is.

SETUP
Each student should have a chair and a small piece of text (Lady Macbeth's speech above or another piece of about ten to fifteen lines).

INSTRUCTIONS
Note that this is a group activity.

1. Students begin by sitting down in their chairs.
2. They begin to speak the piece aloud at their own pace (not in a choral reading fashion).
3. When the students arrive at a period, question mark, or exclamation point, they need to make sure to clearly end the thought.
4. The students then change their position physically before continuing with the text. As the students began by sitting, they would then stand to begin the next section of text.
5. Students speak the text aloud until they come to the next period, question mark, or exclamation point. Again, make sure to clearly end the thought.
6. The students then again change their position physically before continuing with the text. As the students are now standing, they would then sit again to begin the next section of text.
7. Students continue speaking the text in this fashion (changing their position physically by standing or sitting) until they have finished the given text.

Folio Verse Clue: Full Stops—Periods, Question Marks, Exclamation Points

When you have a period, question mark, or exclamation point at the *end* of a verse line, this is called a *full stop* and indicates the end of the character's thought.

A full breath should be taken. We will mark this with an **F**. Take as long as you wish to fill your lungs with air. There is no need to rush. This is a true full stop. If you have a question mark, land the question and, in the full stop, expect the character(s) you are addressing to respond back. It's as if you asked a rhetorical question. If you have a period or exclamation point, land the punctuation, and, in the full stop, formulate your next thought—your next attack—in the full stop.

>LADY.   Was the hope drunk,
>Wherein you drest yourself? Hath it slept since? **F**
>And wakes it now to look so green, and pale,
>At what it did so freely? From this time,
>Such I account thy love. Art thou afear'd   5
>To be the same in thine own Act, and Valour,
>As thou art in desire? Would'st thou have that
>Which thou esteem'st the Ornament of Life,
>And live a Coward in thine own Esteeme? **F**
>Letting I dare not, wait upon I would,   10
>Like the poor Cat i'th'Addage.
>
>MACBETH.   Prithee peace:

Folio Verse Clue: Mid-stops

Full stop punctuation (period, question mark, or exclamation point) is often found in the *middle* of a verse line. This is called a *mid-stop*. Mid-stops indicate the need to finish the thought at the punctuation mark; however, you *do not breathe*. The need to continue is great! You immediately jump to the next thought with a great deal of energy. It's almost as if you were interrupting yourself. Be careful—don't rush. Make sure you complete the first thought and then launch ahead. This is an important part of the technique. We mark this with an **M** above the text where the mid-stop is found.

>LADY.   Was the hope drunk,
>   **M**
>Wherein you drest yourself? Hath it slept since? **F**
>
>And wakes it now to look so green, and pale,
>   **M**
>At what it did so freely? From this time,
>   **M**
>Such I account thy love. Art thou afear'd   5

To be the same in thine own Act, and Valour,
M
As thou art in desire? Would'st thou have that

Which thou esteem'st the Ornament of Life,

And live a Coward in thine own Esteeme? **F**

Letting I dare not, wait upon I would,   10
M
Like the poor Cat i'th'Addage.

MACBETH.   Prithee peace:

When you change your energy and immediately jump to the next thought without a breath, it truly heightens the emotional stakes and the strong drive of this exchange between Lady Macbeth and Macbeth. Shakespeare, through his use of punctuation, creates the emotion that is correct for the speech. Once you feel this in your body by speaking the words aloud, our next step is to pair that up with a verb. Again think, "Why must I use these words now?" Why does Lady Macbeth *need* the mid-stop to effect change in her husband? Brilliant!

Teacher of the Bard Talk

I have students move in some way (weight shift, focal point shift, level change, facing changes, gesture, etc.) for each punctuation mark in their lines. This *forces* them to note/use them. Clearly, students don't keep all the movement, but, by doing all of the movement as an exercise, they find what they need.

—CYNTHIA BURROWS,
Adlai E. Stevenson High School; drama and ELA teacher

Folio Verse Clue: Shared Lines

Did you notice the last two lines from the *Macbeth* text nugget we've been working? This is an example of a shared line. Shared lines in verse contain ten syllables; however, the line is divided between two characters. In this case, Lady Macbeth begins the line with "Like the poor Cat i'th'Addage." Macbeth finishes the line with his phrase, "Prithee peace." They are sharing the line. Shared lines function like a mid-stop; therefore, we treat them as such (which is why we scored this with an **M**). The first actor tosses their line to the second actor, and they, in turn, pick up the energy by immediately speaking their line. Try this. Have two actors speak the following exchange:

LADY.	Letting I dare not, wait upon I would,	10

                                    M

                      Like the poor Cat i'th'Addage.

MACBETH.   Prithee peace:

On the first try, have your students speak the lines without using mid-stop technique. Let there be a pause after Lady Macbeth's line. On the second try, have your students speak the lines; however, this time, use mid-stop technique. The student speaking Macbeth's line should immediately speak after the student speaking Lady Macbeth's line finishes. What you will discover is that, on the first attempt, when you do not use mid-stop technique, the pause between the two lines doesn't feel right. It actually feels like the "air was let out of the tires" of the scene. What you will discover, on the second attempt, is that Macbeth is feeling the "strong push" of Lady Macbeth, and his response "Prithee peace" is a strong, possibly even frustrated, stopping of her drive. The difference is profound. Through the use of mid-stop technique, the high stakes and the emotional content of the exchange is immediately heard and felt.

    Let's try another example from the First Folio version of *Macbeth* (2.2).

MACBETH.   I have done the deed: Didst thou not hear a noise?
LADY.   I heard the Owl scream, and the Crickets cry.

                          M

                Did not you speak?

                            M

MACBETH.   When?

                             M

LADY.   Now.

                                       M

MACBETH.   As I descended?
LADY.   Ay.

                               M

MACBETH.   Hark, who lies i'th'second Chamber?
LADY.   Donalbain.
MACBETH.   This is a sorry sight.

Look what Bill gave us here to reveal the emotional content of the scene. Macbeth has "done the deed." He and Lady Macbeth are on edge and fearful of being caught. One verse line is shared five times between the two characters, followed by another shared line. Try the same process again. Have two students speak these lines without using the mid-stop technique—pausing after each question mark or period. Then, have the students speak these lines while using the mid-stop technique—immediately speaking when one is finished. The results of mid-stop technique are truly remarkable and, again, immediately pull the students into the true heightened feelings and emotions of what these characters are experiencing.

This would be a good time to have students try these two clues by speaking the text (*Mac.* 1.7) aloud in front of the group. Have one student model the text (with your coaching) and then have the entire class repeat the line. When the text is spoken aloud, the technique is activated; therefore, students will immediately see and feel the difference.

> **Teacher of the Bard Talk**
>
> [As a middle school teacher,] I see these early experiences with Shakespeare as a gift to my students. In addition to giving them a leg up on future encounters with the Bard, they are exposed to incredibly rich language, complex characters, and timeless themes. As a student, I felt a powerful sense of mastery when I could make sense of a passage and recite it well, and I see this reflected in my students as they become more willing to read aloud in class.
>
> —JENNIFER BERTACCHI,
> *Carleton Washburne Middle School; ELA teacher*

Iambic Pentameter Guidelines

It's time now for you and your students to resume the role of text detectives or Patrick Tucker's "verse nurses" (39). When we take a deeper look at the structure of a verse line, we are able to piece together evidence that leads us to what Shakespeare possibly intended in his writing. It's an active approach to examining the text. As we know, Shakespeare wrote his verse plays in iambic pentameter. For many students, the study of the verse might stop with the investigation of how punctuation controls the rhythm of a speech or a piece of dialogue. For other students, based on their reading skills and experience with Shakespeare, they will be ready to examine how Shakespeare artfully orchestrates iambic pentameter in his blank verse.

Students will need to know that iambic pentameter contains five feet (a foot consists of one short, or unstressed, syllable and one long, or stressed, syllable) and ten syllables per line. The pattern is: ba-**dum**, ba-**dum**, ba-**dum**, ba-**dum**, ba-**dum**. For example:

```
U   /   U   /   U   /   U   /   U   /
I  went  to  see  a  movie with  my  friend.
```

What students may not realize is this is the natural rhythm of English-speaking peoples. Just as buildings need detailed blueprints and architectural drawings to ensure their stability when built, so does Bill's language. The rhythm provides the blueprint that holds Bill's language together. The underlying rhythm also aids in our phrasing of a particular line. When we explore the rhythm underneath the language, this is called *scansion*. Through the text and his altering of the natural five-foot, ten-syllable line, Shakespeare provides clues as to the character's state of mind or emotional state at a particular moment in the play. Remembering that Shakespeare's characters are living, breathing human beings, it is most effective when we think of scanning as finding the "heartbeat" of the character. When speaking Shakespeare's verse aloud, actually pat your chest with the iambic beat. Try it with this line from *The Two Gentlemen of Verona*:

	U	/	U	/	U	/	U	/	U	/
JULIA.	Oh	hateful	hands,	to	tear	such	loving	words;		

Can you feel her "heartbeat" as she speaks those words? This is the normal iambic pentameter line. This represents the "normal heartbeat" of a character. By investigating the language in this way, we will discover more precisely the emotional state of the character.

Scanning can become quite technical. Once the terms *iamb*, *anapest*, *trochee*, *spondee*, *pyrrhic*, *dactyl*, and more are introduced into the conversation, the "deer in the headlights" look appears from students and actors. They immediately shut down and feel like they are hearing Charlie Brown's teacher instructing them, "Mwa-Mwaaa-Maw-Maw-Waaawmp-Waw-Mawwww." They are lost. But, more important, the point of *why* Bill did what he did is also lost. Honestly, in our combined years of teaching, directing, and coaching students and actors, we can count on one hand the times we have discussed the technical terms of scanning.

Even in the worldwide-respected professional theaters in Chicago that produce Shakespeare's plays on a regular basis, it is extremely rare to hear a conversation about the technical terms of scansion in rehearsals. That's the reason we began our examination of verse with punctuation rather than with strict attention to iambic pentameter. *Versification* is really all about the rhythm—the "heartbeat." This is what we are counting the beats for—to feel the rhythm underneath the language. "My character's heartbeat is normal—they are fine." "Whoa, why did my character's heartbeat just skip?" "Why is my character's heartbeat slowing down?" "Wow! Why are there extra heartbeats in this line? What is up with him/her?" Not only is this helpful to actors, but it is also helpful and more visceral to our students. The rhythm of the language reveals the character's emotional state and the depth of where the character is in this particular situation.

Close Text Analysis: Finding the Verse's Heartbeat

With this in mind, let's take a look at a little section from the First Folio and *Twelfth Night* (see Figure 5.3). Olivia has decided to allow Viola, disguised as the boy Cesario, to speak for Duke Orsino declaring his love for Olivia. While Olivia is tired of Orsino's pleas, she immediately falls head over heels in love with Cesario (Viola). Once Cesario leaves, Olivia confesses to the audience that she has fallen in love with Cesario.

Here are some guidelines and a few versification terms you should stress (pun intended) when working with your students:

- A regular *ten-syllable* line is called a *masculine* line. When you have many masculine lines in a row, Shakespeare is letting you know that the character is levelheaded, coherent, and thinking very clearly.
- An *eleven-syllable* line is called a *feminine* line. Through feminine endings, Shakespeare creates a softer sound, as the line ends with an unstressed syllable. This may signal that something emotional is happening.
- A *twelve-syllable* line is called an *alexandrine*. Shakespeare's use of the alexandrine provides many choices, depending on the emotional state of the character and what the character needs to say. The character requires more than ten beats (which signified normal thought) to state what they are saying. This can raise the emotional or intellectual stakes of the scene. Think about a box that holds only ten golf balls, but you are trying to cram twelve balls into that same box. That's the feeling Bill is trying to create.
- *Incomplete lines* are those in which Shakespeare has deliberately *omitted beats*. Through such a line, Shakespeare is revealing to the actor that there

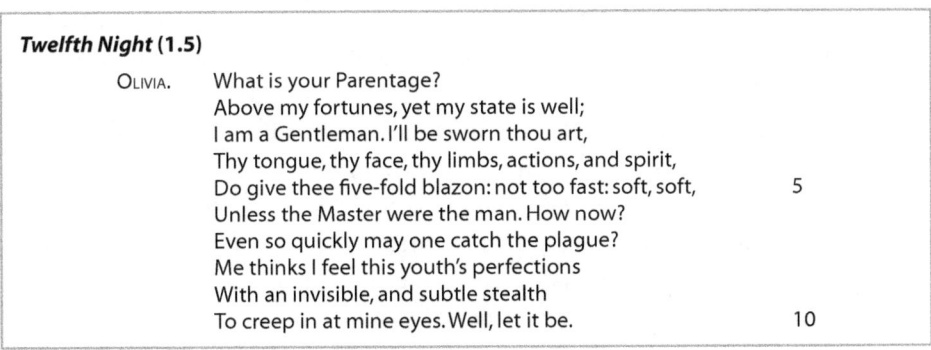

FIGURE 5.3. Speech for analysis: Finding a verse's heartbeat.

should be either a thought or an action. You have the option to place the missing beats at the beginning, middle, or end of the line. This again depends upon the specific intention of the scene and the creative choice of those involved.

- *Rhythm changes* occur when the word's natural stress doesn't fit into the iambic pentameter pattern of a verse line. As you speak the line, you will experience a jolting feeling—everything comes to a halt. Bill is letting us know that not everything is as normal as it should be. The character's heartbeat is off its normal rhythm and we should explore the "why" of that.

Let's now apply these concepts to the text from *Twelfth Night*.

OLIVIA.   What is your Parentage?

Olivia starts right away with an *incomplete line* of only six beats:

```
 U   /   U   /  U  /
What is your Parentage?
```

As stated earlier, incomplete lines provide an opportunity for thought or action. The last lines that Viola/Cesario speaks to Olivia before she/he exits are:

VIOLA.   Love make his heart of flint, that you shall love,
And let your fervor like my master's be,
Placed in contempt: Farewell fair cruelty.

All of Viola's lines are in perfect iambic pentameter. Viola is levelheaded, knows what she is saying, logical, and in control of her speech, thoughts, and emotions. We then have Olivia's six-beat line. There are a multitude of choices here for the four missing beats. One could make the case that the four beats are missing as they allow for Viola/Cesario's exit (action). This is valid. We also could explore using those missing beats for Olivia. After Viola's beautiful "Make me a willow cabin" speech, Olivia is truly falling in love with him (her) and asks the question, "What is your Parentage?" Viola responds, "Above my fortunes, yet my state is well:" so Olivia is reliving this moment at the beginning of the text we are exploring. Have you ever said something to someone you are attracted to, just met, and wish you could take it back because you sounded so "stupid"? I think we all have. What if we try that idea with the missing four beats before Olivia speaks. As there was no "fourth wall" in Shakespeare's time, the second that Viola/Cesario exits, Olivia looks at the audience, mouth open, thinking "What did I just say/do? How stupid!" and then speaks her lines. We've now created a comedic and very human moment based on the fact that Bill gave us four missing beats to explore.

Let's look at another two lines:

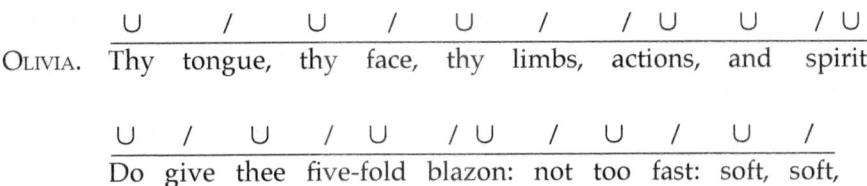

OLIVIA. Thy tongue, thy face, thy limbs, actions, and spirit,

Do give thee five-fold blazon: not too fast: soft, soft,

What fun! Without getting too technical, the first line contains eleven beats and the rhythm is off (thanks to the word *actions*). If you pat your chest as you speak that line, right when you speak "actions, and spirit," your "heartbeat" is all over the place. *That* is the clue from Bill. She is head over heels in love (in all ways) with Cesario. Take a look at the list she goes through (see more on this clue in Chapter 6), and look up *limbs, actions,* and *spirit* on Shakespeare's Words or, more important, in *Shakespeare's Bawdy* (Partridge), and you will discover she is quite bawdy here. Is it any wonder that her heartbeat is off its normal pattern? Next, pat your chest while speaking the second line above and you find that you have twelve beats. The stakes are high for Olivia. Her thoughts and her heart are all over the place, so she's cramming twelve beats into a ten-beat line while telling herself to calm down and get back in control with "not too fast: soft, soft." As we learn in Chapter 6, the colon after *fast* gives her a chance to think. It's almost as though Bill gives her the opportunity for a few panting breaths before she continues. Finally, notice in the next line "Unless the Master were the man. How now?" she is back on a regular ten-beat pattern. She did regain control, but with the mid-stop after *man*, that's a new great discovery and she starts to lose a bit of control again.

Let's explore one more line together:

> **Student of the Bard Talk**
>
> Putting Shakespeare's words and characters into motion tremendously improves my understanding of his work. This is because words I didn't understand before now make sense when paired with a movement. Sometimes, seeing things is what helps to understanding it. It's kind of like in chemistry... an experiment can be explained to me a million times, but, until I see it, I probably won't understand it.
>
> —ABBY SOKOL,
> *Adlai E. Stevenson High School*

```
                      U    /   U   /  U    /      U  /  U
OLIVIA.   Me  thinks  I   feel  this  youth's  perfections
```

Here again, Bill gives us wonderful choices. If you pat your chest while saying this line, you realize that Bill gave us nine beats. Remember that Olivia is a normal, living, breathing woman who is head over heels in love with Cesario. What do you think she is referring to when she mentions Cesario's "perfections"? You got it! She is being quite bawdy and very human. So there is the choice to perhaps place an extra beat of thinking (seeing an image) before she says, "perfections." That would certainly work. But, in Shakespeare, the suffix *-tion* or *-tions* is usually extended to create a normal ten-syllable line. So, in this case, we have the choice to pronounce the word in four syllables: per-FEC-shee-UNS:

```
                      U    /   U   /  U    /     U /  U  /
OLIVIA.   Me  thinks  I   feel  this  youth's  perfections
```

This extension of the word beautifully matches what Olivia is thinking and seeing at the moment. So, in just ten lines, through simply exploring the rhythm of Olivia's speech, we can see how Bill has mapped out her excited, unexpected, and bawdy irregular heartbeat. Thank you, Bill!

One last thought about scansion. There are times in which you may pat your chest while saying a line and feel more than the normal ten beats. The best example used in many books on the subject is Juliet's line from *Romeo and Juliet*:

JULIET.   O *Romeo*, *Romeo*, wherefore art thou *Romeo*?

If you pat your chest while speaking the line, allowing *Romeo* to be pronounced in three syllables, the rhythm is all over the place and you discover fourteen beats and two different ways to pronounce Romeo's name in the same line. However, if we elide *Romeo* (make it two syllables as opposed to three), it is revealed that the line is in regular rhythm with a final extra beat.

```
                 U   / U    / U     /  U    /  U    / U
JULIET.   O   Romeo,  Romeo,  wherefore  art  thou  Romeo?
```

As you can see, there are so many choices in terms of how a line could be scanned. There simply is no "right way" or "one way." Bill gives us a multitude of possibilities. Exploring the heartbeat—the rhythm—of the character is so important. This analysis allows for the freedom of choice based on the rhythm of the language rather than locking into one approach.

Exercise #4: Tap Dancing with the Bard: Iambic Pentameter Step–Heel Exercise

PURPOSE OF THE EXERCISE
To help the students physically discover and explore Shakespeare's use of iambic pentameter.

SETUP
Students should have copies of the lines in Figure 5.4 in order to tap out the iambic pentameter.

INSTRUCTIONS
For students to truly understand and feel the benefits of exploring iambic pentameter in Shakespeare's verse, it is helpful to provide ways in which they can engage with the rhythm of the language through the physical use of their bodies. When learning how to tap dance, one of the very first steps taught is called a "step–heel." The ball of your foot hits the floor first, dropping your heel down next. Your weight is on the ball of your foot, ensuring that you make full contact with the floor before the heel drops down. This is also done with a steady, even tempo. The step looks like this:

R	R	L	L	R	R	L	L	R	R	L
step	heel	step	heel	step	heel	step	heel	step	heel	step heel, etc.

First, just make sure your students are able to accomplish this basic tap dance step by having them walk around the room utilizing the step–heel tap step. Once this is accomplished, it's time to "tap dance with Bill!"

The entire group will now tap dance some lines from Shakespeare. On each unstressed syllable of the line, they should "step." On each stressed syllable, they should drop their "heel." It is suggested that you begin this exercise with a regular iambic pentameter line:

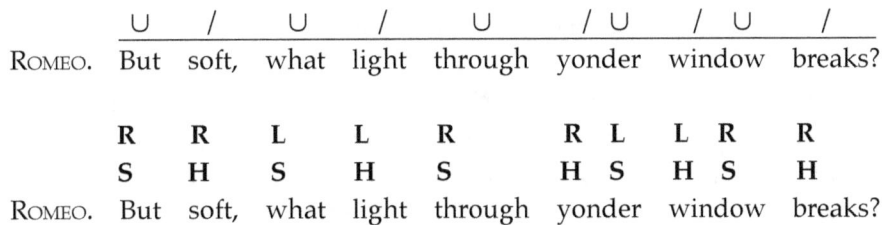

Now try tapping the lines in Figure 5.4.

> - JULIET.   The clock struck nine, when I did send the Nurse, (*Rom.* 2.5)
> - ORSINO.   If Music be the food of Love, play on, (*TN* 1.1)
> - HAMLET.   Oh that this too too solid Flesh, would melt, (*Ham.* 1.2)
> - ANTONY.   Cry havoc and let slip the Dogs of War, (*JC* 3.1)
> - LYSANDER.   The course of true love never did run smooth, (*MND* 1.1)
> - IAGO.   But I will wear my heart upon my sleeve (*Oth.* 1.1)
> - OTHELLO.   It is the Cause, it is the Cause (my Soul) (*Oth.* 5.2)

FIGURE 5.4. Sample step–heel tapping lines.

Once the students have tapped out these lines, ask them the following questions:

- Did you notice something in common with each of the lines above? (If you're lucky, the students will point out that these lines all contain perfect iambic pentameter structure.)
- When tapping out these regular lines, how does it feel physically? Do you feel you are landing on solid ground?
- Try tapping one more line again to feel physically in your body what a regular line of iambic pentameter is like.

Then have them tap the following line:

HAMLET.   To be, or not to be, that is the Question:

Once the students have tapped out this line from *Hamlet*, ask them the following questions:

- What happened physically this time when you tapped the line? (The students should notice that they ended the line with an extra "step.")
- When tapping this irregular line, how does it feel physically? Do you feel you are landing on solid ground this time?

This extra step gives us an "unsure" or "incomplete" feeling. This is the clue from Shakespeare. When confronted with an irregular line, in any fashion, Bill is indicating that the character is feeling uncertain and unsettled in some way. Through this exercise, the students physically feel this same uncertainty, and thus they are feeling the same unsettled feeling that the character is experiencing in this moment of the play. Try tapping these irregular lines:

MACBETH. Is this a Dagger, which I see before me,

VIOLA. I left no Ring with her: what means this Lady?

ROSALIND. Let me the knowledge of my fault bear with me:

Have your students tap dance through any speech line by line and watch them discover the "heartbeat" of the characters. You could also break the students up into pairs, having one student tap dance while another student records the results. The point of this is that, once they have tapped out the rhythm, they should review the speech to see where the rhythm was "off" or irregular. They should then try to figure out *why* the character went off their natural rhythm and what this reveals about their emotional state during the section of a speech or scene they are analyzing.

Shakespeare's Times to Rhyme

We would be remiss not to include a few words about how and when Shakespeare uses rhymes, though, by its very nature, blank verse is unrhymed iambic pentameter. The First Folio and modern editions don't usually differ in how rhymes appear in the text—they just may be spelled differently. Shakespeare actually deviated from earlier drama conventions where rhyme dominated a verse play. He used rhyming couplets to end a scene or the entire play, which was helpful in the absence of a curtain or lighting effects. He also used rhyme to emphasize an idea or image within a scene, where he relied on both internal and end rhymes; for

> **Student of the Bard Talk**
>
> [Physicalizing the verse] helped me understand that the characters in Shakespeare's plays were actual human beings with thoughts, feelings, goals, and motives for everything they do, just like us.
>
> —HAILEY KEENAN,
> *Adlai E. Stevenson H.S.*

example, rhymes were associated with aphorisms, well-worn advice, predictions, and curses (Shakespeare's Globe). Here is an example from *Macbeth* that features both internal and end rhymes:

SECOND WITCH. For a Charm of powerful **trouble**,
  Like a Hell-broth, boil and **bubble**.

ALL WITCHES. Double, **double**, toil and **trouble**,
  Fire burn, and Cauldron **bubble**.

Rhymes can be either strong and "perfect," like *double* and *trouble* in the previous example, or very subtle or inexact. Internal rhymes can be harder to spot, as with this example from *As You Like It*:

> SILVIUS.   Sweet Phe*be* do not scorn *me*, do not Phe*be*

Strong rhymes dominate *Romeo and Juliet* as well as the sonnets, since rhyming is certainly the language of love. Here are a few examples from *Romeo and Juliet* that illustrate a variety of applications, from expressing love to dispensing advice to underscoring their tragedy:

> ROMEO (*on Rosaline*).   She hath forsworn to love, and in that **vow**
>   Do I live dead, that live to tell it **now**.
>
> FRIAR (*to Romeo*).   Young Son, it argues a distempered **head**,
>   So soon to bid good morrow to thy **bed**;
>
> (*Ending the play*)   For never was a Story of more **Woe**,
>   Than this of *Juliet*, and her **Romeo**.

Students might want to think of rhyming as a way to highlight subtly or provide extra importance to a moment in a scene. If you want students to mark rhymes in a speech or scene, highlight them in a color that distinguishes them from the Ecphonesis O.

The Virtues of Verse to Express Emotions

In his *New York Times* article "What Makes a Great Shakespearean?" Charles Isherwood advises:

> Tastes in acting, as in everything else, certainly vary, but a great Shakespearean performance is easy to spot. You know one when you see one, although it's probably more accurate to say that you know one when you *don't* see one: when the language no longer feels remote, when the humanity of the actor and the character seem indivisible, when the emotion being expressed is no longer veiled by poetic phrasing but revealed by it, creating a shock of recognition in your own heart.

Isherwood's assessment is exactly what we are attempting to achieve when we work with the texts of Shakespeare. Bill's characters are living, breathing human beings who *need* the use of heightened language and poetic melody in order to achieve what they want from another character on stage.

Intermediate Folio Clue Card: Versification

Folio Technique Clue	✓	Definition	Scoring the Text
Full Thoughts		A period, exclamation point, or question mark signals a character's **full thought**. <u>Underline</u> or highlight the last three or four words before the period, exclamation point, or question mark.	ANTONY. Thou art the Ruins of the Noblest man That ever <u>lived in the Tide of Times</u>. (JC 3.1)
Full Stops		Periods, exclamation points, and question marks found **at the end of a verse line** signify a full stop. Score these with an **F**. A full breath can be taken. Land the end of the thought.	QUEEN MARGARET. My Lord of Suffolke, say, is this the guise? **F** Is this the Fashions in the Court of England? **F** Is this the Government of Britaines Ile? **F** And this the Royaltie of *Albions* King? **F** (2H6 1.2)
Mid-Stops		Periods, exclamation points, and question marks found **in the middle of a verse line** signify a mid-stop. Score these with an **M** above the mid-stop punctuation. Mid-stops indicate the need to finish the thought at the punctuation mark, then immediately jump to the next thought with a great deal of energy.	CALPHURNIA. **M** What mean you *Caesar?* Think you to walk forth? **F** You shall not stir out of your house today. **F** (JC 2.2)

Shared Lines		Shared lines in verse contain ten or more syllables and the line is divided between two characters. Shared lines function like a **mid-stop**. The first actor tosses their line to the second actor and, in turn, picks up the energy by immediately speaking their line.	ROMEO.
			O that I were a Glove upon that hand,
			                    M
			That I might touch that cheek.
			JULIET. **M**
			                              Ay me.
			ROMEO. She speaks.
			(Rom. 2.2)

Iambic Pentameter Guidelines		1. **A ten-syllable line** is called a **masculine** line. The character's "heartbeat" is regular and thinking is clear.
		2. **An eleven-syllable line** is called a **feminine** line. Line ends with an unstressed syllable. The character's "heartbeat" is off—usually something emotional is happening.
		3. **A twelve-syllable line** is called an **alexandrine**. The character's "heartbeat" is way off. Emotional stakes are ratcheting up.
		4. **Incomplete lines** contain **omitted beats.** This indicates there should be either a thought or an action. This accounts for the "missing" beats.
		5. **Rhythm changes** occur when the word's natural stress does not fit into the iambic pentameter pattern of a verse line.
			1. OPHELIA.
			   O what a Noble mind is here o're-thrown?
			   (Ham. 3.1)
			2. VIOLA.
			   I left no Ring with her: what means this Lady?
			   (TN 2.2)
			3. LADY MACBETH.
			         Come to my Woman's Breasts,
			   And take my Milk for Gall, you murd'ring Ministers,
			   (Mac. 1.5)
			4. HERMIA.
			   Why are you grown so rude?
			   What change is this sweet Love?
			   LYSANDER.
			   Thy love? out tawny Tartar, out;
			   (MND 3.2)
			5. HAMLET.
			   Let me not think on't: Frailty, thy name is woman.
			   (Ham. 1.2)

| Rhymes | Shakespeare used end rhymes for several reasons:
1. to end a scene or end a play
2. to make a prediction or a spiritual curse
3. to make clever or astute observations. | 1. MACBETH.
    I go, and it is done: the Bell invites me.
    Hear it not, *Duncan*, for it is a **Knell**
    That summons thee to Heaven, or to **Hell.**
                          (*Mac.* 2.1)
2. BRABANTIO.
    Look to her (Moor) if thou hast eyes to see:
    She has deceiv'd her Father, and may thee.
                          (*Oth.* 1.3)
3. ORSINO.
    For women are as Roses, whose fair **flower**
    Being once displayed, doth fall that very **hour.**

   VIOLA.
    And so they are: alas, that they are **so**:
    To die, even when they to perfection **grow.**
                          (*TN* 2.4) |

Explore Rhetorical Clues Using the Folio Technique

How Can You Glimpse a Character Cogitating?

In Chapters 4 and 5, we unearthed clues in Shakespeare's texts to help us discover his characters in an immediate and visceral way as they think and speak the words that shape lines of blank verse. Shakespeare's versification strategies reveal the "poetic humanness" of a character. When we activate those verse clues, they unlock a much more believable, understandable, and moving experience for those reading and speaking Bill's texts. While verse stirs our emotions, *rhetoric* appeals to our sense of logic. Advanced Folio technique encompasses rhetorical strategies that employ both the classical notion of rhetoric and a more "actor-ly" form, which includes aspects of diction, syntax, and punctuation to build an argument in the moment, in the same present tense in which the character's emotions also reside. To get closer to Shakespeare's text, especially for novice readers, Graham Watts recommends adopting an actor-ly approach over an academic one—explaining, "an academic will propose an explanation of a line, an actor will seek its motivation" (10)—when applying *rhetorical clues*.

Rhetorical Tradition and Shakespeare's Education

We should begin our examination of Shakespeare's use of actor-ly rhetorical strategies by considering his own academic training. As Simon Callow points out in "Shakespeare's Childhood and Education":

> [In Shakespeare's time t]hey didn't study history, they didn't study mathematics, they didn't study geography, they didn't study science. They studied grammar, from dawn to dusk, six days a week, all the year round. Grammar–Latin grammar. They translated from Latin into English and from English into Latin. At school, ordinary conversation was in Latin; any boy caught speaking English was flogged.

And they mastered the tropes of rhetoric, from *antimetabole* (where words are repeated in inverse order) to *zeugma* (where one verb looks after two nouns). This is the language of power and politics: of the law, of Parliament, of the court, and this is the world of which young Will and his fellow pupils would soon, it was hoped, be part.

As this was the typical educational upbringing for Bill and his contemporaries, those hearing, rather than reading, his plays would have been acutely aware of the language and rhetorical devices he used in order for characters to effect change in his plays. Doug Moston, in his introduction to Routledge's facsimile of the First Folio, notes:

> Elizabethan audiences appreciated rhetoric, listened for it, and there is ample evidence in the texts that Shakespeare was a master at writing it.... It was necessary to a proper education to learn how to structure an argument with logic, passion, and entertainment, balancing word with gesture to make vital points. (xvii–xviii)

Shakespeare's audience might have listened even more intently to see how he used rhetorical strategies and devices within his character's speeches in order for a character to effect change in another character—whether they were using language either to reveal or conceal the truth from other characters. When unearthing these rhetorical devices with your students, investigate them from the viewpoint that characters use language to persuade themselves, another character, or the audience.

First Set of Clues: Rhetoric, Diction, and Syntax

You probably don't have students with the same training in rhetoric of the Elizabethan schoolroom, but they can consider various features of diction and simple syntax as a springboard to rhetorical analysis. Usually, when we examine the power of persuasion, we may look to a political speech or a persuasive essay that has been drafted, revised, and polished until its rhetorical power gleams. Shakespeare's characters usually don't have the luxury of preparation, premeditation, or revision when they argue their case for love, justice, or understanding. Any argument, prepared or extemporaneous, begins with words—the more persuasive, the better.

Folio Rhetorical Clue: Monosyllabic Words

At the heart of Shakespeare's rhetorical strategy is a character's desire not only to inform but also to persuade. The art of persuasion can be intricate and complex, but many of Shakespeare's kings and queens, clowns, and lovers have precious little time to build and land their argument. Bill sometimes chooses monosyllabic lines for a character to express something that is vitally important or difficult to say and possibly to understand. Through the use of monosyllabic words that build key phrases, and even full lines, Bill also can alter the pace of the pentameter with these short words. Often these words add a bit of extra weight and therefore help a character to persuade emotionally as well as intellectually. Let's take a look at a section from Henry V's famous "Feast of Crispian" speech (4.3) from the First Folio to see how monosyllabic words work.

> HENRY. This story shall the good man teach his son:
> And *Crispin Crispian* shall ne're go by,
> From this day to the ending of the World,
> But we in it shall be remembered;
> We few, we happy few, we band of brothers:
> For he today that sheds his blood with me,
> Shall be my brother: be he ne're so vile,
> This day shall gentle his Condition.

King Henry V is trying to inspire his troops, who are significantly outnumbered and face certain death, to fight—and to fight valiantly. He tells them that this day will long be remembered as one of the greatest days of English history and that they will be praised for their courage now and always. His task is not easy at all, yet Shakespeare gives him the persuasive language tools to effect change in his men. Henry uses monosyllabic phrases and even almost full monosyllabic lines of verse in order to effect change. What he is saying is so vitally important for his troops to grasp that it must be spoken slower in order to effect the change Henry desires. He calls them brothers. This is an incredible statement for a king to call a common man his brother. All men who will fight with Henry have been elevated in status rhetorically and are now his brothers. Can you imagine Henry trying to persuade these men to keep fighting with fast-paced phrasing or overly heightened poetic language? That would not work at all. Instead, Bill provides Henry with direct, monosyllabic language creating a measured rhythm. Through the use of all of these monosyllabic words and phrases, he is persuading them on a highly emotional level. This is coupled with the repetitive technique of many monosyllabic words leading up to a polysyllabic word:

> But we in it shall be remembered;
> We few, we happy few, we band of brothers:
> For he today that sheds his blood with me,
> Shall be my brother: be he ne're so vile,
> This day shall gentle his Condition.

This technique billboards a polysyllabic word and makes that image or idea all the more significant and special. Words like *remembered, brothers, Condition,* stand out and are highly persuasive ideas and images. Brilliant. Take a look at the rest of this speech in 4.3 and you will see that Henry uses this monosyllabic technique effectively throughout the entire speech.

Folio Rhetorical Clue: Transitional—or "Big But"—Words

Yes, like rapper Sir Mix-a-Lot, Bill likes *big buts*, we cannot lie, to indicate a change of thought and the direction of an argument. It is then quite appropriate to give *transitional words—but, yet, therefore, however, if, or, so thus,* etc.—greater emphasis. Stressing these words highlights and strengthens the logical relationship between ideas, images, and stages of an argument. That emphasis helps the listener or the reader piece together these thoughts into a coherent persuasive argument. It keeps them on notice as to what is coming next. Characters can persuade successfully, as it is clearer how their ideas fit together. Furthermore, Barry Edelstein, in his book *Thinking Shakespeare,* advises actors (and we should extend that to readers as well) to always stress the words *all, now,* and *long* (100, 241).

When scoring the text to explore the impact of transitions, we box these words:

> ***A Midsummer Night's Dream*** *(2.1)*
>
> HELENA. You draw me, you hard-hearted Adamant,
> But yet you draw not Iron, for my heart
> Is true as steel. Leave you your power to draw,
> And I shall have to power to follow you.

In an attempt to win the favor of Demetrius, Helena has told him about the elopement of Hermia and Lysander and brought him into the woods to stop them. Once in the woods, Demetrius tells Helena again that he does not love her and to leave him alone. Helena then responds to Demetrius with the above four lines. According to the *Shakespeare Lexicon* (Schmidt), an *Adamant* is a stone of impenetrable hardness; the lodestone (15). A lodestone is a stone that strongly attracts something. The Arden Shakespeare Third Series edition of *A Midsummer Night's Dream* provides this note for Helena's line: "Demetrius attracts Helena like adamant, and his heart is as hard; yet he is not like adamant in that he does not draw Helena to him and embrace her, though her heart is true as steel" (162). By stressing the transitional words *But yet,* this strongly matches Helena's persistence and the intensity of her emotional frustration to be wanted and desired by Demetrius, and thus strengthens her persuasive argument. As adamant magnetically attracts iron and steel, so should Demetrius's attraction pull Helena to him, as her heart is like steel. Did you notice that *Adamant* and *Iron* are also capitalized words in the middle of a verse line? From Chapter 4, we learned that these words are "highlighted" through the use of unorthodox capitalization. Helena *really* wants him for *herself*—and not just metaphorically.

In *Henry V* 3.1, Henry is rallying his troops once again—this time, to keep fighting at the siege of Harfleur. As we explored Henry's use of monosyllabic words in the famous "Feast of Crispian" speech, let's now turn to Henry's equally famous "Once more unto the Breach Dear Friends" speech and discover how he effectively uses transitional words to meet his objective to rally his troops:

Henry V

HENRY.   Once more unto the Breach Dear Friends, once more;
         Or close the Wall up with our English dead:
         In Peace, there's nothing so becomes a man,
         As modest stillness, and humility:
         But when the blast of War blows in our ears,
         Then imitate the action of the Tiger:
         . . . .
         Now set the Teeth, and stretch the Nostril wide,
         Hold hard the Breath, and bend up every Spirit
         To his full height.

The use of *Or* so quickly emphasizes that they must keep fighting *or* the gap they created in the fortification will be filled with the bodies of their fellow dead soldiers. Henry then states that, in times of peace, it is admirable to show restraint and even humility. The argument shifts to war and Henry uses the words *But* and *Then,* again stressing the intensity of the moment trying to rouse the men to continue their fighting action. He then states, "Now set the Teeth." We stress the word *Now* so that it is clear he is talking about right now, this very second as he

> **Teacher of the Bard Talk**
>
> I require students [to] put a box around all of what Kevin calls "big but" words, aka transitional words. Doing so (similar to heightening awareness of punctuation) helps students follow...the thought process of the characters as they work toward obtaining their objective in the scene, which encourages [student] engagement.
>
> —CYNTHIA BURROWS,
> *Adlai E. Stevenson High School; drama and ELA teacher*

is speaking to them—not later, not tomorrow, but NOW you must be tigers. The urgency of the moment is made clearer when the word *Now* is stressed.

Folio Rhetorical Clue: Repetition of Words and Phrases

In a famous moment from the 1986 movie *Ferris Bueller's Day Off*, Ben Stein plays an economics teacher taking attendance. Matthew Broderick's character, Ferris Bueller, is absent; however, Ben Stein monotonously continues repeating "Bueller . . . Bueller . . . Bueller . . .," to the great dismay of the other students in the class. Notice that repetition was less than effective in this application. Think about how Martin Luther King Jr. used repetition so effectively in his "I have a dream" speech. He not only inspired a nation with his words, but his use of repetition also enabled everyone to remember the emotionally charged key words and phrases he thought were important.

If you listen to a recording of King's speech, each time he repeats the phrases "I have a dream," "We cannot be satisfied," and "Let freedom ring," he vocally builds on each repetition, giving strong rising momentum and causing the audience to react and cheer. This is the power of repetition. Similarly, in Shakespeare's text, we find powerfully repeated words or phrases. Repetition of emotionally charged words or phrases effectively helps a character announce and possibly achieve their objective. By stressing or treating each repetition differently, whether it is repetition of sounds, words, or phrases, the point made becomes more potent and memorable.

With this in mind, each time you repeat a word or phrase, give it more emphasis and a natural build will occur. We score this by underlining the repeated words or phrases. The first time you read or speak a repeated word, you underline it once. The second time the word occurs, you underline it two times, and so forth. This helps our eye to see the build, and it lets us know how many times we say the repeated word or phrase. Let's also keep in mind that characters are choosing to repeat words in order to effect change in another character—they *need* the repeated words. A good example comes from *A Midsummer Night's Dream* in 3.2. At this point in the play, Lysander and Demetrius (under Puck's spell) are strongly pleading their love for Helena, who believes that they are making fun of her. Hermia then shows up, confused as to why Lysander is now pleading for Helena's love and not her own. Helena believes Hermia is also taking part in mocking her and speaks these words:

A Midsummer Night's Dream

<blockquote>
HELENA.   We *Hermia*, like two Artificial gods,
Have with our needles, created <u>both</u> <u>one</u> flower,
<u>Both</u> on <u>one</u> sampler, sitting on <u>one</u> cushion,
<u>Both</u> warbling of <u>one</u> song, <u>both</u> in <u>one</u> key;
As if our hands, our sides, voices, and minds
Had been incorporate.
</blockquote>

Helena and Hermia are as close as sisters. Helena simply cannot understand why Hermia would join with Lysander and Demetrius in belittling her in such a fashion. In her attempt to make Hermia feel terrible for doing this, Helena repeats the words *both* and *one* again and again. The effect is strong. She argues that the two of them are so close in thought and sisterly love that they act as one. Those repeated words, along with an increase in vocal intensity on each repetition, bring this tactic to a level that is highly persuasive and emotional.

In 5.5 of *Macbeth*, Macbeth has just found out that Lady Macbeth is dead and will soon find out that the castle is under siege, led by Malcom and Macduff. Macbeth realizes that the end of his life is near. Here, the energy in the use of repetition may go in the opposite direction—starting strong and then, with each repeated word, a little less stress and a little less stress, etc. It is an emotionally persuasive tactic that is highlighted physically in the exercise "Stepping It Up with Shakespeare's Lists and Repetition" presented later in this chapter.

Macbeth

<blockquote>
MACBETH.   <u>Tomorrow</u>, and <u>tomorrow</u>, and <u>tomorrow</u>,
Creeps in this petty pace from <u>day</u> to <u>day</u>,
To the last Syllable of Recorded time:
And all our yesterdays, have lighted Fools
The way to dusty death. <u>Out</u>, <u>out</u>, brief Candle,
Life's but a walking Shadow,
</blockquote>

Repetition also occurs between two or more characters. In this way, it's helpful to think that one character hears a word spoken from another character and then purposefully uses that same word in order to effect change in the other character. The build would then happen between the two or more characters.

For example:

A Midsummer Night's Dream (1.1)

HERMIA. God speed <u>fair</u> Helena, whither away?
HELENA. Call you me <u>fair</u>? That <u>fair</u> again unsay,
           Demetrius loves you <u>fair</u>: O happy <u>fair</u>!

A Midsummer Night's Dream (3.2)

HELENA. O excellent!
HERMIA. Sweet, do not scorn her so.
DEMETRIUS. If she cannot <u>entreat</u>, I can <u>compel</u>.
LYSANDER. Thou canst <u>compel</u>, no more than she <u>entreat</u>.
           Thy threats have no more strength than her weak praise.
           Helen, <u>I love thee</u>, by my life I do;
           I swear by that which I will lose for thee,
           To prove him false, that says <u>I love thee</u> not.
DEMETRIUS. I say, <u>I love thee</u> more than he can do.

In each of the examples above, characters are making the conscious choice to *use* the exact word that was just "tossed" at them. They then "throw" the repeated word back at the other character in order to prove *their* point. It's like a tennis match.

Folio Rhetorical Clue: Repetition of Individual Sounds—Assonance, Alliteration, Consonance

Not only does Bill effectively use repetition of words and phrases, but also, like all good poets, he frequently uses repetition of vowel sounds and consonant sounds throughout his plays. Let's take a look at the effect assonance and alliteration have as a character is choosing to use these techniques in order to effect change in another character on stage.

Assonance is the repetition of vowel sounds (e.g., "How now brown cow?"). When the language is very "vowel-ly," this usually indicates heightened emotion in the language.

Romeo and Juliet (4.5)

NURSE.   O woe, O woeful, woeful, woeful, day,
           Most lamentable day, most woeful day,
           That ever, ever, I did yet behold.
           O day, O day, O day, O hateful day,
           Never was seen so black a day as this:
           O woeful day, O woeful day.

When she is speaking the above text, you can hear Nurse's cries through all of the "oh" sounds in her speech. The assonance provided by Bill enables the actor's voice to carry a devastatingly mournful tone. Not to mention, she utters eight Ecphonesis O sounds. As we learned in Chapter 4, the Ecphonesis O sound comes from the Greek theater and it is a cry of passion. Perhaps she is making an audible sound while breathing in at these points. This would match what we hear when someone is in crisis and crying uncontrollably. Have your students speak this piece of text while overemphasizing the vowel sounds. When doing this, it won't sound intelligible and that is OK. This is a quick exercise to feel the power of the vowel sounds and how they contribute to the moment that the character is experiencing on stage. So you will hear something like this:

OH OH	**OH OH-UH**	**OH-UH**	**OH-UH**	**EY**	
O woe,	O woeful,	woeful,	woeful,	day,	

OH	**UH-E-UH-UH**	**EY**	**OH**	**OH-UH**	**EY (etc.)**
Most	lamentable	day,	most	woeful	day,

How does it make you feel when you speak the language this way? It's clear that the Nurse is so upset that she can barely control her emotions and needs to make sure that everyone on stage realizes how devastating it is that Juliet is dead. Thanks to the use of assonance, the text informs us quickly and clearly.

Alliteration is the repetition of initial sounds (e.g., "Peter Piper picked a peck of pickled peppers"). This device can emphasize a key idea or image.

The Tempest (1.2)

ARIEL.   **F**ull **f**athom **f**ive thy **F**ather lies,
          Of his bones are Coral made:

Macbeth (3.2)

MACBETH. Come, <u>s</u>eeling Night,
<u>S</u>carf up the tender Eye of pitiful Day,
And with thy bloody and invisible Hand
Can<u>c</u>el and tear to pie<u>ces</u> that great Bond,
Which keep<u>s</u> me pale.

In the *Macbeth* text nugget that begins with alliteration, we also have examples of *consonance* (repeating consonant sounds in the middle or at the end of words) in the final lines. When speaking the above text by Macbeth, you will hear many "s" sounds. Have your students speak this text while overstressing the "s" sounds. When you speak the text this way, it may sound like you are Harry Potter speaking Parseltongue. How does that make you feel when you speak the language this way? What does the language tell you as to the character and his intent at this moment? Alliteration here is giving us an insight into the core of Macbeth's character at this moment in the play.

Folio Rhetorical Clue: Lists

Another way that Shakespeare builds intensity into the language is by creating *lists*. You will find that Shakespeare uses lists quite frequently throughout all of his plays. Characters may choose to use a listing pattern because the idea expressed is of such great importance that just one word doesn't convey the magnitude of the situation. Or perhaps a character is trying to convince another character, the audience, or themselves that a way of thinking or choice is valid. One example most likely will not work, so they need several examples in order to achieve persuasion. Lists are like stepping-stones for Shakespeare's characters in that there needs to be some type of vocal build when a character is using listing structure.

We score this by numbering the items in the list. Again, this will draw our eye to the list and we can note how long the list is when speaking. In the first example below from the First Folio, the word *Dauphin* is spelled "Dolphin"; the footnote in the Arden Shakespeare edition of the play, edited by T. W. Craik, advises, "Dauphin since 1349 the title of the King of France's eldest son, whose crest was a dolphin" (145).

Henry V (1.2)

1

HENRY. But tell the *Dolphin*, I will keep my State,

>   2   3
> Be like a King, and show my sail of Greatness,
>
> When I do rouse me in my Throne of France.

A Midsummer Night's Dream (3.2)

>   1   2   3
> HELENA.   To vow, and swear, and superpraise my parts,
>   When I am sure you hate me with your hearts.

The Tempest (1.2)

> FERDINAND.   My spirits, as in a dream, are all bound up:
>   1   2
>   My Father's loss, the weakness which I feel,
>   3   4
>   The wrack of all my friends, nor this man's threats,
>
>   To whom I am subdued, are but light to me,

You can couple the attention to lists with parallel structure, which strengthens the regularity of the rhythm of the speech or shared dialogue as well as making the list more memorable and quotable.

Folio Rhetorical Clue: Antithesis

Antithesis is the setting up of opposites in the text to help convey meaning to the audience. Antithetical phrases strengthen the persuasive argument of the character by the use of contrasting words, phrases, or ideas. This device can also employ listing to dramatic and memorable effect. As a result, antithesis helps make clear the intent of a character in a remarkable way:

- It was the best of times, it was the worst of times. (Charles Dickens, *A Tale of Two Cities*, vol. 1)
- That's one small step for man, one giant leap for mankind. (Neil Armstrong)
- It is our choices, Harry, that show what we truly are, far more than our abilities. (Spoken by Dumbledore in *Harry Potter and the Chamber of Secrets* 352)
- You're hot then you're cold / You're yes, then you're no / You're in, then you're out / You're up, then you're down (Katy Perry, "Hot n Cold")

Characters utilizing antithesis set up their viewpoint in direct contrast to an opposing viewpoint or position. This makes the case that what they think or feel is correct and should be clearly understood by all. As Cicely Berry, voice director from the RSC, in her book *The Actor and the Text* states:

> The actor has to be in tune with this way of thinking, and he has to be able to lift these opposites so that they catch the attention of the hearer, for it is through this rhetorical device that the argument is presented. And this is what gives the writing so much vigour, because it is between extremes that a character operates and thinks. (90)

We score the antithetical words or phrases by circling the opposite ideas and tie them together with an arched line, like this:

Hamlet (1.1)

HORATIO. This Spirit (dumb) to us, will (speak) to him:

In this first example, Horatio emphasizes that, to overcome the muteness of the apparition, he and his companions will need to speak first. In the second example, we have Orsino speaking with Viola, disguised as Cesario, about love. Orsino is deeply in love with Olivia; however, she continues to reject his love throughout the play.

Twelfth Night (2.4)
ORSINO. . . .   if ever thou shalt love
           In the (sweet) (pangs) of it, remember me:

As Charles Boyce observes in *Shakespeare A to Z*, "Utterly involved in his self-image as a brooding, rejected lover, Orsino cannot accept the fact that his passion for Olivia is misplaced" (469). He is a self-indulgent, melancholy, and melodramatic character. All of this is strikingly revealed through Bill's use of the two-word antithesis above when Orsino describes love: sweet/pangs. As John Barton states in his book *Playing Shakespeare*, "And of course the contrast and clash between 'sweet' and 'pangs' needs bringing out because it tells us about Orsino. Love is sweet to him and he is in pain, but he loves it" (151).

Folio Rhetorical Clue: Inversion Strategies

Inversion strategies rely on one of three devices: (1) *anastrophe*, changing the order of the words; (2) *anaclasis*, a substitution of a variant foot; and (3) *antime-

tabole, from a Greek term meaning "turning in the opposite direction." When students encounter an inverted line such as "The Castle of Macduff, I will surprise" in *Macbeth*, it confirms for them the oddness and unnaturalness of Shakespeare's language, but, if they are fans of *Star Wars*, they should be familiar with this technique. Jedi Master Yoda is a true master of straight-up inverted syntax. He is famous for making these statements, among many others:

- Strong am I in the Force. (*Return of the Jedi*)
- Much to learn have you. (*The Phantom Menace*)
- Truly wonderful, the mind of a child is. (*Attack of the Clones*)

His use of simple inverted statements adds to his role as a sage and guru. His syntax sets him apart from the other characters in the saga. So, if students approach inversions as "Yoda speak," they will find the technique less intimidating and more familiar (McKinney). You may choose not to introduce the technical terms for the three patterns, but simply ensure that your students can recognize the patterns and how they function in a scene or a speech. Let's explore those functions.

Usually, when Shakespeare employs inverted syntax, he essentially highlights a statement or a phrase, since the basic syntactical pattern of subject–verb–object is disrupted. *Romeo and Juliet* offers many examples of anastrophe, which thematically makes sense since the star-crossed lovers themselves are disrupting the social order of Verona through their clandestine liaison. Let's look at two examples and tag lines featuring inverted syntax with an upside-down "i": ¡.

Romeo and Juliet (1.5)

NURSE. Her Mother is the Lady of the house,
  And a good Lady, and wise, and Virtuous, ¡

Romeo and Juliet (4.5)

NURSE. Never was seen so black a day as this: ¡

In the first example, the Nurse emphasizes that Juliet's mother is not only a "good lady" but "and wise and virtuous" as well by placing that adjectival phrase at the end of the line, giving those two descriptors greater importance. The second example, uttered upon the discovery of the dead lovers, relies on inversion to underscore the shocking discovery.

Inverted syntax is also used in Shakespeare's plays and sonnets to fit either the iambic pentameter rhythm or to create a rhyme, but its most important

Explore Rhetorical Clues Using the Folio Technique

application advances a thematic pattern. The most famous example of anaclasis is found at the beginning of Hamlet's most famous speech:

Hamlet (3.1)

HAMLET.   To be, or not to be, that is the Question: !

Here, Shakespeare substitutes a *trochee* in an iambic line. The first line of *Richard III* begins with emphasis on the first word:

Richard III (1.1)

GLOUCESTER.   **Now** is the Winter of our Discontent, !
               Made glorious Summer by this Son of York:

That single word, *Now,* sets in motion Richard, Duke of Gloucester's audacious plans to assume the throne as Richard III by any means necessary, as his opening soliloquy lays out his grievances and ambitions.

The final inversion technique, antimetabole, creates memorable idioms and quotable quotes by repeating a phrase in reverse order:

- When the going gets tough, the tough get going. (Knute Rockne, American football coach)
- Eat to live, not live to eat. (Socrates, qtd. by Plutarch)
- Ask not what your country can do for you, ask what you can do for your country. (John F. Kennedy, "Inaugural Address")

Shakespeare uses this technique to great effect in prophecies or incantations:

Macbeth (1.1)

WITCHES.   fair is foul, and foul is fair,

as well as in riddling wisdom dispensed by the most unlikely of sources:

Twelfth Night (1.5)

CLOWN.   virtue that transgresses, is but patch'd with sin, and sin that amends, is but patch'd with virtue.

This type of inversion occurs less commonly than the other two, but it does point out that things may not be as they seem, or underscore a moment with a touch of sarcasm. Also, at its best application, it can sum up an argument in a single pithy statement.

Exercises to Physicalize Rhetoric, Diction, and Syntax

Since these clues provided Shakespeare's actors access to the complexities of the characters they are playing in an immediate way, let's work through some exercises so that your students can, like Bill's actors, gain immediate access to the power of basic rhetorical strategies.

Exercise #1: Stepping It Up with Shakespeare's Lists and Repetition

Purpose of the Exercise
To help the students successfully build in voice and intensity when utilizing list structure with a simple physical exercise.

Setup
The students need a copy of any text that employs listing structure. Work in a location where you have access to a staircase.

Instructions
Begin by explaining the concept of lists, and why they are needed by a character in order to effect change.

- Shakespeare builds intensity into the language by creating lists.
- Characters *choose* to use a listing pattern because the idea expressed is of such great importance that simply using one word or example will not suffice.
- Lists are like stepping-stones for Shakespeare's characters in that there needs to be some type of vocal build when a character is using listing structure.

Say to students: Let's return to the example from *Twelfth Night* highlighted in Chapter 5. Olivia, who has fallen in love with Cesario (Viola) at first sight, confesses this to the audience in this speech:

Twelfth Night (1.5)

OLIVIA.   What is your Parentage?
            Above my fortunes, yet my state is well;
            I am a Gentleman. I'll be sworn thou art,
            Thy tongue, thy face, thy limbs, actions, and spirit,
            Do give thee five-fold blazon: not too fast: soft, soft, 5
            Unless the Master were the man. How now?

Say to students: Score the text by placing numbers above the list employed by the character speaking. In this case, Olivia is categorizing Cesario's (Viola) physical aspects that attract her.

        1   **2**   **3**   **4**   **5**
Thy tongue, thy face, thy limbs, actions, and spirit,

Say to students: Speak the text aloud, making sure to account verbally for the listing structure.

Say to students: At a location with a staircase and with this text in hand, begin again and, when you get to each item in the list, step up to the next step. With each step up, build in vocal intensity until you finish the list. This simple physical exercise immediately will help you to understand and "feel" the power of listing structure.

This exercise works well when the listing structure needs to build in intensity. It also works when the build needs to move in the opposite direction.

SIDE COACHING

As classes can be large, it might be safer to introduce this exercise with one student demonstrating while others watch. Then split the class into small groups and have them explore the "Stepping It Up with Shakespeare's Lists and Repetition" exercise.

Macbeth TEXT NUGGET: REPETITION

Say to students: Now let's try this same exercise, utilizing repetition, which will support the build moving in the opposite direction, using the following speech from *Macbeth*:

Macbeth (5.5)

MACBETH.   Tomorrow, and tomorrow, and tomorrow,

> Creeps in this petty pace from day to day,
> To the last Syllable of Recorded time:
> And all our yesterdays, have lighted Fools
> The way to dusty death. Out, out, brief Candle,
> Life's but a walking Shadow, a poor Player,
> That struts and frets his hour upon the Stage,
> And then is heard no more. It is a Tale
> Told by an Idiot, full of sound and fury
> Signifying nothing.

Say to students: This time, start at the top of the staircase. And, when repeating the word *Tomorrow*, take one step down; do this as well each time you repeat the words *tomorrow, day,* and *out*.

Say to students: The emotional state of Macbeth at this moment is made clearer through his use of repetition, and, when walking down the steps on each repeated word, you will physically feel the weight of his words and his situation. How did adding physical movement to the speech help you follow Macbeth's line of thought and attempt to convince himself he is taking appropriate, yet dangerous, action?

Exercise #2: Tossing Pizzas Topped with Antithesis

Purpose of the Exercise
To help the students successfully identify antithesis and vocally highlight the opposing ideas when speaking the work of Shakespeare.

Setup
The students need a copy of the text from *Romeo and Juliet* (4.5) presented below, or any text that is rich in showcasing antithesis.

Instructions
Say to students to preview the activity: Have you had the opportunity to visit your local pizza parlor and watch as the chefs make pizza? A chef stretches the pizza dough over their fists, and then, in one fantastic moment, they toss the dough high into the sky in a circular, twirling motion. The dough then comes down and the chef catches it again with their fists. This is a great analogy for how we need to vocally set up antithetical words, phrases, and ideas so that our audience can follow the textual argument. We need to vocally "toss" the first part of the antithetical idea strongly up into the air so that it clearly rings in the ears of our

audience, and then vocally pull the second part of the antithetical idea back down with great energy so that the opposition is also clear in the audience's ears. In this exercise, you not only verbally "toss" the ideas into the air, but physically you will replicate the motion of tossing up pizzas and then catching them when they land. We will create vocal pizzas!

SIDE COACHING

You may want students to practice the vocal and physical toss with simple antithetical phrases like "What goes up must come down" before exploring the technique with the following piece of Shakespearean text.

> *Romeo and Juliet* (4.5)
>
> CAPULET. All things that we ordained Festival,
> Turn from their office to black Funeral:
> Our instruments to melancholy Bells,
> Our wedding cheer, to a sad burial Feast:
> Our solemn Hymns, to sullen Dirges change:
> Our Bridal flowers serve for a buried Coarse:
> And all things change them to the contrary.

You might need to provide a bit of context for students before they work this speech: Juliet's family, along with Friar Laurence, arrives to take Juliet to her wedding with Paris, when they discover that the Nurse was unable to wake her. All believe that Juliet is dead. Here, Shakespeare's use of sharp contrasting antithetical ideas in Juliet's Father's language brings out his deep grief that his daughter is dead. The positive and happy ideas associated with weddings are starkly contrasted with ideas of deep mourning that happen with funerals.

Now, prep the students with the following anticipatory activities:

1. Begin with a discussion of what antithesis is and how it is used. *Say to students:* Score this piece of text noting the antithetical ideas by circling them and connecting them with a line:

> CAPULET. All things that we ordained (Festival,)
>
> Turn from their office to black (Funeral:)

2. Review the concept of verbally tossing pizzas set out in the introductory instructions.

3. Then move on to these verbal instructions:
    - Speak the text and, when you get to the first part of the antithetical idea, toss the word/idea vocally and physically up into the air.
    - Continue speaking and, when you get to the second part of the antithetical idea, vocally and physically pull down the idea from the sky.

SIDE COACHING

We have experienced times when student participants attempt this exercise in a lackluster way. If they "put in junk, junk will come out." Stop the process; coach the students to fully commit to the exercise, and then restart. Join your students in this exercise. Once everyone fully commits vocally and physically, the point of the exercise is revealed. It really does work.

EXTENDING THE ACTIVITY

Have the students add in knowledge they have already gained. In those seven lines from *Romeo and Juliet* (4.5), students can unearth, score, and apply the following clues:

- transitional words
- capitalized words
- repetition of words and phrases
- lists
- monosyllabic phrases/lines.

DEBRIEFING THE ACTIVITY

- When finished, ask the students how they felt speaking the lines employing all of these various clues.
- When "tossing pizzas," does the antithesis become clearer to the audience who is hearing the play?
- Did any words or ideas stand out when speaking the text employing these techniques?

Teacher of the Bard Talk

A student favorite is "toss the pizza" when reciting antithetical words and phrases. Students really seemed to feel in their speech and in their bodies the "high and low" of such comparisons. I noticed that, near the end of the unit, some students were able to tune in automatically to opposites, even in sections they had not marked.

—JENNIFER BERTACCHI,
Carleton Washburne Middle School; ELA teacher

- How does language help reveal character in this sense?

This is a great exercise for the entire class. Have fun. Participate with your students. Be silly with your students. Exaggerate the pizza toss movements physically and vocally. If you can find pieces that have multiple antithetical ideas, you and your students will have more fun as you will need to toss several pizzas in the air at the same time.

> ### Teacher of the Bard Talk
>
> I use the antithesis "pizza toss" activity with *Romeo and Juliet* 1.4. The [students] playing Romeo, Mercutio, and Benvolio have a lot to do, as the scene is filled with repetition and antithesis! I used Romeo's speech as an example: "I am too sore empiercéd with his shaft / To soar with his light feathers, and so bound / I cannot bound a pitch above dull woe: / Under love's heavy burden do I sink" (19–22). Once the students became familiar with all the rich repetition and antithesis in this speech, I had the student playing Romeo take the actions a step further by letting his knees fall out from under him every time there was a repeated or "antithesis" word, to emphasize both Romeo's angsty pouting and Shakespeare's brilliant wordplay, forcing Benvolio and Mercutio to catch him, and resulting in some hilarious physical comedy. I received such comments as "I never realized how funny Shakespeare was!" and "I had read *Romeo and Juliet* a couple times before and I never understood it until now!"
>
> —Kate McDuffie,
> *Wolcott School; choral and drama teacher*

Exercise #3: Working Inverted Syntax with Master Yoda and Bill the Bard

Purpose of the Exercise

To have students manipulate a set of words drawn from the *Star Wars* film canon and Shakespeare's plays to examine how subject–verb–object can be inverted to create greater impact and meaning.

Setup

Snip apart each of the quotations provided in Figure 6.1. Place the snipped-up words in individual envelopes. Separate the Yoda Speak set from the Shakespeare Speak set and the Challenge set. Begin with the Yoda Speak quotations and move on to the Shakespeare Speak set.

Instructions

1. Have student volunteers come up in front of the class to work through their set of words, or divide them into groups based on the number of words in their phrase set (specified in parentheses).

2. Begin by modeling one of the Yoda sentences with volunteers to work out the phrase in front of the class. Pass out a word to each group member. Take care that they are not distributed in their "correct" order.

3. Ask students to read their words in a round-robin fashion. Once that is done, have them line up to assemble their phrase in its grammatically correct form.

4. Once that is accomplished, have students physically rearrange themselves in a line to form an inverted syntax version using the same words.

5. After you have worked through the Yoda Speak sentences, follow the same steps with the Shakespeare Speak set.

Debriefing

- How does inverting syntax change which words are emphasized in a phrase or sentence?
- How does inverting the syntax change the meaning of the phrase or sentence in any way?
- How does inverting the syntax change how you read the phrase or line? To what extent do you speed up or slow down the reading?

Yoda Speak

- To question, no time there is. (6)
- Always in motion is the future. (6)
- Mourn them, do not. Miss them, do not. (8)
- Truly wonderful the mind of a child is. (8)
- Not if anything to say about it, I have. (9)

Shakespeare Speak

- Rude am I, in my speech, (5) (*Oth.* 2.3)
- Came he not home tonight? (5) (*Rom.* 2.4)
- Weeds of *Athens* he doth wear: (6) (*MND* 2.2)
- The Castle of *Macduff*, I will surprise. (7) (*Mac.* 4.1)
- From that place, I shall no leading need. (8) (*Lr.* 4.1)
- Younger than she, are happy mothers made. (7) (*Rom.* 1.2)
- More needs she the Divine, than the Physician: (8) (*Mac.* 5.1)
- Repays he my deep service with such contempt? (8) (*R3* 4.2)
- So foul and fair a day I have not seen. (10) (*Mac.* 1.3)
- Vexed I am of late, with passions of some difference, (10) (*JC* 1.2)

FIGURE 6.1. Inverted syntax lines.

Second Set of Clues: Rhetoric, Punctuation, and Breath

Examining the impact of punctuation and how it guides a character's delivery enables the reader, viewer, or actor to see and to feel how an argument is being constructed or a moment of persuasion is being executed. From a rhetorical strategies perspective, these clues help students understand how Shakespeare expertly builds in "thinking time" for characters who are living in the *perpetual present tense*. Rhetorically, they are thinking and speaking on their feet—and the stakes can be enormous, in both tragic and comic terms.

Folio Rhetorical Clue: Commas

When speaking the texts of Shakespeare (or any text aloud, for that matter), *intonation* is vitally important. Various intonation patterns utilized by a speaker will send out verbal signals to the listener. These signals will affect the meaning a listener attaches to the verbal message. One of the most common intonation mistakes occurs at the ends of verse lines when a comma is present. Many times, the speaker will utilize a "down-glide" intonation pattern at the end of every verse line. This not only confuses the listener, but also weakens the character's rhetorical argument. We have associated a down-glide intonation pattern when the end of a sentence (period or exclamation point) is present. Commas, however, indicate phrases or section of thought. Commas indicate thinking and the continuation of a thought. If a comma is found at the *end* of the verse line, keep the energy up, vocally lift your voice up at the end of the verse line (as opposed to a down-glide), and take a quick catch-breath to propel yourself into the next phrase. We will mark this with **cb** to remind us to "catch breath" as we speak or read. In this way, we are continuing to capture the ear of the listener who is "waiting" to hear the down-glide intonation to receive the verbal signal that the thought has ended with a period or exclamation point. You must continue to drive your energy through to the period, question mark, or exclamation point. In this way, the audience will receive the entirety of the rhetorical argument and the needed intent of the language will be clearly understood.

There are times when you will find a comma in the *middle* of the verse line. We have to remember that Bill's characters are *living in the perpetual present tense*. In a performance, an actor is fully memorized and knows what text is coming next; however, the character does not. Characters are not clairvoyant. They don't know they *need* the next bit of text until they discover that what they have been speaking up to a certain point has not been working.

To achieve the ability to live in the perpetual present tense, the skill of how to use commas in the middle of the verse line becomes vital. Let's apply this understanding of the importance of commas to this piece of Romeo's speech in *Romeo and Juliet* (3.3):

> Hadst thou no poison mixed, no sharp ground knife, **cb**
> No sudden mean of death, though ne'er so mean, **cb**
> But banished to kill me? Banished?

Notice the commas in the middle of the verse line after *mixed* and *death*. Instead of breaking up the verse structure by breathing after the commas in the middle of the verse line, let's stick with the idea of Romeo *in the perpetual present tense*. Romeo doesn't know any of this list beforehand. Just as in life, he's coming up with these ideas *in the present tense*. Even though the actor knows what is ahead in the plot, Romeo doesn't know he is going to come up with the idea of the knife until he speaks the last sound in the word *mixed*. When the commas are in the middle of the verse line, think of them, as John Basil does, as trampolines (71). We *will not take a breath* at these commas. Doing so breaks up the verse structure so much that those listening become lost. Rather, try to speak the text as if nothing is coming next after the word *mixed*. Then the next new thought of "sharp ground knife" comes in. So, *bounce* on the comma to help bring in this new thought. You should take quick catch-breaths after *knife* and *mean*, because those commas are at the end of the verse line. When you do this, you are matching how we speak as humans. Most important, you are acting and living in the *perpetual present tense*. It's truly a remarkable way of speaking the text. Romeo is trying to get Friar Laurence to understand how horrible banishment is and that death would be a far better punishment. Romeo then uses language to try to achieve this goal. The energy created by bouncing on the commas in the middle of his verse lines create the spontaneous and emotional outbursts he is experiencing while trying to find image after image to make the Friar understand his horrible predicament. Without this technique, the language would not contain the drive and spontaneity of this young man in crisis. This would be another time to have the students put the clues into action. Have one student speak Romeo's text above aloud with your coaching. Then have the entire class speak the same lines.

Let's apply the comma technique to another character in a deeply emotional crisis. Presented below is a text nugget from *Hamlet* (1.2), along with scoring full stops and mid-stops. As a quick review, when we encounter a period, exclamation point, or question mark at the *end* of the verse line, this is called a full stop. The text then is scored with an **F**. This is a full stop of the delivery of the text and a significant breath can be taken. If a period, exclamation point, or question mark is found in the *middle* of the verse line, this is called a mid-stop and we score the text with an **M**. The need to speak is great. Make sure to land the full thought, but, because the punctuation is in the middle of the verse line, you immediately launch into the next thought without taking a breath.

> Oh that this too too solid Flesh, would melt, **cb**
> Thaw, and resolve itself into a Dew:
> Or that the Everlasting had not fixed
> His Cannon 'gainst Self-slaughter. **M** O God, O God! **F**
> How weary, stale, flat, and unprofitable   5
> Seems to me all the uses of this world? **F**
> Fie on't? **M** Oh fie, fie, 'tis an unweeded Garden
> That grows to Seed: Things rank, and gross in Nature
> Possess it merely. **M** That it should come to this:
> But two months dead: Nay, not so much; not two, **cb**   10
> So excellent a King, that was to this
> *Hyperion* to a Satyr: so loving to my Mother, **cb**
> That he might not beteem the winds of heaven
> Visit her face too roughly. **M** Heaven and Earth
> Must I remember: why she would hang on him, **cb**   15
> As if increase of Appetite had grown
> By what is fed on; and yet within a month? **F**
> Let me not think on't: Frailty, thy name is woman. **F**

Notice the full stop after Hamlet speaks line 6, "Seems to me all the uses of this world?" The next time there is a full stop isn't until line 17, when he says, "By what is fed on; and yet within a month?" Through the use of mid-stops and commas, the drive of Hamlet's speech in this section is moving rapidly. He is using these strong rhetorical devices to make sure that the audience is as devastated as he is about his current situation. Commas in the middle of the verse give him the opportunity to search quickly for the next image that he can then use to devastate them. The urgency is written into the language. When we keep our voices lifted at those end-of-line commas, his drive continues. The audience listens intently, anticipating the full scope of the argument as they have not heard the down-glide of a period.

Folio Rhetorical Clue: Colons and Semicolons

Colons and semicolons signify the end of a phrase or section of thought, but do not signify the end of the *full thought*. Only periods, question marks, and/or exclamation points signify that. Through colons and semicolons, Shakespeare lets the actor know that a new thought is coming and that there will need to be a shift of energy that is equal to a shift in rhetorical strategy. To make this change clear to the audience, the actor takes a quick "thinking" breath to accomplish this "gear shift" from thought to thought. We mark this with a **T**. Working this way propels the thought forward as you move through various ideas toward the period, question mark, or exclamation point. Our score at this point would then look like this:

> Oh that this too too solid Flesh, would melt, **cb**
> Thaw, and resolve itself into a Dew: **T**
> Or that the Everlasting had not fixed
> His Cannon 'gainst Self-slaughter.^M O God, O God! **F**
> How weary, stale, flat, and unprofitable   5
> Seems to me all the uses of this world? **F**
> Fie on't?^M Oh fie, fie, 'tis an unweeded Garden
> That grows to Seed:^T Things rank, and gross in Nature
> Possess it merely.^M That it should come to this: **T**
> But two months dead:^T Nay, not so much;^T not two, **cb**   10
> So excellent a King, that was to this
> *Hyperion* to a Satyr:^T so loving to my Mother, **cb**
> That he might not beteem the winds of heaven
> Visit her face too roughly.^M Heaven and Earth
> Must I remember:^T why she would hang on him, **cb**   15
> As if increase of Appetite had grown
> By what is fed on;^T and yet within a month? **F**
> Let me not think on't:^T Frailty, thy name is woman. **F**

Student of the Bard Talk

Paying attention to the punctuation plays a major role in [understanding] Shakespeare. Let the students know the [function of] each punctuation mark because that will have a great impact on understanding the character. [Equally important] is re-reading with the emphasis on each punctuation mark in the line. This activity had improved [my understanding] overall because, with such emphasis, something has to change in a character.

—DZIYANA BALAKIR,
Adlai E. Stevenson High School

Teacher of the Bard Talk

Before we workshop, students must highlight or circle all of their punctuation. We discuss how the punctuation serves like road signs—encouraging the speaker to adjust vocal speed via inflection required by comma, semicolon, colon, period, question mark, exclamation point, etc. (like driving speed depends on the condition, shape of a road). That in and of itself changes a great deal in their [understanding].

—CYNTHIA BURROWS,
Adlai E. Stevenson High School; drama and ELA teacher

Folio Rhetorical Clue: End-of-Verse Lines

In our daily lives, we are constantly trying to persuade people to do something, whether it's to convince someone to go traveling with you, get someone to help you with yard work, coax someone into buying you that new car, and so on. You quickly realize that, to persuade someone to do something they do not want to do, it takes several attempts. You realize this in the present moment and search for each new idea or example that you can use to convince someone of what you need them to do. You say, subtextually, in your head, "What can I use/say that would convince her. . .?" AH! You find it and then "toss that idea" to the person you are trying to persuade, hoping it will work. We want to zoom in on that moment when we are thinking and searching for another way to present an idea. It's in that moment of searching that we are alive and in the present tense.

How does this apply to Shakespeare's work? When you encounter the end of a verse line without punctuation, this is akin to the moment described above. Shakespeare is giving his characters this moment to find language that is needed in order to effect change in another character. It's a quick moment of searching or finding. However, when confronted with end-of-verse lines missing punctuation, many chose to continue speaking the text straight through without pausing. This is called *enjambing*. When the practice of enjambing is employed, speakers are actually breaking down the verse structure Bill gave us and turning his verse into prose. Remember, if Shakespeare wanted his characters to speak in prose at any moment, he would have written the text that way. Bill typically did not use prose. Seventy-five percent of the First Folio is written in verse, while only 25 percent is written in prose. He kept most characters in the heightened verse structure for a reason; therefore, we need to honor that reason and avoid enjambing the text. Barry Edelstein, in his book *Thinking Shakespeare*, calls these instances "magic Mamet moments":

> Shakespeare was aware of what he was doing when he split lines. As he wrote, he made an endless series of choices about how to deploy iambic pentameter, the form he chose for the overwhelming majority of his output. . . . The modern master David Mamet uses a device that provides an exceptionally useful way for a Shakespearean to begin phrasing with the verse line. Here [is a] speech from Mamet's controversial play *Oleanna*:

> "You are to be disciplined. For facts. For *facts*. Not 'alleged,' what is the word? But *proved*. Do you see?"

Midway through [the above lines], Carol [a university student speaking to her professor] takes the briefest moment to ask herself how she's going to continue to articulate her thought. "What is the word?" she wonders, before finding it: "proved." . . . Mamet, like Shakespeare, knows that people speak spontaneously. They do not recite prewritten speeches. They think in the moment and then find language needed to reveal what is on their minds. So, Mamet writes Carol's thinking into her lines. (Edelstein 164–65)

As we apply the "magic Mamet moment" aspect of the Folio technique, Edelstein instructs us to ask "What?," or "How?," or "When?" at the ends of verse lines without punctuation. This creates the opportunity for that very quick thought as described above. The answer then to these imaginary questions is the next line of verse. In addition, the Folio technique requires that we should not take a breath. When we do this, we are honoring the verse line and the verse structure of what Bill wrote. When we correctly utilize the "magic Mamet moments," we are again keeping the character in the perpetual present tense. The character is *alive* and *thinking* in the present tense. Working this way will truly transform the way you think about the texts of Shakespeare. Try it. First, let's score the text from *Hamlet* (1.2), addressing the end-of-verse lines without punctuation:

```
Oh that this too too solid Flesh, would melt,
Thaw, and resolve itself into a Dew:
Or that the Everlasting had not fixed (What?)
His Cannon 'gainst Self-slaughter. O God, O God!
How weary, stale, flat, and unprofitable (What?)         5
Seems to me all the uses of this world?
Fie on't? Oh fie, fie, 'tis an unweeded Garden (What?)
That grows to Seed: Things rank, and gross in Nature (What?)
Possess it merely. That it should come to this:
But two months dead: Nay, not so much; not two,          10
So excellent a King, that was to this (What?)
Hyperion to a Satyr: so loving to my Mother,
That he might not beteem the winds of heaven (What?)
Visit her face too roughly. Heaven and Earth (What?)
Must I remember: why she would hang on him,              15
As if increase of Appetite had grown (How?)
```

By what is fed on; and yet within a month?
Let me not think on't: Frailty, thy name is woman.

Just by scoring all of the ends of verse lines with the questions "What?" or "How?," we can visually see how much Hamlet is *thinking in the moment*. It is unbelievable to him that his mother would marry his uncle so quickly after his father's death. He then goes on to imagine the specifics of their relationship and it is appalling to him. He is trying to describe how appalling it is to him through this soliloquy to the audience. Hamlet does not take the stage knowing exactly what he is going to say for the next three minutes. He is trying to find the language he needs *in the moment* (and ends of verse lines without punctuation) to make the audience understand how horrifying this situation really is. Speaking the text utilizing these quick moments of thought (as opposed to enjambing, which gives a sense that he knows what he is going to say) will truly open up the text in new and exciting ways to you and your students.

Exercises to Physicalize a Character Thinking in the Moment

Let's explore these new aspects to experience characters thinking on their feet through three further exercises.

Exercise #1: Snapping (the Commas) with Shakespeare

PURPOSE OF THE EXERCISE
In order to achieve the ability *to live in the perpetual present tense*, the skill of how to use commas in the middle of the verse line becomes necessary.

SETUP
Print the text below from *Romeo and Juliet* (3.5) (see Figure 6.2).

INSTRUCTIONS
Inform the students that characters in Shakespeare's plays (and any play, for that matter) don't know beforehand what they are going to say. They find the language they need in the moment to effect change. Just as in life, they are coming up with these ideas *in the present tense* (even though the actor knows what is ahead in the plot and has their lines memorized). Shakespeare replicates this concept by his use of commas in the middle of verse lines.

> **Romeo and Juliet (3.5)**
>
> CAPULET. God's bread, it makes me mad:
> Day, night, hour, ride, time, work, play,
> Alone in company, still my care hath been
> To have her matched, and having now provided
> A Gentleman of Noble Parentage,   5
> Of faire Demeans, Youthful, and Nobly Allied,
> Stuffed as they say with Honourable parts,
> Proportioned as one's thought would wish a man,
> And then to have a wretched puling fool,
> A whining mammet, in her Fortunes tender,   10
> To answer, Ile not wed, I cannot Love:
> I am too young, I pray you pardon me.
> But, and you will not wed, I'll pardon you.
> Graze where you will, you shall not house with me:
> Look to't, think on't, I do not use to jest.   15

FIGURE 6.2. Making the most of those mid-line commas.

Distribute Capulet's speech (Figure 6.2) and have the students score the text for commas, end-of-verse lines, and lists. In this way, the skill of commas in the middle of the verse lines will effectively come into play.

At this point in the play, Juliet has informed her parents that she doesn't want to marry Paris. Capulet is enraged that she would boldly refuse the man he has chosen for her. He demoralizes her with this speech. Notice how Bill beautifully scores the text to match how furious Capulet is through his use of commas in the middle of verse lines, along with lists and end-of-line clues. This reveals how Capulet is grasping for image after image (in the present tense) to effect change in Juliet.

It's always best to define words and phrases that are unfamiliar to your students. Capulet *needs* these *particular* words *now* to *effect change* in Juliet (see the Teacher Note at right).

To accurately capture Capulet's intense searching for image after image, we have all of these commas in the middle of verse lines combined with listing structure. See the scoring:

Teacher Note

Although we are only scoring here for a few clues, this is a great piece of text to use as a capstone piece to score everything students have learned thus far. Use the clue cards in Chapters 4 through 6 to guide the students in their work.

Teacher Note

In the First Folio, *ride* in line 2 is usually changed to *tide* in many modern editions. In addition, *Demeans* in line 6 is usually changed to *demesnes*. Please feel free to make this adjustment for your students.

CAPULET. God's bread**,** it makes me mad:
         1   **2**   **3**   **4**   **5**   **6**   **7**
Day**,** night**,** hour**,** ride**,** time**,** work**,** play,
  8   **9**
Alone in company**,** still my care hath been **(What?)**

To have her matched**,** and having now provided **(What?)**
       1
A Gentleman of Noble Parentage,   5
      2   **3**   **4**
Of faire Demeans**,** Youthful**,** and Nobly Allied,
  5
Stuffed as they say with Honourable parts,
  6
Proportioned as one's thought would wish a man,
    1
And then to have a wretched puling fool,
  2   **3**
A whining mammet**,** in her Fortunes tender,   10
   1   **2**
To answer**,** Ile not wed**,** I cannot Love:
   3   **4**
I am too young**,** pray you pardon me.

But, and you will not wed**,** I'll pardon you.

Graze where you will**,** you shall not house with me:

Look to't**,** think on't**,** I do not use to jest.   15

Speak the text aloud and, each time you get to a comma (which we have placed in bold and underlined), *snap* your fingers—as if you've come up with another idea. If you are unable to snap, you could also clap.

Do not breathe at the commas in the *middle* of the verse lines. *Do* breathe at the commas at the *end* of the verse lines. You might feel slightly out of breath and even frustrated that you don't have enough breath. Thank you, Bill! This is his acting clue—Capulet feels the exact same way. Bill manufactured this idea in your body by affecting when and where you can or cannot breathe.

Remember, this is happening in the perpetual present tense. So, as you are working through the language, try not to anticipate what is coming next. Try to *discover* each new image at the mid-line commas. As there are many lists, build on each item in the list in vocal intensity. Without even trying, you are living in the moment as Capulet.

Icing on the Cake

If you can also incorporate other aspects of the technique we have covered, the piece will work even more strongly for you:

- Notice that lines 1, 2, 7, 8, 12, 13, 14, and 15 all contain mostly *monosyllabic* words (see technique clue above).
- There is some great *alliteration* in line 1: **m**akes **m**e **m**ad
- There is some great *assonance* in line 9: p**u**ling f**oo**l
- In lines 5, 6, 7, 10, and 11, there are *capitalized words* in the middle of verse lines that are not proper nouns (see technique clue in Chapter 4).
- Look for the *repeated words* and build on the repetition.
- Look for the *transitional words*. Stress them.

Exercise #2: Walking with Shakespeare's Colons and Semicolons

Purpose of the Exercise
To obtain a true sense of what the character's thoughts are and how rapidly they move from one thought to the next.

Setup
Make sure Hamlet's speech from 1.2 is correctly scored for colons and semicolons (see Figure 6.3). These are the *thinking breaths* and this exercise will highlight this aspect of the Folio technique with one of the Bard's great thinkers.

Instructions

1. Using Hamlet's speech, begin to speak the text aloud while moving throughout the room in one direction.
2. When you arrive at a colon or semicolon, change the direction in which you are moving (maybe take a sharp turn to the right).
3. Continue speaking the text walking in this new direction until you get to another colon or semicolon.
4. Again, change the direction in which you are moving (perhaps you make an about-face and walk back).
5. Continue to do this throughout the piece.

This amazingly simple exercise helps students physically discover how

> **Hamlet (1.2)**
>
> HAMLET. Oh that this too too solid Flesh, would melt,
> Thaw, and resolve itself into a Dew:
> Or that the Everlasting had not fixed
> His Cannon 'gainst Self-slaughter. O God, O God!
> How weary, stale, flat, and unprofitable   5
> Seems to me all the uses of this world?
> Fie on't? Oh fie, fie, 'tis an unweeded Garden
> That grows to Seed: Things rank, and gross in Nature
> Possess it merely. That it should come to this:
> But two months dead: Nay, not so much; not two,   10
> So excellent a King, that was to this
> *Hyperion* to a Satyr: so loving to my Mother,
> That he might not beteem the winds of heaven
> Visit her face too roughly. Heaven and Earth
> Must I remember: why she would hang on him,   15
> As if increase of Appetite had grown
> By what is fed on; and yet within a month?
> Let me not think on't: Frailty, thy name is woman.

FIGURE 6.3. Scoring Hamlet's thinking breaths.

quickly new thoughts come into a character's mind, as well as the length of each of these thoughts, as they are trying to work their way toward the end of their full thought (a period, exclamation point, or question mark).

Exercise #3: To Enjamb or Not to Enjamb, That Is the Question

PURPOSE OF THE EXERCISE
To help the students realize the power of *not* enjambing the text of Shakespeare.

SETUP
The students need a copy of the text from *Hamlet* (1.2) as well as Capulet's speech from *Romeo and Juliet* (3.5) used in the previous exercises (Figures 6.2 and 6.3).

1. Begin by explaining Barry Edelstein's concept of "magic Mamet moments" to your students, using the description above.
2. Have the students score their text, writing the questions "What?" and "How?" (as described above) next to the end of each verse line without punctuation.

3. Have one student speak the text aloud; however, let them enjamb all of the lines. In other words, don't apply this Folio technique clue.

4. Now you can be a text master and emulate how Barry Edelstein coaches this idea with his actors. We have used this technique again and again and the results are quite profound. Have the same student speak the text again, but, this time, when they get to the end of a verse line without punctuation, ask them the questions "What?" or "How?" as scored. Make sure they truly "hear" you ask the question—then they should continue speaking, answering your question of "What?" or "How?"

5. When finished, ask the students the following questions:
   - After hearing the text spoken both ways, which way did you believe the most?
   - What does applying the Folio technique of not enjambing but using these as a moments to "search for the correct language needed" do for us as listeners?
   - Which aspects of this exercise help you feel the character is more human, more "in the moment," and more invested in the true given circumstances of the play and the moment?
   - What helps you feel more connected to Hamlet when utilizing this approach to examining a speech?

Extending the Experience
Now try the same exercise with Capulet's speech (Figure 6.2).

Prose as a Rhetorical Strategy

When we look at Shakespeare's canon, we discover that 75 percent of his work is written in verse while 25 percent is written in prose. Shakespeare's prose is just as rich and complex as his verse; therefore, many of the Folio technique clues we have been exploring directly apply to the speaking of prose. The only difference clue-wise between verse and prose is that prose does not contain the structured poetic meter that verse does. This gives us a bit more freedom in terms of where the full stop and mid-stop techniques can be applied. However, the other clues are present and fully apply. Edelstein, in *Thinking Shakespeare*, states:

> Shakespeare's prose is as artfully composed and meticulously crafted as is his verse. It can communicate elevated thought as well as simple sentiment, swooping from one to another and back again in a flash. Indeed, some of Shakespearean prose is as rich and complex as his most celebrated verse. (394)

He then provides the example from *Hamlet* (2.2) below, ending with the thought, "Hamlet's famous speech may be prose, but it most certainly isn't prosaic" (Edelstein 394):

> What a piece of work is a man! how Noble in Reason? how infinite in faculty? in form and moving how express and admirable? in Action, how like an Angel? in apprehension, how like a God? the beauty of the world, the Paragon of Animals; and yet to me, what is this Quintessence of Dust?

In the above example, we can see full thought punctuation (periods, exclamation points, and question marks) throughout. Are they full stops or mid-stops? This is freely up to the speaker and their particular interpretation. Other verse clues that can be effectively applied include capitalized words that are not proper nouns, semicolons, the comma "in the middle of verse line" technique, repeated words, repeated phrases, listing structure, "big but" words, assonance, and alliteration.

There are many times when a character speaks in verse, switches to prose, and then switches back to verse again. This can also occur in the opposite way: prose to verse and then back to prose again. When this happens, this is a *major* clue from Bill. We need to explore *why* a character *needs* to shift out of their normal way of speaking to a different way of speaking and then back again. Investigating why a character needs to do this reveals remarkable insights into Bill's characters.

Exercise: Prose Example to Analyze

Let's take a look at an interesting example of this idea of switching from verse to prose through the character of Lady Macbeth in *Macbeth*. Distribute the text in Figure 6.4 to your students. Begin your discussion by letting the students know that, throughout the play, Lady Macbeth speaks almost entirely in verse. Verse is her "vernacular." However, when we get to her famous sleepwalking scene, let's take a look at what Bill has done.

> **Macbeth (5.1)**
> LADY.   Out damned spot: out I say. One: Two: Why then 'tis time to do't: Hell is
>   murky. Fie, my Ford, fie, a Soldier, and afear'd? what need we fear?
>   who knows it, when none can call our power to accompt: yet who would
>   have thought the old man to have had so much blood in him.
> DOCTOR. Do you mark that?
> LADY.   The Thane of Fife, had a wife: where is she now? What will these hands
>   ne're be clean? No more o'that my Lord, no more o'that: you mar all
>   with this starting.

FIGURE 6.4. Parsing the prose.

Pose the follow questions to your students:

- Why would Shakespeare choose to have his characters speak in verse as their normal way of speaking?
- Why do you think Shakespeare has Lady Macbeth speaking in a way that is not "normal" to her under these circumstances? What does that reveal about her character and her state of mind at this point in the play?

Discussion could center on the fact that prose is a strong indicator to the actor that she is sleepwalking; thus, the change in her language.

- It could mean that she, as a character, is unraveling due to guilt over what she has done and thus her language is also unraveling.
- Perhaps she is slowly transitioning into madness and this is reflected in her switch to prose.

Explore and discuss other rhetorical techniques found in this excerpt that may reveal clues to her state of mind:

- alliteration
- monosyllabic words and phrases
- transitions/"big but" words
- repetition
- capitalized words that should not be capitalized

- even though this is prose, some of the question marks could indicate a mid-stop—which ones? Why? How does the application of mid-stop technique help reveal the emotional state of Lady Macbeth?

There are many possibilities and all can be supported by her use of language, rhetorical devices, and the definitive fact that she is now speaking in prose as opposed to verse. She is not dealing with the situation at hand as she has done in the past.

Minding the Reasons for the Rhetoric

Bill's use of rhetorical devices immediately provides clues to help the actor and the audience discover the true essence of his characters and why they need each specific device to effect change within the present moment. Characters employ classic rhetorical devices, masterfully planned by Shakespeare, to persuade or influence other characters—sometimes even themselves. When we identify, score, and understand the rhetorical techniques Bill used, not only do we immediately discover the inner life of the character in the moment, but also scenes and entire plays become clearer. We innately respond to what we hear and how the words are delivered. When attention is given to the "why" of what device is used by this particular character in this particular moment to achieve this particular result, we will be able to communicate the persuasive argument in a way that is clear and meaningful to our audience and other actors on stage.

\multicolumn{4}{c}{**Advanced Folio Clue Card: Rhetorical Strategies**}			
Folio Technique Clue	✓	**Definition**	**Scoring the Text**
Monosyllabic Words		Verse lines that contain a string of single syllable words. These are the "whole notes" of Shakespeare. Slow down. These reflect the weight of the character's thought.	ORSINO. If Music be the food of Love, play on, Give me excess of it: (*TN* 1.1)
Transitional Words "Big But" Words		Transitional words such as **but, yet, therefore, if,** *so*, etc. are like gear shifts in the language. They indicate that a character's thought is changing direction. Give these words more emphasis. Always stress *all, now,* and *long*. Score these words with a box.	HELENA. O spite! O hell! I see you are all bent To set against me, for your merriment: If you were civil, and knew courtesy, You would not do me thus much injury. (*MND* 3.2)
Repeated Words, Phrases, and Sounds		Underline each word, phrase, or sound (alliteration, assonance, consonance) as they are repeated.	JULIET. O Romeo, Romeo, wherefore art thou Romeo? (*Rom.* 2.2)
Lists		Characters *choose to use* lists because the idea they are expressing is of such great importance. There needs to be some type of vocal build when a character is using a listing structure. Score this by numbering the items in the list.	HENRY. Now set the Teeth, and stretch the Nostril wide, Hold hard the Breath, and bend up every Spirit To his full height. (*H5* 3.1)
Antithesis		Antithesis is the setting up of opposites in the text to help convey meaning to the audience. "Toss your pizza" in the air by vocally stressing the antithetical ideas.	HELENA. And will you rent our ancient love asunder, To join with men in scorning your poor friend? (*MND* 3.2)
Inversion		**Anastrophe** = changing the order of the words **Anaclasis** = a substitution of a variant foot **Antimetabole** = turning in the opposite direction Mark these with an inverted **i**.	MACBETH. The Castle of *Macduff*, I will surprise, ! (*Mac.* 4.1)
Commas at the *End of a Verse Line*		Commas indicate thinking and the continuation of a thought. If a comma is found at the *end* of the verse line, keep the energy up, vocally lift your voice up at the end of the verse line, take a catch-breath, and propel yourself to next line. Score with **cb**.	JULIET. Had she affections and warm youthful blood, **cb** She would be as swift in motion as a ball, **cb** My words would bandy her to my sweet Love, **cb** And his to me, (*Rom.* 2.5)

Commas in the *Middle of a Verse Line*	No breath. Bounce on these commas "receiving" the new piece of thought that comes into the character's mind *in the perpetual present tense*.	HAMLET. How weary, stale, flat, and unprofitable Seems to me all the uses of this world? *(Ham.* 1.2)
Colons and Semicolons	These signify the end of a phrase or section of thought. Take a quick *thinking* breath to accomplish this "gear shift" from thought to thought. We will mark this with a **T**.	JULIET. The clock struck nine, when I did send the Nurse, In half an hour she promised to return, Perchance she cannot meet him: **T** that's not so: **T** Oh she is lame, Loves Harald should be thoughts, Which ten times faster glides then the Suns beams, Driving back shadows over lowering hills. *(Rom.* 2.5)
Avoid Enjambing No Punctuation at the Ends of Verse Lines	Keep your characters in the *perpetual present tense* by taking time for a very quick thought at the ends of verse lines without punctuation. Quickly ask yourself, "What?" or "How?" or "When?" Do not take a breath.	ROMEO. 'Tis Torture and not mercy, heaven is here **(Where?)** Where *Juliet* lives, and every Cat and Dog, And little Mouse, every unworthy thing **(What?)** Live here in Heaven and may look on her, But *Romeo* may not. *(Rom.* 3.3)

7

Create Abridgements and Cue Scripts

To Cut or Not to Cut: Why Use an Abridged Text?

As much as we would like students to read every word of *Romeo and Juliet*, *Macbeth*, or *A Midsummer Night's Dream*, some students are just not ready to read an entire play. Those same students can develop the skills as well as the reading stamina to tackle a Shakespeare play by reading a carefully abridged version. We don't want fledgling or novice readers to drown in a sea of too much text. Two British educators we met at a conference advised that they introduce their lower-elementary students to the Bard with a short speech from *King Lear* and then revisit those classes year after year with increasingly longer excerpts from a variety of plays, relying on active drama approaches to maximize student engagement and understanding. Struggling readers and ELLs "can still enjoy Shakespeare's work if it is packaged in a more accessible format" (White). When considering an abridgement, we must keep in mind that "the goal with Shakespeare . . . is to move the student away from abridgements and into the real thing as [soon] as possible," which is advice from a home-schooling mom who hasn't shied away from including the Bard in her custom-made curriculum (Rollins). In this chapter, we present a series of text options and supporting activities if you feel using an abridgement would serve your students best as their primary text or as a way to preview the full text.

As we have described how the Folio technique can be incorporated in your approach to Shakespeare, we have maintained that his plays are performance-based texts peppered with clues so they can be successfully performed with minimal rehearsal time. Shakespeare was writing for the actor; however, he always had his audience in mind. Like any good theater practitioner, he would do whatever was needed to make his plays work in performance for his audiences. As we learned by examining the two endings of *King Lear* back in Chapter 2, Shakespeare and his actors did a bit of revising and cutting of the text themselves. Brian Kulick, a former artistic director of Classic Stage Company, assures us that modern adapters have license to abridge the plays thoughtfully and purposefully:

> I don't think the text is sacrosanct. I believe, when you look at the various quartos and the folio, that these plays were constantly revised for different occasions. When you look at the work that a lot of scholars have done with *Othello* and *Lear*, you can see that Shakespeare kept revising these plays, kept adding and subtracting, based on his opportunities of experiencing the text with an audience. I've always felt that the initial performances of these plays probably used less text than what we might find in the quarto or folio. I have this somewhat elaborate imaginary scenario in my mind where Shakespeare gets into these endless arguments with Burbage about cuts and paraphrases, I can see him screaming, "I can't take this! You put, 'To be, or not to be' *where*?" And, in this imaginary scenario of mine, Richard Burbage responds, "Bill, you can't do that. It's too much, it's endless! Save it for the book. *This* is what we're going to do." In this respect, I am not a purist, I don't think these plays were meant to be treated that way. They were meant to be manhandled; it is part of their textual DNA. (qtd. in Ney 143)

Teacher of the Bard Talk

I don't think it is necessary for a teacher to teach an entire play word by word. My advice to teachers is to create contexts where students experience the text in active ways, focus on key scenes that are vivid and compelling to students—a teacher can summarize and skip over longer portions. Too often, I think teachers think that, if they skip over a scene, the students will miss something crucial. That just isn't true. What is crucial is that students learn to have a strong, exciting, and smart experience within their learning.

—Mark Onuscheck,
Adlai E. Stevenson High School; director of curriculum, instruction, and assessment

With this in mind, we can give ourselves permission to trim the Bard, or allow a published abridgement to do it for us. It really is OK. The Bard seems to have done it himself. *Hamlet*, if not cut, would most likely play for more than four hours. If you have seen Kenneth Branagh's film adaptation of the play, you know well its playing time is indeed that long. Trimming and cutting for length is a valid reason, but this practice also brings great clarity to the piece as well. We consider here how cutting for clarity can help your students become better readers of any play. We also examine how to use an abridgement as a motivational strategy to introduce a play that students will read in full.

Narrative and Animated Abridgements to Preview a Play

A narrative abridgement is a useful tool with which to prepare students to read an entire play. A well-crafted summary usually does the trick to give students a broad outline of plot and introduce the dramatis personae. To begin the study of any play in her classroom, home-schooling parent Cindy Rollins recommends "reading aloud a synopsis of the play from either Lamb's *Tales from Shakespeare* or Edith Nesbit's *Beautiful Stories from Shakespeare*." Many children's book adaptations combine a manageable abridgement of the plot with colorful illustrations. Even the most sophisticated high school eleventh and twelfth graders enjoy a return to "storytime."

The BBC School Radio series Shakespeare Retold offers an abridgement of ten of the plays that are created by well-known British authors of children's books. Several of these adaptations tell the central story of the play from a minor character's point of view; for example, Pistol recounts the wartime exploits chronicled in *Henry V*. Other episodes feature an elementary school student passing along the bloody tale of *Macbeth*, or Shakespeare himself telling his son the story of *Hamlet*. For *A Midsummer Night's Dream*, the scenario is shifted to a modern summer camp setting. These fifteen-minute podcast episodes are available online along with teaching tips at www.bbc.co.uk/programmes/p03dwshd/episodes/player. These retellings are aimed at elementary students, but they can work effectively with middle and high school students who love a good story told well.

Shakespeare: The Animated Tales, which debuted (retitled as *The Animated Shakespeare*) on HBO in 1992, makes reading a summary pale in comparison to viewing an engaging twenty-five-minute film adaptation, and thereby successfully appeals to visual and auditory learners. The series features twelve plays, including *Macbeth*, *Romeo and Juliet*, *The Tempest*, *Hamlet*, *A Midsummer Night's Dream*, and *Julius Caesar*, as well as a few other comedies, another romance, and a history play. These films draw on a variety of animation techniques, including the traditional cel process, paint on glass, and stop-motion puppets. Leading British actors from the RSC lend their voices to characters and a bit of prose narration. These films are available as a DVD box set from Ambrose Video and can often be found on YouTube.

We have used these films as a prereading activity for students who benefit from a plot overview to guide their reading of the full text. To stress that an abridgement gives students only the bare bones of plot and characterization, have them follow a particular character as presented in the abridgement using the questions listed in Figure 7.1, and ask them to write a brief summary about the importance of that character to the plot as a whole. Students then can become an "expert" on that element of the play over the course of a unit. Then, in turn, they can use that focus to gain control over one aspect of the text and share it with their classmates or scene partners. This attention to a single character usually becomes the focus of a capstone essay or project.

> **Student Handout: Character Focus**
>
> The character I am tracking is: _____
>
> What is this character first presented doing or saying?
> _____
>
> Jot down the ways the character participates in the action:
> _____
>
> How does this character facilitate, support, or prevent the actions of others?
> _____
>
> After viewing the film, how can you tell if this character is playing a main or supporting role in the action?
> _____
>
> List any questions you have about your character that might be answered by reading the play in full:

FIGURE 7.1. Viewing focus for *Shakespeare: The Animated Tales* series.

For students who could dive into a play without any overview of plot or character, screen the animated short at the end of a unit. For a viewing focus in this summative application, ask students to generate a list of characters and plot elements omitted from the abridgement. Viewing the film at the end of a unit serves as a playful review of plot and characterization, as well as a tool to assess comprehension when students share their lists of what is "missing." You can then ask students to evaluate the abridgement and how the animation technique suits the genre and mood of the play.

"Professional" Print Abridgements

If you decide an abridged version of a play would provide the best reading and study experience for your students, compared to handing them a Folger or Cambridge School edition of the entire play, you might find yourself at a loss as to how to select the optimum abridged edition. The following suggestions are available in a paperback edition or as a pdf, and all these editions are affordably priced.

Shorter Shakespeare: Globe Education

At present, this is the most well-appointed series of abridgements. The text is based on the Shakespeare's Globe Globe Education project's student productions and it "fillets" each play by a third while retaining all the important elements—the tastiest bits—of plot and characters (Shakespeare, *Globe Education Shorter Shakespeare: A Midsummer Night's Dream* 5). Early Modern English words are not changed, and useful footnotes clarify difficult vocabulary, idioms, and allusions. Each volume includes many full-color photographs from a variety of Globe productions and a smattering of supplemental activities. The format is reminiscent of the Cambridge School Shakespeare editions discussed in Chapter 2. The series includes *Romeo and Juliet*, *Macbeth*, *A Midsummer Night's Dream*, *Twelfth Night*, and *Much Ado about Nothing*, with other titles on the way as new productions are mounted. When you read these adaptations, even a play you know well, you will be hard-pressed to discern what is missing.

Shakespeare Shorts for Schools and Performance

This series, edited by K. J. O'Hara, offers abridgements of *Hamlet*, *Macbeth*, *Romeo and Juliet*, *A Midsummer Night's Dream*, *The Merchant of Venice*, and *Twelfth Night*. O'Hara is an English and drama teacher who created these adaptations for Antic Mind Theatre Company's touring productions and for classroom study. The abridgement of *Hamlet* reduces the text by about 40 percent, leaving all the essentials of plot, characterization, and theme intact, which actually compares in length (or the rough percentage of the original text retained) to Zeffirelli's 1990 film adaptation. This edition doesn't include footnotes or any other introductory or supporting materials. The text's large-page format gives students lots of space for annotation. This edition works best when most of the reading is completed in class. Students should have access to other print editions or online reference sites when they need to consult footnotes or a Shakespeare dictionary.

30-Minute Shakespeare

This series by Nick Newlin currently includes eighteen plays. Each abridgement focuses on the essentials of plot and character development while relying on a narrator to link the heavily edited scenes together. This approach is most suitable for students performing a version of the play rather than for close study of Shakespeare's language, plot, and characterization. These texts are available in paperback or downloadable pdf form.

> **Teacher of the Bard Talk**
>
> The way an edition is presented can help the student reading experience in ways that can help with understanding and visual interest. Texts that offer some annotations or paraphrasing can help build stronger reading confidence, and can help the student develop a greater capacity to handle more complex levels of thinking.
>
> —Mark Onuscheck,
> *Adlai E. Stevenson High School; director of curriculum, instruction, and assessment*

Creating Your Own Custom Cut: Key Scenes and Speeches

If an abridgement would benefit your students but you don't have the budget to purchase a set of a professional abridgement, you can consider creating your own. If you teach the same play often or every year, the time investment is certainly worth the long-term use. With a limited amount of time in class to study a play, cutting the text will help you immediately get to the heart of what you feel is most important for your particular group of students. In this way, you will have more time to create meaningful connections with Bill and his plays rather than just "getting through" the play because there isn't really enough time for deep learning. The old adage "less is more" truly comes into play here. So, let's remember Bill's own words from *Romeo and Juliet* (1.0):

> Chorus. The fearful passage of their death-marked love,
> And the continuance of their Parents' rage:
> Which but their children's end naught could remove:
> Is now the two hours' traffic of our Stage.

Taking a Stab at Abridgement: Tips for Cutting a Scene

When an adapter cuts a text, those edits dramatically reshape the story, spotlighting certain characters, interactions, and events that provide a highly selective view and understanding of the play. When director and adapter Marti Lyons created a seventy-five-minute adaptation of *Romeo and Juliet* for Chicago Shakespeare Theater, she trimmed the interactions between Juliet and her parents to focus more intensely on interactions between the teenage lovers and the two adults who directly facilitated their clandestine plans, Juliet's Nurse and Friar Laurence. Lyons was most interested in those adults' culpability in the wake and aftermath of the couple's tragic fate, even though they thought they were acting in the lovers' best interest and they might heal their families' long-standing animosity. The compelling question for Lyons became, "Shouldn't the Nurse and Friar Laurence have known better than to act against such ingrained social norms?" She began her production with the Nurse and Friar Laurence speaking the prologue that foregrounded their presence in the tragedy. By shifting the prologue to those characters, Lyons deliberately underscored that the play's action is a flashback. Juliet's parents, especially her mother, were still present to push along Paris's pursuit of Juliet, but not to the same extent that they are in the original text. Lyons shifted the focus to bring forward supporting characters who were not kin but critical confidantes.

If you are ready to take a stab at adaptation, there really aren't any solid rules for how, why, and what to cut with respect to the texts of Shakespeare, but here are a few guidelines observed by most directors and adapters in their editing process:

Teacher of the Bard Talk

[Abridging a text] is a fantastic way to approach Shakespeare for ELLs! I am not a "purist" with Shakespeare. I cut out scenes or sections that are not essential to understanding characterization or the major themes (such as some scenes with the Nurse and Peter's "sail" or preparing for the party/wedding).

—JENNIFER ARIAS,
Adlai E. Stevenson High School; ELL and ELA teacher

- First and foremost, the story the adapter wishes to tell must determine what is cut. The cuts are made to clarify the storytelling while still maintaining the complexity of character and situation. You will need to consider how much of the play—start to finish—your students will be able to read, understand, and analyze without feeling overwhelmed.
- Try to maintain as much of the poetry (including extended metaphors, rhythm patterns, and rhyme). When possible, try to cut entire lines of verse or perhaps half lines of verse that, when merged with the next piece of text, will create a complete verse line.
- Look for full-thought punctuation (periods, exclamation points, or question marks). Cuts work well when employed after a character's full thought has been expressed.
- Many times you will find quite a bit of repetition of the same idea throughout Bill's texts. This is a good place to cut. As opposed to a character expressing the same idea five different ways, cutting down to one or two laser-focused examples works better and will be clearer for the audience to grasp.
- If a passage or section of text is too obscure (i.e., something that you feel no one will successfully grasp on one hearing), this is a good section to consider cutting. A modern audience's or reader's cultural literacy or general frame of reference is much different from that of the audience of 400 years ago.
- Just remember that the works of Shakespeare are not sacred. Nor is any particular beloved or famous passage exempt from being cut. The clarity

of the story being told is most important. Consider that you are "shaping a text," rather than cutting it, to serve the needs of your students and to whet their appetite for a fuller, more complete experience in the future.

Barbara Gaines, artistic director of Chicago Shakespeare Theater, makes the following point about adapting Shakespeare:

> Orson Wells said: "We all betray Shakespeare." I begin there with an apology to William. Since the text is a living organism and Shakespeare was an actor, a man of the theatre, I freely adapt the script, if there's a good reason to do it—for theatre is an interpretive art. (Ney 140)

Well, we may not want betray the Bard, but we will use *A Midsummer Night's Dream* (3.2) to model the cutting process, observing the guidelines offered above. The actual text is based on the First Folio edition found on the Internet Shakespeare Editions website (internetshakespeare.uvic.ca/doc/MND_F1/scene/3.2/), which allows you easily to cut and paste it into your own file for editing. In this wonderful seventeen-line speech, Helena is belittling Lysander and Demetrius, who are now, thanks to Puck's magic, declaring their undying love for her:

HELENA. O spite! O hell! I see you are all bent
To set against me, for your merriment:
If you were civil, and knew courtesy,
You would not do me thus much injury.
Can you not hate me, as I know you do,   5
But you must join in souls to mock me to?
If you are men, as men you are in show,
You would not use a gentle Lady so;
To vow, and swear, and superpraise my parts,
When I am sure you hate me with your hearts.   10
You both are Rivals, and love *Hermia*;
And now both Rivals to mock *Helena*.
A trim exploit, a manly enterprise,
To conjure tears up in a poor maid's eyes,
With your derision; none of noble sort,   15
Would so offend a Virgin, and extort
A poor soul's patience, all to make you sport.

Lysander has told Helena he loves her and that he wants to be her knight. Right before this speech, Demetrius praises her as a goddess, perfect, and divine, and wishes to kiss her. They are both ready to partake in an actual fistfight to prove their love for her. In lines 7–10, Helena is repeating what the audience has just seen and heard, and these four lines represent a complete thought. Therefore, it makes sense that we could cut lines 7 to 10. We now have a speech that is thirteen lines long, until we take a hard look at the last five lines. While including some great language, they are actually another repetition of Helena's main argument. These five lines are also a complete thought and could be cut as well:

O spite! O hell! I see you are all bent To set against me, for your merriment: If you were civil, and knew courtesy, You would not do me thus much injury. Can you not hate me, as I know you do, 5 But you must join in souls to mock me to? ~~If you are men, as men you are in show,~~ ~~You would not use a gentle Lady so;~~ ~~To vow, and swear, and superpraise my parts,~~ ~~When I am sure you hate me with your hearts.~~ 10 You both are Rivals, and love *Hermia*; And now both Rivals to mock *Helena*. ~~A trim exploit, a manly enterprise,~~ ~~To conjure tears up in a poor maid's eyes,~~ ~~With your derision; none of noble sort,~~ 15 ~~Would so offend a Virgin, and extort~~ ~~A poor soul's patience, all to make you sport.~~	O spite! O hell! I see you are all bent To set against me, for your merriment: If you were civil, and knew courtesy, You would not do me thus much injury. Can you not hate me, as I know you do 5 But you must join in souls to mock me to? You both are Rivals, and love *Hermia*; And now both Rivals to mock *Helena*. A trim exploit, a manly enterprise, To conjure tears up in a poor maid's eyes, 10 With your derision; none of noble sort, Would so offend a Virgin, and extort A poor soul's patience, all to make you sport.

After our cuts, we are now left with a speech that is eight lines long:

> HELENA. O spite! O hell! I see you are all bent
> To set against me, for your merriment:
> If you were civil, and knew courtesy,
> You would not do me thus much injury.
> Can you not hate me, as I know you do,   5
> But you must join in souls to mock me to?
> You both are Rivals, and love *Hermia*;
> And now both Rivals to mock *Helena*.

Create Abridgements and Cue Scripts

As you can see, this abridged version still maintains the original spirit of the longer seventeen-line version while also clarifying the storytelling of this moment. It's cleaner, clearer, and students will have more confidence tackling this focused eight-line version as opposed to the thirteen-line version.

While the above example of cutting is helpful, it represents only a single character's speech focusing on repeated ideas and complete thoughts. Let's take a look at a significant portion of this scene with all four characters to see how to effectively cut exchanges between several characters while still maintaining the essence, drive, and intent of the original full-length version. In the following columns, on the left is the complete text for 3.2, with strike-throughs for possible cuts. On the right are explanations for the cuts. Please remember there isn't one way to cut the text. The cuts listed are suggested based on the guidelines above; however, they are just guidelines—not hard rules.

DEMETRIUS.	I say, I love thee more then he can do.	
LYSANDER.	If thou say so, withdraw and prove it too.	
DEMETRIUS.	Quick, come.	
HERMIA.	*Lysander*, whereto tends all this?	
LYSANDER.	~~Away, you *Ethiop*.~~	*Ethiop* is a derogatory term; cutting is appropriate.
DEMETRIUS.	~~No, no, Sir, seem to break loose;~~ 5 ~~Take on as you would follow,~~ ~~But yet come not: you are a tame man, go.~~	Let's just get right to the chase and cut to Lysander asking Hermia to let go of him.
LYSANDER.	Hang off thou cat, thou burr; vile thing let loose, Or I will shake thee from me like a serpent.	
HERMIA.	Why are you grown so rude? 10 What change is this sweet Love?	
LYSANDER.	~~Thy love? out tawny *Tartar*, out;~~ Out loathed medicine; O hated poison hence.	*Tartar* is another derogatory term; worth cutting.
HERMIA.	~~Do you not jest?~~	Let's keep the storytelling tight. We know the men are fighting for Helena. No need to repeat it again here. In keeping the story tight, cut the "do you jest" exchange, as the idea is repeated in line 26. After Lysander says "hated poison," a good place to pick up is Hermia saying "Hate me." We cut six full thoughts.
HELENA.	~~Yes sooth, and so do you.~~	
LYSANDER.	~~*Demetrius*: I will keep my word with thee.~~ 15	
DEMETRIUS.	~~I would I had your bond: for I perceive~~ ~~A weak bond holds you; I'll not trust your word.~~	
LYSANDER.	~~What, should I hurt her, strike her, kill her dead?~~ ~~Although I hate her, I'll not harm her so.~~	
HERMIA.	~~What, can you do me greater harm then hate?~~ 20	

	Hate me, wherefore? O me, what news my Love?
	Am not I *Hermia*? Are not you *Lysander*?
	I am as fair now, as I was ere while.
	Since night you lov'd me; yet since night you left me.
	Why then you left me (O the gods forbid) 25
	In earnest, shall I say?
LYSANDER.	Ay, by my life;
	And never did desire to see thee more.
	Therefore be out of hope, of question, of doubt;
	Be certain, nothing truer: 'tis no jest,
	That I do hate thee, and love *Helena*. 30
HERMIA.	O me, you juggler, you canker-blossom,
	You thief of love; What, have you come by night,
	And stol'n my love's heart from him?
HELENA.	Fine i'faith:
	Have you no modesty, no maiden shame,
	No touch of bashfulness? What, will you tear 35
	Impatient answers from my gentle tongue?
	Fie, fie, you counterfeit, you puppet, you.
HERMIA.	Puppet? why so? Ay, that way goes the game.
	Now I perceive that she hath made compare
	Between our statures, she hath urg'd her height, 40
	And with her personage, her tall personage,
	Her height (forsooth) she hath prevail'd with him.
	And are you grown so high in his esteem,
	Because I am so dwarfish, and so low?
	How low am I, thou painted Maypole? Speak, 45
	How low am I? I am not yet so low,
	But that my nails can reach unto thine eyes.
HELENA.	I pray you though you mock me, gentlemen,
	Let her not hurt me; I was never curst:
	I have no gift at all in shrewishness; 50
	I am a right maid for my cowardice;
	Let her not strike me: you perhaps may think,
	Because she is something lower then myself,
	That I can match her.
HERMIA.	Lower? hark again.
HELENA.	~~Good *Hermia*, do not be so bitter with me,~~ 55
	~~I evermore did love you Hermia,~~
	~~Did ever keep your counsels, never wronged you,~~
	~~Save that in love unto *Demetrius*,~~
	~~I told him of your stealth unto this wood.~~

	~~He followed you, for love I followed him,~~	60
	~~But he hath chid me hence, and threatened me~~	
	~~To strike me, spurn me, nay to kill me too;~~	
	~~And now, so you will let me quiet go,~~	
	~~To *Athens* will I bear my folly back,~~	
	~~And follow you no further. Let me go.~~	65
	~~You see how simple, and how fond I am.~~	
HERMIA.	~~Why get you gone: who is't that hinders you?~~	
HELENA.	~~A foolish heart, that I leave here behind.~~	
HERMIA.	~~What, with *Lysander*?~~	
HELENA.	~~With *Demetrius*.~~	
LYSANDER.	~~Be not afraid, she shall not harm thee *Helena*.~~	70
DEMETRIUS.	~~No sir, she shall not, though you take her part.~~	
HELENA.	O when she's angry, she is keen and shrewd,	
	She was a vixen when she went to school,	
	And though she be but little, she is fierce.	
HERMIA.	Little again? Nothing but low and little?	75
	Why will you suffer her to flout me thus?	
	Let me come to her.	
LYSANDER.	Get you gone you dwarf,	
	You *minimus*, of hindering knot-grass made,	
	You bead, you acorn.	
DEMETRIUS.	~~You are too officious,~~	
	~~In her behalf that scorns your services.~~	80
	~~Let her alone, speak not of *Helena*,~~	
	~~Take not her part. For if thou dost intend~~	
	~~Never so little show of love to her,~~	
	~~Thou shalt abide it.~~	
LYSANDER.	Now she holds me not,	
	Now follow if thou dar'st, to try whose right,	85
	Of thine or mine is most in *Helena*.	

Cut for maximum storytelling. This section, while fun, is a repeat of exposition that we have already seen recently played out. To keep the tension that has built between Hermia and Helena, cutting lines 55–72 achieves this and adds to this tension.

This line indicates that Hermia is rushing to attack Helena. This suggests that Lysander is holding Hermia back while Demetrius is protecting Helena.

With the image then of Hermia being stopped by Lysander, then maybe grabbing him in order to "keep" him, let's tighten up the storytelling and keep the tension strong by cutting half of 79 through half of 84. We then create a full line of verse. Lysander pushes her off and continues.

DEMETRIUS.	Follow? Nay, I'll go with thee cheek by jowl.
	Exit Lysander and Demetrius.
HERMIA.	You Mistress, all this coil is long of you. Nay, go not back.
HELENA.	I will not trust you I, 90 Nor longer stay in your curst company. Your hands then mine, are quicker for a fray, My legs are longer though to run away.

Once we apply the cuts above, we have trimmed the text from ninety-three lines down to fifty-eight lines. In doing so, we've kept the essence of the scene, intent of the characters, and physical action required of this scene; however, the storytelling is tighter and more focused. See what you think:

DEMETRIUS.	I say, I love thee more then he can do.	
LYSANDER.	If thou say so, withdraw and prove it too.	
DEMETRIUS.	Quick, come.	
HERMIA.	*Lysander*, whereto tends all this?	
LYSANDER.	Hang off thou cat, thou burr; vile thing let loose, Or I will shake thee from me like a serpent.	5
HERMIA.	Why are you grown so rude? What change is this sweet Love?	
LYSANDER.	Out loathed medicine; O hated poison hence.	
HERMIA.	Hate me, wherefore? O me, what news my Love? Am not I *Hermia*? Are not you *Lysander*? I am as fair now, as I was ere while. Since night you lov'd me; yet since night you left me. Why then you left me (O the gods forbid) In earnest, shall I say?	10
LYSANDER.	Ay, by my life; And never did desire to see thee more. Therefore be out of hope, of question, of doubt; Be certain, nothing truer: 'tis no jest, That I do hate thee, and love *Helena*.	15
HERMIA.	O me, you juggler, you canker-blossom, You thief of love; What, have you come by night, And stol'n my love's heart from him?	20

Create Abridgements and Cue Scripts 163

HELENA.	Fine i'faith:	
	Have you no modesty, no maiden shame,	
	No touch of bashfulness? What, will you tear	
	Impatient answers from my gentle tongue?	
	Fie, fie, you counterfeit, you puppet, you.	25
HERMIA.	Puppet? why so? Ay, that way goes the game.	
	Now I perceive that she hath made compare	
	Between our statures, she hath urg'd her height,	
	And with her personage, her tall personage,	
	Her height (forsooth) she hath prevail'd with him.	30
	And are you grown so high in his esteem,	
	Because I am so dwarfish, and so low?	
	How low am I, thou painted Maypole? Speak,	
	How low am I? I am not yet so low,	
	But that my nails can reach unto thine eyes.	35
HELENA.	I pray you though you mock me, gentlemen,	
	Let her not hurt me; I was never curst:	
	I have no gift at all in shrewishness;	
	I am a right maid for my cowardice;	
	Let her not strike me: you perhaps may think,	40
	Because she is something lower then myself,	
	That I can match her.	
HERMIA.	Lower? hark again.	
HELENA.	O when she's angry, she is keen and shrewd,	
	She was a vixen when she went to school,	
	And though she be but little, she is fierce.	45
HERMIA.	Little again? Nothing but low and little?	
	Why will you suffer her to flout me thus?	
	Let me come to her.	
LYSANDER.	Get you gone you dwarf,	
	You *minimus*, of hindering knot-grass made,	
	You bead, you acorn.	
LYSANDER.	Now she holds me not,	50
	Now follow if thou dar'st, to try whose right,	
	Of thine or mine is most in *Helena*.	
DEMETRIUS.	Follow? Nay, I'll go with thee cheek by jowl.	
	Exit Lysander and Demetrius.	
HERMIA.	You Mistress, all this coil is long of you.	
	Nay, go not back.	

> HELENA. I will not trust you I, 55
> Nor longer stay in your curst company.
> Your hands then mine, are quicker for a fray,
> My legs are longer though to run away.

Please do note that this is only one option of how to cut text to meet the needs of your particular students within the particular time frame you have to teach the play. The ways of cutting the text are endless. No one way is "right." Knowing this, we hope you work with confidence as you cut and adapt the text for your students. Doing so will not only give you more time for valuable instruction, but you also have the opportunity to shape the text to meet what you feel is important for your particular students in your particular class. Just like professional theaters across the country, where directors adapt and cut the text to meet their particular vision for a particular theater's audience, you are doing the exact same thing for your "audience." If you are ready to create your own cut of a scene, an act, or an entire play, you may also want to take a look at Fiona Banks's *Creative Shakespeare: The Globe Education Guide to Practical Shakespeare* (31–38, 172–74) and at Simon Rodberg's "Cutting Antony's Speeches" lesson plan available on the Folger Shakespeare Library Education Department's website (www.folger.edu/cutting-antonys-speeches).

Reading–Viewing for Micro and Macro Understanding

Another approach to cutting a play combines reading key scenes and speeches with viewing a film adaptation. This reading–viewing approach had its genesis in the very early days of using video in the classroom. The Stevenson High School ninth-grade team methodically would take students through Act 1 of *Romeo and Juliet* while they listened to key speeches on a recording of the play. Reading and listening should have enhanced their understanding, but students glazed over as the speeches were declaimed on a scratchy, worn, hard-to-cue record. The team decided to combine reading the play and watching a film adaptation

Student of the Bard Talk

I think another good tactic to learning Shakespeare is to watch a version. In every English class I've been in where we read Shakespeare, we've watched a movie version. It is very helpful to see what I'm reading for me because sometimes it can go over my head. Seeing it furthers my understanding.... Considering how the language in Shakespeare is so different from the language we use now,... if a character says they're sad, using that Shakespearean language, a reader might not pick up on that. While watching [that scene on film], the [actor will] be crying ..., allowing the reader, or viewer, to understand how the dialogue conveys that emotion.

—ABBY SOKOL,
Adlai E. Stevenson High School

incrementally act by act, since the audiovisual department had recently acquired Zeffirelli's film version on VHS tape. After students read and discussed Act 1, the class screened the equivalent of that act in the film to promote discussion of difficult aspects of character, plot, and language they encountered during the reading process. Seeing one visual interpretation of the characters, their actions, and the world of the play gave students the ability to create a movie in their heads as they continued to read the play. This approach works particularly well if students are reading key scenes and speeches and applying the Folio technique to explore them in depth.

Choosing the read–view approach is especially helpful when working with ELL students. Moreover, Abbas Pourhosein Gilakjani claims that "the potential pedagogical value and rationale for using classroom media . . . are as follows:

- to raise interest level—students appreciate (and often expect) a variety of media
- to enhance understanding—rich media materials boost students' comprehension for complex topics
- to increase memorability—rich media materials lead to better encoding and easy retrieval. (58)

In Chicago Shakespeare Theater's teacher handbooks available online for seasons 2013 through 2019 (see www.chicagoshakes.com/education/teaching_resources/teacher_handbooks), an abridgement feature focuses on scenes that either take students through the major plot threads of an entire play or focus on key relationships that can be contextualized by watching a film adaptation. If you take the key relationships approach, it is important to select scenes and speeches that run the gamut of the play. When abridging *Macbeth* in this way, you might, for example, decide to explore the Thane of Cawdor's relationship with the Weird Sisters and with his Lady wife:

Macbeth and the Weird Sisters: Planting and Nurturing the Seeds of Ambition

- "When shall we three meet again?"—setting the stage to incite conflict (1.1)
- "All hail Macbeth, that shall be the king hereafter"—providing catalyst (1.3)
- "How did you dare/To trade and traffic with Macbeth"—facing Hecate's rebuke (3.5)

- "Fire burn, and cauldron bubble"—predicting future consequences for Macbeth (4.1)

Macbeth and Lady Macbeth: Partners in Unbridled Ambition

- responding to the Witches' prophesies (1.5)
- resolving to execute the plan to remove Duncan (1.7)
- killing the king, shifting blame (2.2)
- securing the throne, eliminating another threat (3.2)
- confronting Banquo's ghost and consequences of ambition (3.4)
- sleepwalking and the pangs of conscience (5.1)
- responding to loss (5.5)

You also can combine those scenes with Macbeth's soliloquies and asides:

Macbeth's Key Asides, Soliloquies, and Speeches: Tracking Psychological Development

- "Two truths are told"—processing, responding (1.3.126–41)*
- "The Prince of Cumberland: that is a step"— brooding, dissembling (1.4.48–53)
- "If it were done, when 'tis done"—equivocating, hesitating, resolving (1.7.1–28)
- "Is this a dagger which I see before me"—taking action (2.1.33–64)
- "To be thus is nothing/But to be safely thus"—facing consequences (3.1.49–73)
- "Time, thou anticipat'st my dread exploits"—making plans (4.1.143–55)
- "Bring me no more reports, let them fly all "—trusting prophecy (5.3.1–10)
- "She should have died hereafter"—grieving, brooding (5.5.17–27)

(*Line numbers correspond to the Cambridge School Shakespeare edition of *Macbeth*)

Depending on how you contextualize these scenes and speeches with the animated short or a feature film version viewed act by act, you could pull a single thread—witches, the Macbeths, or Macbeth's private moments—one set at a time, or you could merge all three sets to address them in chronological order. Focusing on each set separately allows for a closer look at the importance of supporting characters, interactions between central characters, and the function of the soliloquy in dramatic character development. Merging the three sets works best with screening a film treatment incrementally and chronologically.

Students can certainly gain much from watching professional actors interpret a role on screen, but the spirit of the Folio technique embraces students physically trying on a character. A deep dive into key scenes and speeches would pair nicely with students trying out how Shakespeare's actors discovered their characters literally in bits and pieces through cue scripts.

Creating and Using Cue Scripts: Exploring Key Scenes through Performance

As mentioned at the beginning of Chapter 4, the actors during Shakespeare's day did not have rehearsal time equivalent to our modern-day rehearsal process. At the Globe:

> A repertory system was used and no play was given two days in succession. The actor played a different part every night and he had no opportunity to settle into a comfortable routine while the lines of the part became second nature to him. (Chute 90)

These men were putting up a different play every afternoon. With this type of rigorous repertory performance schedule, "rehearsals" consisted of meeting in the morning for a quick brush-up of fights, songs, and dances. Basic entrances and exits were also established. Then, in the afternoon, the men performed. Peter Quince and his troupe of amateur actors in *A Midsummer Night's Dream* (1.2) give us a glimpse of the challenges of such limited rehearsal:

> QUINCE. Here is the scroll of every man's name, which is thought fit through all *Athens*, to play in our Interlude before the Duke and Duchess, on his wedding day at night.
>
> BOTTOM. First, good *Peter Quince*, say what the play treats on: then read the names of the Actors: and so grow on to a point.
>
> QUINCE. Marry our play is the most lamentable Comedy, and most cruel death of *Pyramus* and *Thisbe*.

BOTTOM. A very good piece of work I assure you, and a merry. Now good *Peter Quince*, call forth your Actors by the scroll. Masters spread yourselves.

. . . .

QUINCE. . . . But masters here are your parts, and I am to intreat you, request you, and desire you, to con them by tomorrow night: and meet me in the palace wood, a mile without the Town, by Moonlight, there we will rehearse: for if we meet in the City, we shall be dog'd with company, and our devices known. In the meantime, I will draw a bill of properties, such as our play wants. I pray you fail me not.

BOTTOM. We will meet, and there we may rehearse more obscenely and courageously. Take pains, be perfect, adieu.

When we speak about an actor and their *role*, that term comes from the scroll or *rolled* parchment that contained the entirety of an actor's part. Patrick Tucker, a proponent of using cue scripts in the classroom, presents this scene from *A Midsummer Night's Dream* in *Secrets of Acting Shakespeare: The Original Approach* as an example of the rehearsal process and characterizes it as a "quick technical rather than a textual get-together" (29). He reveals other fascinating information about the *original practice* Shakespeare and his company used in their rehearsal and acting techniques too:

> I chose 1595 as a date by which Shakespeare himself might have started writing and began digging around. I found that the Elizabethan companies presented an enormous number of plays in a short time. It was quite common to have more than 20 plays in repertoire and to play six different plays in the six days of the week. Plays would drop in and out of the repertoire at short notice, and companies would introduce new plays at an average of one every two weeks. . . . From the schedule, it looked as if an actor's life would consist of learning or relearning lines in the mornings and performing in the afternoons, with no time left for what we call rehearsal—which made putting on a play very puzzling. (26–27)

With the demands of the repertory system, it is obvious that a company of actors did not have the luxury of our modern-day three- to six-week rehearsal process. Therefore, Shakespeare created a system that quickly and efficiently provided an actor with the entirety of their character, which put the Folio technique into practical action.

We must remember that complete copies of Bill's plays were the property of the company and were highly protected. The company would not want to provide the full play for fear that a disgruntled or jealous actor might take the complete text to a rival theater or even to a local printer in order to seek revenge. In addition to this, there were many practical reasons (printing costs, difficulty of transcribing individual copies) for not providing a complete copy to each actor. Instead, actors were given *cue scripts* containing their lines and the three- or four-word cue that proceeded their speaking of each line. The playwright would have read the complete play once only to the shareholders of the company. Therefore, unless the actor was a shareholder, he probably would have experienced the complete play for the first time during the first full performance in front of the Globe audience. Even if an actor was a shareholder, imagine trying to capture and understand all of the complexities and intricacies of *Hamlet* in one hearing.

Figure 7.2 presents an example of a cue script for Hermia in a short section of 3.2 of *A Midsummer Night's Dream*. Unlike actual cue scripts, the cue speaker is indicated here in parentheses.

(*cue from* HELENA) _____ **O excellent!**
(character's line) Sweet, do not scorn her so.

(*cue from* DEMETRIUS) _____ **Quick, come.**
Lysander, whereto tends all this?

(*cue from* LYSANDER) _____ **like a serpent.**
Why are you grown so rude?
What change is this sweet Love?

(*cue from* LYSANDER) _____ **poison hence.**
Do you not jest?

(*cue from* LYSANDER) _____ **harm her so.**
What, can you do me greater harm then hate?
Hate me, wherefore? O me, what news my Love?
Am not I *Hermia*? Are you not *Lysander*?
I am as fair now, as I was ere while.
Since night you lov'd me; yet since night you left me.
Why then you left me (O the gods forbid)
In earnest, shall I say?

FIGURE 7.2. Sample cue script: Hermia (*MND* 3.2).

As you can see, the Globe actor who played Hermia has all of the character's lines, but just the three- or four-word cues that precede the speaking of his lines. Once the actor heard the cue, he knew to speak. Let's explore what that means a little bit more. The first cue listed in our short excerpt is, "O excellent!" Who says it? Relying on the original cue script, the actor doesn't know. When do they say it? The actor doesn't know. All the actor does know is that he has to stay truly focused and present so that, when he hears the cue "O excellent!," he then knows to speak. Using cue scripts with students provides a practical activity that rewards and hones listening skills as well as relies on careful collaboration to solve a problem unlike anything they probably have encountered in small-group work.

You still may be thinking, "How can this possibly work?" It does—and the results are surprising, truly in the moment and honest. This practice actually is still in use today. If you ever have played in a band, you know the members are not given the full conductor's score for each piece performed. Each player receives only their particular part. All the members are playing music from their musical cue scripts. However, when they all play together from their cue scripts, all the parts fit together and the music happens. Also, if you have performed in a musical, one particular publisher does not send complete scripts for all the actors. They send *sides* for each speaking role, which contains all of a character's lines along with the cue lines. Only the director and the stage manager have complete copies of the script. Both of these examples are the modern equivalents of the cue scripts from Shakespeare's time.

Shakespeare's actors had another tool that helped them perform effectively in light of these challenging circumstances. When they performed, a *platt* for each production was created. This was a large sheet of paper attached to a board and hung in the wings on the day of performance. The platt briefly outlined what happened in the play scene by scene. Each scene listed noted each actor involved, what character they were playing in the particular scene, when they enter, and what props were needed.

Using cue scripts with students has a number of benefits. First of all, it allows for an in-depth interaction with a key scene. You might select a scene for exploration to preview a key interaction before students read it in its proper context. Putting a brief text nugget in front of students allows them to apply the Folio clues they are either testing out for the first time or

Student of the Bard Talk

When you are comfortable with acting and performing in front of people, physically acting Shakespeare's plays out is very helpful. When I was just reading it at first, the words seemed flat and boring, and they did not have much meaning because I had no idea what they meant…When I understood what I was saying, it made working on Shakespeare so much more enjoyable for me and for the audience.

—Hailey Keenan,
Adlai E. Stevenson High School

activating yet again. To make a scene work using a cue script, students have to carefully collaborate with one another since only the *keeper of the book* or the *prompter* has all the lines. The cue script is a literary jigsaw puzzle that has to fit together just so. To perform from their scripts, students need to listen carefully to one another to pick up their cues. So working with cue scripts fosters critical analysis of the text, requires strong collaboration in pairs or small groups, and sharpens both listening and speaking skills.

Activity: Exploring A Midsummer Night's Dream *(3.2) with Cue Scripts*

The directions outlined below are adapted from the exercise "Cue Scripts" found in *Creative Shakespeare: The Globe Education Guide to Practical Shakespeare* by Fiona Banks, an excellent resource to have on your bookshelf.

PURPOSE OF THE EXERCISE

Working with cue scripts helps students put into practice the elements of the Folio technique from Chapters 4, 5, and 6, enabling them to experience firsthand how Shakespeare "directs" his actors through the use of his textual clues.

SETUP

Provide students with pertinent clue cards from Chapters 4–6; printed cue scripts for each character (see Appendix B), one for each student; a printed master script for the keeper of the book or stage manager; two unsharpened pencils per student, in order to create a rolled cue script; and a large enough space for students to rehearse and eventually present their work to the class.

INSTRUCTIONS

1. Break the students into groups of five, assigning the roles of Demetrius, Helena, Hermia, and Lysander. Assign the fifth student to be the *keeper of the book* or the stage manager to help the actors sort out cues, create the master score of the text, and make suggestions for staging the action before the scene goes up in front of the class.
2. Distribute the individual cue scripts based on each student's assigned character (see Appendix B).
3. Students will then create their own *roll* (their cue script formatted as a scroll). Have students tape their cue script pages together to create

one long strip. Then tape each end of the long strip onto an unsharpened pencil. After that, roll the paper up to create a roll (or scroll). Roll each cue script up in such a way that the words are on the outside so that the cue scripts can be read as the students are rehearsing, holding them in their hands.

4. Distribute the Shakespeare clue card(s) on pages 89, 111, and 149. Students then collaboratively analyze and score their text utilizing appropriate Folio clues from Chapters 4, 5, and 6. The keeper of the book will record the definitive scoring of the scene for all the characters.

5. Using the cue scripts they created, analyzed, and scored, students then conduct a read-through of the scene in their group. At this stage, students should focus only on the words and not any action they would add to illustrate those words.

Side Coaching

Remind students to speak strongly, clearly, and immediately when they hear their cue line spoken. You might want to use a vocal warm-up activity found in Chapter 3, especially a tongue twister or two.

6. Now that they have spoken the scene aloud once or twice, they have a basic idea of the scene. Have the students read the scene aloud several times focusing on movement that the text requires or suggests. Here are some instructions you might offer to students from reading to reading during a brief rehearsal process:

   - Walk to the character you are speaking to—even if it means moving other people out of the way. If it's not clear whom you are talking to, address your lines to the character that gave you your cue.

   - Let the words help you. Most of your needed physical action will be spoken within the text. Simply follow suit.

   - Remember, Bill knew what he was doing, so take in everything that happens as your character. If things seem confusing working this way, excellent. This may be the clue from Bill that things are confusing for the characters on stage and he created that confusion for his actors as well. Perhaps your groups as actors find out some shocking discovery you didn't know about, as you only have a cue script. Let that shocking discovery also be your character's shocking discovery.

7. After several run-throughs, the scene groups should now perform for the class. As students view different versions of the same text, have them discuss the choices each group made in speaking the text and adding movement.

Creating Your Own Cue Scripts

If you want to use a cue script for plays other than *A Midsummer Night's Dream* we suggest that you log on to the Internet Shakespeare Editions website (internet shakespeare.uvic.ca) and (1) choose "Shakespeare's Works"; (2) from the "Texts" tab at the top of the screen, choose the play; (3) from the "Texts of this edition" list, choose Folio 1, 1623 ("old-spelling transcription," which you would edit to regularize variant spelling); (4) print the scene in relation to which you wish to create a cue script for your students; (5) then cut, paste, and edit cue scripts for each character, using the format we model here for *A Midsummer Night's Dream*; and (6) retain the complete scene as the master version. Note that you can bypass the Folio edition of the play and use another edition that regularizes the Early Modern spelling and internal capitalization, if activating those Folio clues is not important for your students.

Creating cue scripts on your own might be a bit labor intensive, so you can explore ready-made cue scripts that are available online for a user's fee. Some fees, though, make taking advantage of the ready-made option difficult. Patrick Tucker created short cue scripts for a variety of plays in his book *Shakespeare Cue Script Scenes for the Classroom*, which is out of print but may be sitting on the shelf of a public or academic library near you.

Finding the "Right Size" Text

The classroom teachers and theater practitioners included in this chapter and elsewhere in this book have emphasized the importance of creating an experience for students to engage with Shakespeare's works that suits their present reading skills and prior experience navigating challenging texts. The one-size-fits-all or "let's all read the entire text" approach might not be the best fit. And, as with most things, that first experience will color students' ability to understand and enjoy the Bard. Rely on either professional adapters or on your own familiarity with a play to shape the text that allows your students not just to read it but also to experience, understand, and enjoy it, applying the appropriate range of Folio techniques.

Connect Shakespeare to YA Fiction, Contemporary Literature, and Media Texts

How Can Shakespeare's Plays "Talk" to Contemporary Texts?

When textbooks organized by genre, theme, or cultural timeline dominated our classrooms, curriculum design tended to be prescribed by the editors of those tomes. Generally, it was a matter of which texts to include or to exclude, since it was impossible to cover everything offered in the comprehensive table of contents. Shakespeare always had his place in those textbooks, as he represented a durable genre, mined significant themes, and held a prominent position on both the British and the world literature timelines. Now Shakespeare is unfettered in many ways, since a textbook is not necessarily the peg on which we hang curricular decisions. As we consider how Shakespeare fits within a curricular framework shaped by national, state, and local standards, Mark Powell, the associate director of the Salisbury Playhouse, offers the following counsel:

> Our schools are full of Shakespeare, but often in completely the wrong places. Old uncle Bill has become the relative that we invite to family gatherings out of habit, not because we actually want to. He sits there in the corner sharing his stories with anyone who'll listen; the adults lend a patient ear out of a sense of duty and most of the kids have no concept of the vitality of his youth.

Shakespeare can be as vital, relevant, and engaging as we want, and that depends on how we frame a particular play within a unit by selecting carefully orchestrated reading, speaking, composing, and viewing activities. This chapter offers approaches to texts and activities for building out a unit with one of Shakespeare's plays as an anchor or supplemental text.

When designing curricula, it is crucial to examine how texts "talk" to one another in significant ways. Sometimes we think students fully understand why and how we combine different works in a course syllabus. Most times, however, our thoughtful rationale and planning are lost on them. When we take Shakespeare out of Powell's corner, his work is often viewed as the "good" (but

> **Teacher of the Bard Talk**
>
> For many reasons, teaching Shakespeare can seem a little intimating to some teachers. This hesitation is particularly true when teachers are working with what they view to be struggling or resistant readers. Or they might think that Shakespearean texts will be viewed as boring or too difficult. The important point in teaching Shakespeare is to make sure there is a compelling reason or "why." For purposes of curriculum, extending students to experience complex text and complex ideas is central to making sure Shakespearean texts are a fixture in curriculums, as we work to balance our curriculum choices in connected ways to other text selections.
>
> —Mark Onuscheck,
> *Adlai E. Stevenson High School; director of curriculum, instruction, and assessment*

bad-tasting) medicine we apply to our students when we get the chance. Susan Spangler reminds us:

> While the works of Shakespeare may be amazing, too many students fail to appreciate those works the way their teachers do, and I fear that our adoration prevents us from letting students engage the texts rather than simply *revere* them. (130)

If Shakespeare's place on a cultural pedestal isn't enough to gain our students' attention and admiration, we need to consider what role one of his plays should play in a unit: as an anchor text supplemented by other works, or in an abridged form to supplement a contemporary anchor text.

We offer strategies for basic unit design mindful of Gardner's multiple intelligences and how students engage in texts in a variety of ways. We address the following questions:

- Will a Shakespeare play be the anchor or a supplemental text in my unit plan?
- How much of the Folio technique will I incorporate effectively before, during, and after reading a play in its complete or abridged form?
- How do I set the stage with the right balance of previewing and prereading activities?
- Which literary or popular culture text(s) will partner well with a Shakespeare play?
- Which media texts will complement the selected Shakespeare play?
- What kind of formative and summative activities will demonstrate student growth and support a unit's design (text edition, active drama approaches, Folio technique, viewing experiences)?

Also, we consider how you can introduce active drama approaches and supplemental texts if you follow a fairly prescribed curriculum that makes innovation a challenge.

"The Play's the Thing": Choosing to Anchor or to Supplement

Of all the decisions you make, this may be the most provocative one. Since we spent Chapter 7 extolling the virtues of using excellent, ready-made abridgements or encouraging you to create your own custom cut of a play, bringing this up again really shouldn't come as a surprise. You may not have a choice to abridge the play. It may be prescribed as the anchor for an established unit. Case closed. In that case, the experiences you build around that play will be crucial to students' overall engagement, understanding, and enjoyment. So you may want to move ahead to the next section.

If you have the opportunity to move *Romeo and Juliet*, *Macbeth*, or *Hamlet* out of the anchor role in a unit, then you will need to consider if hitting the highlights or key scenes of a Shakespeare play will serve to illuminate specific themes, conflicts, or character relationships in the selected anchor text. Using a Shakespeare play as a supplemental text is an excellent strategy with which to introduce students to the Bard who might not have great success navigating the language and the play's length the first time through.

> **Teacher of the Bard Talk**
>
> What makes a "good fit," then, revolves around these four criteria:
>
> 1. age and maturity level of the students
> 2. curricular context—what the students have studied in history that may enhance their comprehension
> 3. teacher excitement over key themes of the play
> 4. teacher comfort with the schemes, tropes, and structure of Shakespearean text, especially as these skills are reinforced in other areas of the curriculum
>
> —STEPHEN HELLER,
> *Adlai E. Stevenson High School; ELA teacher and AP language consultant*

You could build a unit connecting a Shakespeare play with several short nonfiction texts to strengthen students' ability to read and understand informational and persuasive texts. A quick Google search for short nonfiction titles to complement *Romeo and Juliet*, for example, yields "Why Teenagers Are So Impulsive" (Underwood); "'Romeo and Juliet' Has Led Us Astray," an op-ed piece by Andrew Trees; plus many appropriate TED Talks. The tale of star-crossed lovers in Renaissance Verona takes on contemporary resonance as students recognize their plight spans the centuries and cultures.

If you are introducing students to techniques of persuasion, Shakespeare's works brim with examples of characters trying to persuade themselves or other characters to act. Though excerpts from Shakespeare might not immediately come to mind as exemplar texts to teach persuasive techniques, incorporating Hamlet's "To be or not to be" speech or Iago manipulating Roderigo to join him against Othello places a manageable text nugget in front of students in advance of reading a complete play later in the curriculum. In Appendix C, you will

Teacher of the Bard Talk

I have taught *The Taming of the Shrew, The Comedy of Errors, A Midsummer Night's Dream*, and *Macbeth*. *Macbeth* is by far my favorite to work on with eighth graders, with *Midsummer* running a close second. Initially, I thought that *Midsummer* would be the best fit, but, actually, *Macbeth* is far more accessible to this [middle school] age group. The witches and acts of violence are compelling to them, and the linear nature of the story is easier for students to follow than, say, that of *Midsummer*. They enjoy …the clever unraveling of the witches' prophesies and engaging in conversations about where the responsibility lies in terms of Macbeth's downfall.

—Jennifer Bertacchi,
Carleton Washburne Middle School; ELA teacher

find a stand-alone activity through which to examine Hamlet's "Oh that this too too solid Flesh, would melt" soliloquy. The excerpt students examine in November might be from the play read in March, allowing them to retrieve something they learned, something they know to apply then to its original context.

We discuss here how Shakespeare can be complemented by a YA novel, and we consider using a Shakespeare play as the anchor text and a YA novel supplementing its study—but you could flip that pairing strategy by using excerpts from the play to illuminate key elements of the novel; for example, John Green's *The Fault in Our Stars*, which takes its title from *Julius Caesar*, resonates well with *Romeo and Juliet*. Providing students with scenes from *Romeo and Juliet* to explore parallels with that YA novel connects a canonical text with an emerging, contemporary one. It makes Shakespeare more vital and relevant to today's popular culture landscape.

"All the [Classroom's] a Stage": Integrating the Folio Technique

When you embark on integrating bell ringer warm-ups, active drama approaches, and the Folio technique, you need to consider how *active* your classroom really is. If you have spent time long before starting a unit on Shakespeare getting students up on their feet in large and small groups, and perhaps individually, the introduction of Folio technique speaking activities will not seem so odd or threatening. You can look at the Folio technique as a souped-up annotation protocol to foster deeper critical reading and analysis and use it in that way, but we would assert that you are not making the most of the natural engagement aspect of reading and studying a work of drama: hear the words, see them in action. Those hearing and seeing dimensions work wonderfully for examining text nuggets that are not very long. And those Folio technique activities should be placed strategically over the breadth of the unit.

When you consider adding the Folio technique to a play you already teach, think back to the obstacles students have experienced in getting close to the Early Modern English language and blank verse structure. What have you spent the most time explaining or interpreting for students? Use that as your guide to select the most pertinent Folio clues to present. If your students are Shakespeare novices, you may be focusing exclusively on the language clues presented in Chapter 4, with a few verse clues added midway through the unit. Students who have read Shakespeare more than once may only need a quick review of the basic language clues with greater time spent on the impact of verse. More accomplished students who demonstrate a high level of mastery will be more comfortable tackling clues in all three categories. You are certainly free to mix and match the clues as they suit your students and the play. You may recall that we focused quite a bit on antithesis in *Romeo and Juliet* in Chapter 6, as the main characters' relationship challenges Verona's social norms, while inversions are prevalent in *Macbeth*, as that rhetorical strategy reflects the language of the supernatural and incantations. Let the play dictate the initial pool of clues you want to introduce to get at character and theme. Then consider which linguistic and syntactical hurdles your students will need to navigate to normalize Shakespeare's way of writing and his character's way of speaking.

Moreover, consider adding John Basil's *How to Act Shakespeare in 21 Days* to your resource shelf. It may seem too theater-class focused, but it complements our chapters on the Folio technique nicely and offers other ways to structure the introduction of the various clues along with additional text nuggets.

"What's Past Is Prologue": Previewing the Play's Essentials

Textbooks generally introduce an author using a short biographical sketch and some contextual information about the time period that produced a particular work. For Shakespeare, editors also will provide information about the Globe Theatre and how his plays were staged there. If students have studied more than one play, they have probably encountered much the same information to introduce the Bard. With YouTube, Shakespeare apps, and plenty of Shakespeare-themed websites, we have many more choices regarding how to introduce students to a particular play, learn about Shakespeare and his theater, or build a case for his relevance in contemporary, popular culture. The following sections present a few examples of how to start a unit with a media text or two.

Thug Notes

With over one hundred episodes available on YouTube, *Thug Notes* provides a quick summary of most of the plays you would use in your classroom. The producing website Wisecrack bills the series as "classic literature, original gangster." And the series' host, Sparky Sweets, PhD, provides a quick summary and a bit of analysis in a video that runs under five minutes. Sweets's engaging and irreverent manner may be suitable for most, but not all, classrooms. You will find some versions of the original videos labeled "clean" on YouTube. If you cover a play that currently is not part of *Thug Notes,* you can have students develop their own *Thug Notes* episode for that play or create another format that isn't reliant on rap music and culture.

TED-Ed Shakespeare Videos and Lesson Ideas

You can access a lesson plan from TED-Ed for using the *Thug Notes* "Macbeth" episode at ed.ted.com/on/et0ddHix, which organizes the experience around a "watch, think, dig deeper, and discuss" approach (Cadeño). TED-Ed also offers a series of animated videos that pose the question: Why should you read Shakespeare's [*Title of Play*]?. Typing in "TED-Ed Shakespeare videos" to a search engine will take you to the latest titles in the growing collection.

The Clash of the Film Clips: Is It Shakespeare?

If they don't need a plot summary preview, you might want to engage students in considering that Shakespeare was a popular culture star of his time. You can present a series of film clips illustrating various treatments of the same play to pose the question: "Is it Shakespeare?" Students view each clip and place it on a continuum with "Shakespeare" on the far left and "Not Shakespeare" on the far right. The activity begins with a discussion of the question: "How do you know Shakespeare when you read it, hear it, or see it?" The aim here is to tease out students' preconceived notions of what makes Shakespeare feel either remote or accessible to them. Depending on their previous engagements with the Bard, it might be more remote and inaccessible than a welcome return. You can also introduce the dichotomy of "high" versus "low" culture, to move the discussion toward how Shakespeare shifted from popular culture star to high art icon over time.

Use the following film adaptations to introduce and examine treatments of *Romeo and Juliet*. Screen the equivalent of the opening skirmish between the Montagues and Capulets or the balcony scene from all of the following in this order:

1. Baz Luhrmann's *Romeo + Juliet* (1996)
2. *Shakespeare: The Animated Tales*, "Romeo and Juliet" episode (1992)
3. *Warm Bodies* (2013)

4. Franco Zeffirelli's *Romeo and Juliet* (1968)
5. *West Side Story* (1961)

As students view each clip, have them discuss the markers present in each example that makes an approach to "Shakespeare," or not (e.g., language, time period, costume, acting style). Students may have to move an individual clip around on the "Shakespeare or Not" continuum as they view other clips in the set. You can substitute clips based on their YouTube availability—and the supply of substitutions is incredibly vast. Notice, in the suggested *Romeo and Juliet* set of clips, students will be evaluating a traditional approach to language and costume, a modern-day setting of the text, an animated version of the text, a YA zombie apocalypse adaptation, and a musical. Three of the five clips use Shakespeare's language, but their visual style is very different. Two of them don't use Shakespeare's language and represent two different adaptation genres.

By engaging students in this discussion and analysis, Shakespeare will seem less remote as students consider his position in the popular culture of his time and in the present day. Extend this activity with students gathering information about Shakespeare's evolving reputation over the centuries and the emergence of "bardolatry" in the nineteenth century. Refer to Appendix D for suggestions of clips that complement introducing *Hamlet* and *Macbeth* as well as questions to guide discussion of any clip set.

Demystifying Shakespeare is the crucial element of any previewing process. Reading his work is challenging, but it should be selected, framed, and orchestrated in a unit that is both manageable and pleasurable for the student. We need to move him out of Mark Powell's metaphorical corner in our classroom and off his pedestal as Susan Spangler urges. And we need to ask him to sit alongside our students as a collaborator helping students make meaning of his text. We should strive to create reading, writing, critical thinking, and low-risk performing activities that invite students to make strong connections between Shakespeare's characters and their conflicts as much as possible.

Teacher of the Bard Talk

[To help them to connect better with characters and their conflicts,] students focus on a key topic at the heart of the scene…to situate its content in their minds. If we are reading Helena's and Hermia's dialogue in 1.1 of *A Midsummer Night's Dream*, my "Do Now" [previewing task would] ask students to reflect on a time they had an argument with a close friend about a love interest and the multitude of emotions that they experienced during the face-to-face conversation. To take it a step further, I may ask students how this dialogue would be different if conducted over a text message.

—Rita Göndöcs,
World Language Academy; ELA teacher

"Unclasp'd to Thee the Book": Selecting Companion Novels and Plays

YA Fiction

Pairing a Shakespeare play with a YA novel might be the best engagement tool for many middle and high school students. Some of the novels plunge their modern-day protagonists into the world of a play or Shakespeare's times and theater company: for example, *The Shakespeare Kid*, *Dreamers Often Lie*, *Kissing Shakespeare*, *Saving Hamlet*. Other titles focus on how being cast in a production of a play reveals parallels between the protagonists' lives and the play itself: *Speak of Me as I Am*, *Swimming in the Monsoon Sea*, *Illyria*, *Saving Juliet*. Some novels reveal the next chapter of the story (the *Still Star-Crossed* book and television series pertains to *Romeo and Juliet* among others), shift the perspective (*Ophelia/Hamlet*), reverse the original plot (*The Taming of the Drew/The Taming of the Shrew* or *Juliet Immortal/Romeo and Juliet*), develop a whodunit (*Something Rotten*, a Horatio Wilkes mystery/*Hamlet*), create a zombie apocalypse (*Warm Bodies/Romeo and Juliet*). The titles and genres in all these categories go on, and you can easily find vetted recommendations online. For many of the plays commonly taught at the middle and high school grades, there are so many options that you could make several novels available for students to self-select titles and form literary circles.

Hogarth Shakespeare Series

There are many contemporary and canonical novels based on Shakespeare's plays, from *King Lear* in Jane Smiley's *A Thousand Acres* to *The Tempest* in Aldous Huxley's *Brave New World*. In 2015 the Hogarth Press launched a series of novels that set eight of Shakespeare's plays in modern contexts, each written by a bestselling writer, including Margaret Atwood, Gillian Flynn, Anne Tyler, and Tracy Chevalier. The series has debuted titles twice a year since the initial offering of *A Gap in Time*, Jeanette Winterson's adaptation of *The Winter's Tale*, and it will conclude with Gillian Flynn's take on *Hamlet* in 2021. These novels are aimed at the readers of the selected authors, so, for the most part, they can fit easily into most high school classrooms. As with the YA adaptations of Shakespeare, the series draws on a variety of genres, from family melodrama to romantic comedy to a time-traveling yarn. The standouts for classroom use include Atwood's *Hag-Seed*, which brings *The Tempest* into a prison where inmates perform their version of the romance and who would best play Caliban; Chevalier's *The New Boy*, where *Othello* plays out on a middle school playground in the DC area during the 1970s; and Tyler's *Vinegar Girl*, which reframes *The Taming of the Shrew* as a sweet romantic comedy set in a college town where a defiant daughter is paired with her father's research assistant who is in need of a wife and a green card.

These novels can be read in their entirety or in excerpt form. For example, in *Hag-Seed*, the inmate-actors engage in lively discussions of *The Tempest*'s themes and character relationships as well as the approach their director, Felix, applies in order to get revenge on a few government officials. For a table work discussion, Felix presents his company with a way to think about the characters that is a particularly useful approach to offer students. He posits that all the characters in the play at one point or another are prisoners contained in physical confinement by a specific jailer: Ariel/pine tree/Sycorax. He asks his actors to identify "eight unique incarceration events" that are fairly easy to discern and then challenges them to uncover a ninth (Atwood 130). Chapter 21, "Prospero's Goblins," offers the inmates' lively discussion of their discoveries about forms of imprisonment in the play and what makes Prospero a tyrant. Students could read the chapter to respond to and then evaluate Felix's approach. This activity would set the stage for reading more traditional literary criticism, or allow students to create their own critical approach for analyzing character relationships in the play.

Contemporary Plays

Most teachers who pair contemporary drama with Shakespeare will include *Rosencrantz and Guildenstern Are Dead* (1966) with *Hamlet*, but Tom Stoppard presents many challenges for student readers, so a search for other companion plays may stop there. There are other choices for other Shakespeare plays that are rich and accessible texts to illuminate themes, conflicts, and relationships developed by the Bard. We offer a few options for reading more dramatic texts.

In *Dunsinane* (2010), David Greig dramatizes what happens after the death of Macbeth and imagines that Lady Macbeth, here known as Gruach, has survived Macbeth's coup. Here, she is the mother to a son from her first marriage. This play could stimulate a comparison of the English nation-building efforts in eleventh-century Scotland to contemporary events in Afghanistan and Iraq (Billington). A unit could be built around first reading Shakespeare's *Macbeth* and investigating why the Bard chose to write about a legendary Scottish king when King James sat on the throne, then shifting the unit's focus to the contemporary

Teacher of the Bard Talk

I think pairing *Macbeth* with contemporary (or even historic) leaders is a really interesting way to develop richer conversations about power and ambition. I think students need to understand why we read fiction and what we can learn from fiction. This happens best when they see relevant connections with their lived experiences.

—MARK ONUSCHECK,
Adlai E. Stevenson High School; director of curriculum, instruction, and assessment

play that extends the narrative and contextualizes it amid modern invasion and colonization (Jones).

Aimé Césaire's *Une Tempête* (*A Tempest*) shifts the focus of Shakespeare's *The Tempest* to the indigenous inhabitants of the island, Caliban and Ariel. Published in 1969, the drama centers on Caliban's and Ariel's approaches to the colonial oppression of Prospero. Caliban, a black slave who would prefer to be called "X," speaks for revolution by any means necessary, while Ariel, characterized as mixed race, champions a nonviolent approach against colonial oppression. As the founder of the Négritude movement, a black consciousness initiative, Césaire used theater as a tool to disseminate its ideology and provide a critique of canonical literature that examined the virtues and vices of colonialization through an Early Modern lens. Relying on Shakespeare's *The Tempest* as a starting point, students can trace the ambitions of colonialization during the Age of Exploration through to its unraveling in the twentieth century. Supplemental texts could include excerpts from historical exploration narrative from Shakespeare's time; Michel de Montaigne's essay "Of Cannibals" (1580); and primary texts from the Négritude movement.

Another group of plays dramatizes events in Shakespeare's own life and times, in the vein of the film *Shakespeare in Love* (the screenplay was cowritten by Tom Stoppard and Marc Norman), which has been adapted into a stage play by Lee Hall. Selecting one of these plays will bring students closer to Shakespeare the man as playwright, father, and literary legend in the making. Here are some other options that would make for entertaining and informative reading in high school classrooms:

- *The Book of Will* (2017) by Lauren Gunderson—Condell and Heminges set out to compile and publish the First Folio.
- *A Cry of Players* (1968) by William Gibson—Young Will Shakespeare struggles between domestic responsibility and his ambitions in the theater.
- *The Beard of Avon* (2001) by Amy Freed—Both Shakespeare and Anne Hathaway become involved with Edward de Vere, a secret playwright in Elizabeth's court, who might be the "real" Shakespeare.
- *Equivocation* (2009) by Bill Cain—Did Shakespeare actually write the plays attributed to him? Here he receives a royal commission to adapt a narrative about the Gunpowder Plot.
- *The Herbal Bed* (1996) by Peter Whelan—Susanna Shakespeare is accused of adultery and must defend her actions as English society grows more and more puritanical.

These plays allow students to explore aspects of Shakespeare's life, career, and legacy with varying levels of historical accuracy, so focused research activities should encourage students to fact-check the characters and circumstances presented.

Shakespeare: All Mashed Up, Chosen as an Adventure, without a Filter, in Fourteen Pictures, as a Folktale, or as a Literary Travelogue

> **Student of the Bard Talk**
>
> To me, it is important to give the credit Shakespeare deserves. He is a revolutionary writer, and, while it may be difficult for high schoolers, very important to understand. But, I do think that there should be a reason why you read whatever play you read. If not, you have nothing to tie it back to, nothing to create a big picture for the students.
>
> —Hailey Keenan,
> *Adlai E. Stevenson High School*

Our final set of suggested texts presents Shakespeare's influences, works, and characters in unusual formats. Many of these adaptations can serve as motivational tools or as exemplars for students to create their own adaptations. You should display books like these during a Shakespeare unit as a literary "petting zoo" to encourage students to browse these unorthodox takes on the Bard.

Deadpool Does Shakespeare

At several points in his dubious career as an irreverent superhero, Deadpool has found himself trapped in narratives that parallel those penned by the Bard. This special collection features Issues #26 and #27 of the comic, which find the "Merc with a mouth" enmeshed in a star-crossed Valentine's romance, and then "Much Ado about Deadpool," a "tragical–comical" parody in five acts (Duggan and Doescher). Like characters in Shakespeare, Deadpool breaks the fourth wall to address his readers directly. This collection comes with a "parent advisory" warning, so it will be suitable for some, but not for all, students.

William Shakespeare's Much Ado about Mean Girls, William Shakespeare's Get Thee . . . Back to the Future, MacTrump

Ian Doescher's fertile imagination has mashed up the Bard's blank verse and five-act structure with more contemporary cinema after having his way with the Star Wars franchise, beginning aptly enough with *William Shakespeare's Star Wars*. He tackles political satire, too, with *MacTrump* leaning on both Macbeth and Hamlet for inspiration.

Kill Shakespeare

Created and written by Conor McCreery and Anthony Del Col. Billed on the comic's back cover as a "dark take on the Bard [pitting] his greatest heroes

(Hamlet, Juliet, Othello, Falstaff) against his most menacing villains (Richard III, Lady Macbeth, Iago) in an epic adventure to find and kill a reclusive wizard named William Shakespeare." The Kill Shakespeare series has grown to include four volumes of twelve issues.

To Be or Not to Be and *Romeo and/or Juliet*
Ryan North reformats two of the greatest tragedies of all time into a lively, crazy, engaging "choose your own adventure" format.

OMG Shakespeare
This series helps us imagine how Shakespeare's memorable characters would make the most of social media in *srsly Hamlet, YOLO Juliet, Macbeth #killingit*, and *A Midsummer Night #nofilter* (Carbone; Wright).

Classics Unfolded
Imagine an entire Shakespeare tragedy—*Romeo and Juliet* (Bryksenkova)—encapsulated in fourteen illustrations on the front and back of a folded sheet of heavy paper that measures thirty-three by nine inches slipped into a cardboard case less than one inch thick. Each image is captioned with a line from the play, and the reader gets a thirty-second plot summary and five-word description of the play (genre, themes, players, action) to introduce the image sequence.

Shakespeare and the Folktale: An Anthology of Stories
In Chapter 1, we discussed how two UK educators framed their introduction of *King Lear* with its connections to common fairy tale tropes and conventions. Charlotte Artese brings together well-known folktales that could have been Shakespeare's inspiration and source material for *King Lear* and *The Merchant of Venice*. The anthology also presents forty tales related to eight of the Bard's plays drawn from a variety of world cultures and folklorists, including the Brothers Grimm and Zora Neale Hurston.

World's Elsewhere: Journeys around Shakespeare's Globe
The nonfiction suggestion in this set, *Worlds Elsewhere: Journeys around Shakespeare's Globe*, reveals to students how Shakespeare has evolved into a global superstar—the Bard of Avon. If you would like to supplement reading any play with some engaging nonfiction, Andrew Dickson offers an array of anecdotes about his investigation of the Bard's penetration of American culture, from the names of cities and towns to barnstorming actors blazing a trail across the frontier, as well as Shakespeare's presence on the world's stages and screens, from Europe (beyond the UK) to South Africa, India, and China. The book's chap-

ters are easy to excerpt and the index is comprehensive and helpful for the efficient selection of an appropriate passage or two for above grade-level readers. Dickson reveals the importance of Shakespeare sustaining and inspiring prisoners incarcerated at Robben Island, and one in particular: Nelson Mandela. In a lighter vein, we are particularly partial to the segment on cities named after Shakespearean characters since we live in Illinois, not too far from the town of Romeoville, which is near the city of Joliet—at one time, thought to be christened "Juliet" and not named for the explorer Louis Joliet.

How Shakespeare Changed Everything

Obviously, the best way to motivate students to read, understand, and enjoy Shakespeare is to show them he has never left the cultural conversation. One last recommendation for the Shakespeare "petting zoo" display would be Stephen Marche's *How Shakespeare Changed Everything*. Dedicate bulletin board or online space for students and yourself to post references to the Bard and his work as they appear in print, music, movies, and television. You really can't escape Bill in popular culture!

Making and Evaluating Connections with Literary and Popular Culture Companions

With any of the companion texts recommended here, students should focus their analytical and critical attention on how a novel or play uses its Shakespearean source material in creative, illuminating, and entertaining ways. What are the markers that announce the parallels or connections to source material? Students should also examine how well a narrative "stands alone" as an enjoyable reading experience as well as how understanding the source material enhances that experience even further. Students can pose the question: "Will this companion to one of Shakespeare's great plays stand the test of time and remain relevant and readable one hundred years from now?" By considering that question, they can tease out what makes Shakespeare's works endure and appeal.

"Such Stuff / As Dreams Are Made Of": Pairing Shakespeare Plays with Media Texts

If we decide to incorporate a viewing activity to complement the study of a play, we will probably choose to screen a theatrical-release film to give students the experience of seeing a play in action. As dramatic texts, Shakespeare's works were meant to be seen and heard. That impulse then is certainly a good and productive one, but there are other viewing experiences that can be used before, during, or after the reading process. Mary Ellen Dakin's *Reading Shakespeare Film First* is an excellent and comprehensive resource for integrating feature-length films into your unit, and we recommend that you also add her book to your teacher resources. We make a few recommendations of our own to consider in addition to screening a feature film adaptation.

Shakespeare Uncovered

This BBC series came to the United States on PBS. These fifty-five-minute episodes feature an actor or director exploring a single play or several plays within a single genre. Over three seasons, the series has covered nineteen plays, including many that find their way into ELA curricula: *Macbeth*, *Hamlet*, *Othello*, *A Midsummer Night's Dream*, *Julius Caesar*, and *Romeo and Juliet*. An episode provides an excellent previewing activity in place of screening one of the abridgements from *Shakespeare: The Animated Tales*, if students do not require an overview of a play's plot. Actually, a Shakespeare Uncovered episode incorporates enough narrative context to provide a brief plot summary, since it doesn't presume that the viewer is necessarily steeped in the play. Episodes also can be easily excerpted to provide students with helpful interpretive information that might be best introduced during the reading process.

American actor Ethan Hawke hosts the "Macbeth" episode and uses his preparation for the role as the framework for his inquiry. He seeks out scholars, historians, master actors, and film versions to answer his questions about Macbeth's historic origins, motivations, and actions in Shakespeare's tragedy, as well as the influence of the Weird Sisters and Lady Macbeth on his behavior. The program is exceptionally well focused on the supernatural aspects in the play by posing the following questions: "Did witches corrupt Macbeth, or his own ambition?" "Did Macbeth always have the desire to seize the crown or did the witches plant that notion in his mind?" Students can use Hawke's questions to focus their reading and to spur their own inquiry. Other episodes help students focus their reading and critical analysis in similar fashion.

Shakespeare Retold

Here is another excellent BBC miniseries that includes ninety-minute episodes updating four plays. The scripts modernize Shakespeare's language. Each adaptation repositions the tragedy or comedies into a new milieu. The *Macbeth* episode casts James McAvoy as an ambitious chef who takes over a toney restaurant with the assistance of his ruthless wife, seasoned with liberal dashes of murder and madness. *The Taming of the Shrew* enters the political world; *Much Ado about Nothing* lands in the broadcast news business; and romantic entanglements emerge at an engagement party in *A Midsummer Night's Dream.*

Shakespeare's Globe Theatre on Screen

The productions of Shakespeare's plays mounted at the Globe since 2010 have been filmed for an initial release in movie theaters. Now they are available for use in the classroom in two formats: on DVD and via streaming through the Globe Player website and app. The productions feature well-known actors in iconic roles, including Mark Rylance as Olivia and Eddie Redmayne as Viola in an all-male production of *Twelfth Night*. They also make use of original practice staging at the Sam Wanamaker Playhouse in the Globe complex. The Globe Player offers the full-length productions, Globe to Globe productions in various languages, and silent film versions of the Bard for a fee, as well as some interviews from the Muse of Fire project and documentary content at no charge.

Having a copy of a production from this series on hand allows you to screen excerpts that help students visualize characters and actions performed on a replica of Shakespeare's own playhouse. Students can experience the interaction of the actors with the audience, especially in the comedies. If you are using the read–view approach mapped out in Chapter 7, texts in these productions are not edited all that much.

Many film adaptations feature serious cuts to a text as well as a reordering of scenes that make any read–view application challenging. The Shakespeare's Globe productions make relatively few cuts. We also recommend two other theater production series, those of the Royal Shakespeare Company and of the Stratford Festival (Ontario, Canada), which are likewise available on DVD. Several of the RSC productions are set in various time periods, which invites students to compare and contrast different directorial and design approaches to a play. The RSC also publishes print editions of ten plays (available in the United States through the Modern Library) that complement those videotaped productions. These paperback editions offer a good deal of engaging supplemental material aimed at students, not scholars.

Companion Documentaries: Performing Shakespeare in Schools, in Prison, in Nursing Homes, on the Stage

Viewing documentaries that follow student, professional, and nonprofessional actors can provide a rich and rewarding engagement tool, especially if your students don't view themselves as performers. They can see actors getting a text on its feet and experience their struggle and victories to make meaning of a challenging text. In addition to documenting a rehearsal process or acting master class, all of these films include valuable insights into their featured plays.

Romeo Is Bleeding (2015)
Spoken word poet Donté Clark collaborates with teens at a drop-in arts center in Richmond, California, to craft a rap version of *Romeo and Juliet*, called *Té's Harmony*, to address the gang violence that has permeated the community for decades. Blueshift Education offers a robust curriculum guide at www.blueshifteducation.com/romeo-is-bleeding.

My Juliet: Romeo and Juliet *for a New Generation* (2005)
Baz Luhrmann, the director of *Romeo + Juliet*, serves as a mentor to a British actor who is casting a community theater production of the play from a pool of non-actors in a working-class neighborhood of London.

Rwanda and Juliet (2016)
More than twenty years after the genocide that resulted in a million Tutsi deaths, an Ivy League professor directs a production of *Romeo and Juliet* cast with Tutsi and Hutu students.

Midsummer in Newtown (2016)
In the aftermath of the Sandy Hook shooting, a group of New York theater artists come to Newtown to create a musical version of *A Midsummer Night's Dream* with students who were touched by the tragedy, with the hope that engagement in the artistic process will contribute in some small way to the community's healing process.

Shakespeare behind Bars (2006)
Director Hank Rogerson follows the rehearsal process for *The Tempest*, which marked the seventh production mounted by inmates at a correctional complex in Kentucky under the guidance of Curt L. Tofteland.

Still Dreaming (2014)
Hank Rogerson documents the rehearsal and performance of *A Midsummer Night's Dream*, this time with retired professional actors at the Lillian Booth Actors Home outside of New York City.

Discovering Hamlet (1990)

This documentary follows Derek Jacobi directing a young Kenneth Branagh in 1988. It features interviews with the cast, designer, and scholars, which are very accessible to student viewers. The two-disc DVD edition (2011) includes three hours of additional material that can be easily excerpted, as can the documentary.

Shakespeare High (2011)

This film follows students from various schools in California preparing to compete in a Shakespeare Festival supported by some of Hollywood's most well-known actors and Shakespeare enthusiasts.

Playing Shakespeare (2009)

John Barton's miniseries from 1982 showcases a series of master classes he conducted with RSC actors, including Patrick Stewart, Judi Dench, Ian McKellen, and Ben Kingsley, among others. The nine episodes offer easily excerpted segments to focus on verse, language, character, and themes in the plays.

As with all viewing experiences, make sure you set a viewing focus for students as they watch any of these documentaries.

YouTube and Online Video Gems

Poking around the internet can be time well spent if you are searching for short videos to integrate into a unit as part of the previewing and while-reading strategies. That's how we discovered *Thug Notes*. With all online discoveries, it is important to preview videos for classroom appropriateness and to fact-check any information presented. Typing in a play's title will take you to a variety of sources, such as Macmillan Education, which offers the Shakespeare for Life series that includes the work of the Hip-Hop Shakespeare Company (see www.macmillandictionary.com/learn/shakespeare-for-life/). As previously mentioned, TED-Ed maintains a robust video library, including "Insults by Shakespeare" and "Shakespeare's Dating Tips," linked to short lesson plans that invite students to "watch, think, dig deeper, and discuss." You can pick up segments from the Reduced Shakespeare Company's *The Complete Works of William Shakespeare Abridged*, such as their football-themed, madcap recap of the history plays. Finally, look out for engaging and informative videos produced by students, teachers, and other lovers of the Bard. For example, Terry M. Moore-Porter created "Reinventing Shakespeare" for a Technology in Education class. In a little over three minutes, she makes an excellent case that Shakespeare's influence is alive and well in contemporary popular culture, and that he is not as culturally remote as many students might fear or imagine. You can task your students with their own YouTube search for videos related to Shakespeare, his theater, and the play being studied. Provide students with criteria for selection and see what they discover.

Need More Viewing Suggestions?

Chicago Shakespeare Theater's teacher handbooks provide recommendations for using Shakespeare on film and video to prepare students for attending one of their productions. This feature includes a "film finder" feature for each play, highlighting the top five films you should consider screening in whole or in part, as well as all the film adaptations of a specific play, loose adaptations and contemporary update films, animated versions, play-specific documentaries, and "film curiosities" such as avant-garde silent film versions. You can access those handbooks at www.chicagoshakes.com/education/teaching_resources/teacher_handbooks.

"Our Revels Now Are Ended"—Or Almost So: Developing Meaningful, Active Assessments

Paraphrasing

Both our teacher and student partners have extolled the virtues of paraphrasing to improve understanding. Teachers who have used parallel text editions and SIB (i.e., Shakespeare in Bits) versions recommend providing students with a short "cold" text nugget to paraphrase in order to determine how well students understand Shakespeare's language and syntax.

ELA instructor David Noskin, who routinely uses Folger Shakespeare editions, shared that when he works with his sophomores who are reading at or above grade level:

> I use the 50, 60, 70, 80, 85 rule. When we begin Act 1, we're hoping to understand about half of what we read. This encourages them to work with the text, as it mitigates the fear that they are not getting all or most of it. By the middle, I expect about three-quarters comprehension. By the end of the act, some students will reach a plateau (the reason for 85 percent, rather than 90 or 100).

He frequently checks for understanding by using short paraphrasing activities in the midst of reading or discussing a scene or as short formative assessments:

During Act 1, after we read a short scene, I model paraphrasing and then summarizing. I then say to the class that I would expect us to get around 50 percent of the content.... The main reason I do that is so students don't feel pressure to get everything or even most lines; instead, students should be reading for a general understanding. Psychologically, students relax and focus more on the plot and the figurative language (that I point out sparingly).

> **Student of the Bard Talk**
>
> The paraphrase activity was so helpful and so useful and so necessary because it gave me an opportunity to look at every single one of my lines and understand them.... This would be helpful to non-actors in an English class because it would help them to understand the confusing and really not modern language of the play. As one understands the words better, they will understand the plot better, as a result.
>
> —ABBY SOKOL,
> *Adlai E. Stevenson High School*

Noskin recommends students should have the opportunity "to share their techniques for emergent understanding," since reading strategies have varying success in a class and students need to create their own toolkit of "go-to" strategies. Keep in mind that many Folio technique clues work nicely with the paraphrasing process.

Producing

Throughout this text, we have highlighted how graphic, animated, and filmic texts work so effectively in concert with traditional print editions of Shakespeare, as well as to support the implementation of the Folio technique. Many students have shifted from merely consuming those texts to creating them, so it makes sense that a capstone activity would involve students creating a response to a play using one of those visual forms. High school ELA teacher Laura L. Brown has her students create a "coming attractions" trailer to distill the most important elements of *Macbeth*. Students can also create public service announcements using characters from a play to advocate a theme or topic that emerges from their study of the play. These public service announcements can be either serious or comic in tone. Developing a sequence for a comic book edition of a play can focus on situating a play in a different time period as many of plays in the Manga Shakespeare series do. Students can create their own versions of any visual formats that they encounter in a unit as models.

In a film studies class, a student's video project fell apart miserably in the editing process. He had no time to reshoot scenes to salvage his original idea, so, to meet the deadline, he created a short film in which he offered tips on how to make a successful film to meet all the requirements of the project. That happy accident gave life to the "recommendation film project," which could involve the entire class scripting, shooting, editing, and performing. The film would be used the following year to brief students before they embarked on studying the same play. It could be built around a "top ten list" of "what to expect when you read [*add the title of the play*]."

No matter what form a video or graphic text production project takes, it allows students to respond to a play using a variety of composing skills: words, sounds, and images. Not that far removed from the tools Shakespeare used himself.

Performing

We have not emphasized "finished product" performing when we have discussed implementing the Folio technique or cue scripts. Those performance-based techniques have been all about developing students' ability to read and understand Shakespeare's work in an active and dynamic way, not to transform them necessarily into stage performers. But you may find students at the end of the unit are eager to showcase their burgeoning performance skills. If that is the case, then creating a festival of scenes would be a good choice as a capstone activity. And this could be a good place to screen a segment of the documentary *Shakespeare High*. Students certainly can perform scenes they have memorized, present polished performances using cue scripts, original hip-hop interpretations of key speeches or scenes, as well as improvised scenes setting a play in the modern day or in a different genre (comedy becomes tragedy and vice versa). To lessen performance anxiety, students can put their scenes on video and present them to the class for discussion and critique, or they can be uploaded to an online site where students view them and provide constructive comments.

But Where's the Literary Analysis Essay?

For students with newly emerging skills in reading, understanding, and analyzing Shakespeare, a formal literary analysis essay might not be the best means to assess their development. If you decided to have students create a video, graphic text excerpt, or performance, you should have them document their process in a series of journals, blog posts, or an essay. You then can focus on their writing skills. Any of these projects would allow students to tackle the following topics:

- Which part of the play did you choose to adapt or perform?
- Why did you choose that speech or scene?
- What challenges did you face in fully understanding that piece of text in order to adapt it and/or perform it?

- Which Folio clues helped you better understand Shakespeare's words and intentions?
- What did you learn from working with that piece of text in this way that you didn't fully understand when you first read it?

You should consider giving students, working independently or in groups, a series of options so they can play to their strengths along Gardner's multiple intelligences spectrum to increase their level of confidence and virtuosity—although it isn't out of the question to stretch students to test the waters with new forms of expression and analysis. We encourage you and your students to decide what will be the best measure of their growth within the context of your curriculum's goals and objectives.

Start Planning Your Next Experience Teaching the Bard

We have stayed away from offering a traditional unit framework because we know and believe that each student population and curriculum have their own objectives, rhythms, and outcomes. One size doesn't fit all. What we encourage you to do is review what you do now with your students and the play(s) you teach:

- What works well?
- What would you like to do better?
- How would adding active drama approaches and the Folio technique help to improve activities and strategies that aren't working as well as you would like?
- How might changing the way you use video enhance student engagement?
- Is it time to replace those worn paperback editions of the play?
- If so, which paperback or digital edition of the play might you use going forward that fits your students' needs and the book replacement budget?

Once you have taken yourself through that reflection on your current practices, it is important to set realistic goals to shift your instructional style. Appendix E provides a list of one essential resource mentioned in each of our chapters to aid planning your unit.

If you are a part of a curriculum planning team, you may find that your desire to implement the Folio technique, add video content, or include a supplemental text to an existing unit rests with the support and sanction of your colleagues. The teachers featured in Chapter 2 who use the SIB series of apps are part of a curriculum team that needed to adopt the same edition of *Macbeth*. One team member, an early adopter of technology in the classroom, tested SIB with her students and made recommendations for its use across the team. Their school's recent introduction of a one-to-one iPad program made using the SIB system an easy sell to teachers and administrators at that point across the team. You might implement an aspect of the Folio technique, a short video, or an excerpt from a supplemental text that doesn't take much time away from your team's lesson plan and report back about how it worked for your students. Consider carefully the buy-in needed for your team to adopt new strategies for their Shakespeare skills toolkit. You should invite them into your classroom to observe how an activity or strategy actually works—seeing helps with believing.

And whatever changes you make to your approach, engage the students in evaluating any new strategies, activities, or texts. Sometimes you can tell how something new is working from students' observable behavior and assessment data, but students can be extremely helpful providing focused anecdotal information as well. Be creative. Be patient. Be reflective. You will be surprised at how changes, great and small, can make your students' and your own efforts so much more impactful and rewarding well beyond your classroom encounters with the Bard.

Epilogue

KEVIN LONG

The RSC's John Barton, in his groundbreaking video series and companion book *Playing Shakespeare*, stated:

> simply that the clues in the text are much richer and more numerous than at first appears. And though the possibilities are infinite, we can only sift the fruitful from the perverse by getting our teeth into the text and the verse itself. If the textual points are ignored, then it's pretty certain that Shakespeare's intentions will be ignored also or at least twisted.... [I]f [one] ignores the verse it leads to an alternative to and not a realization of Shakespeare. (167–68)

Almost twenty-five years ago, I was drawn to this work with the Folio technique because I saw productions produced by Shakespeare Repertory (now called Chicago Shakespeare Theater) directed by Barbara Gaines. Each time I saw a production, the text was crystal clear. What were they doing? After reading an article in the *Chicago Tribune* about Barbara and Shakespeare Repertory, she mentioned the term *Folio technique* and the use of the First Folio when preparing the text for performance. "Aha!" I thought, "I must learn this groundbreaking technique." I contacted Barbara and she introduced me to Kate Buckley, the Shakespeare Repertory's First Folio text coach. Kate taught me the technique. It was life changing. My initial investigation with the Folio technique began with a quest to become a stronger actor when playing Shakespeare. However, my mission soon changed from self-improvement to attempting to change the Shakespeare experience of as many people as I could. I, like you, encounter people of all ages who make statements such as, "Oh, I just don't understand Shakespeare at all!" or "Ugh, him again!" or "Shakespeare is so boring!" To which I say, "Just give me an hour of your time and an incredible door will be unlocked for you. You will 'crack the code' of Shakespeare, and, in the process, not only understand his plays in a much clearer and visceral way, but you too will have a fire lit within you as you develop a true love for his plays."

On May 19, 2018, I attended the graduation ceremonies at Harper College, where I currently teach. Our keynote speaker was David Coleman, the president and CEO of the College Board. David's commencement speech was one of the best commencement speeches I have ever heard. He and his team had spent quite a bit of time interviewing students and faculty from our college in preparation for it. He then used those words gathered from our community to create a speech that drew lessons to be taught and shared. It was uniquely a Harper's graduation speech. His final point to the graduates and loved ones in attendance was to "Be a Harper." This was drawn from the name of our college; however, the word also comes from Old English, meaning the harpists who carried music from town to town sharing the news and the stories of their time. The role of the Harper was to inspire others. As documented in the article "Graduates Celebrate at Harper College's 50th Commencement Ceremony," David finished his speech with these words:

> If you want to make the world better, to be a light against darkness, be a Harper. ...Think about whom you have inspired or will inspire. For that's what being a Harper means. Creating that spark in others, lifting them up with your stories and your successes, encouraging them and showing them how to keep moving forward. (Harper College News Bureau)

Thanks to the words of David Coleman, I consider myself a Harper for Shakespeare. I hope that, when you read these chapters, you become inspired and that a spark will be lit within you to try some new techniques with the texts of Shakespeare and share them with your students. Who knows, we may end up with an entire symphony of Harpers for Shakespeare. This, I know, would make Bill proud!

Appendix A

Speeches for Further Study

Presented here are several well-known soliloquies that will serve as excellent vehicles for your students to apply their working knowledge of the Folio technique. Each soliloquy is, of course, taken from the First Folio and is presented with regularized spelling; however, the text still preserves Shakespeare's authorial intention (grammar, capitalization, punctuation, etc.). Each soliloquy featured is rich with text clues that your students will enjoy digging into. Consider using one of these soliloquies to measure student learning after introducing basic, intermediate, or advanced Folio clues (see also the cue cards in Chapters 4–6).

As students analyze one of the following speeches, activating the targeted Folio clues, remind them to:

- look up each soliloquy by its act and scene in *Shakespeare A to Z* (or a similar online or print resource) in order to provide context for the speech as needed
- use their "magic" index cards to move through the speech, speaking it line by line
- refer to either Schmidt's *Shakespeare Lexicon* (available online at www.perseus.tufts.edu/hopper/text?doc=Perseus%3Atext%3A1999.03.0079) or the "Glossary" on the Shakespeare's Words website (www.shakespeareswords.com/Public/Glossary.aspx) to define the unfamiliar words
- rely on selected clue cards to score the text for targeted Folio clues

Romeo and Juliet (2.5)

(Source: internetshakespeare.uvic.ca/doc/Rom_F1/scene/2.5/.)

JULIET. The clock struck nine, when I did send the Nurse,
In half an hour she promised to return,
Perchance she cannot meet him: that's not so:
Oh she is lame, Love's Herald should be thoughts,
Which ten times faster glides then the Sun's beams, 5
Driving back shadows over lowring hills.
Therefore do nimble Pinion'd Doves draw Love,
And therefore hath the wind-swift *Cupid* wings:
Now is the Sun upon the highmost hill
Of this day's journey, and from nine till twelve, 10
Is three long hours, yet she is not come.
Had she affections and warm youthful blood,
She would be as swift in motion as a ball,
My words would bandy her to my sweet Love,
And his to me, but old folks, 15
Many feign as they were dead,
Unwieldy, slow, heavy, and pale as lead.

Macbeth (1.5)

(Source: internetshakespeare.uvic.ca/doc/Mac_F1/scene/1.5/.)

LADY. The Raven himself is hoarse,
That croaks the fatal entrance of *Duncan*
Under my Battlements. Come you Spirits,
That tend on mortal thoughts, unsex me here,
And fill me from the Crown to the Toe, top-full 5
Of direst Cruelty: make thick my blood,
Stop up th' access, and passage to Remorse,
That no compunctious visitings of Nature
Shake my fell purpose, nor keep peace between
Th' effect, and it. Come to my Woman's Breasts, 10
And take my Milk for Gall, you murdering Ministers,
Wherever, in your sightless substances,
You wait on Natures Mischief. Come thick Night,
And pall thee in the dunnest smoke of Hell,

> That my keen Knife see not the Wound it makes, 15
> Nor Heaven peep through the Blanket of the dark,
> To cry, hold, hold.

Macbeth (5.5)

(Source: internetshakespeare.uvic.ca/doc/Mac_F1/scene/5.5/.)

> MACBETH. She should have died hereafter;
> There would have been a time for such a word:
> Tomorrow, and tomorrow, and tomorrow,
> Creeps in this petty pace from day to day,
> To the last Syllable of Recorded time: 5
> And all our yesterdays, have lighted Fools
> The way to dusty death. Out, out, brief Candle,
> Life's but a walking Shadow, a poor Player,
> That struts and frets his hour upon the Stage,
> And then is heard no more. It is a Tale 10
> Told by an Idiot, full of sound and fury
> Signifying nothing.

Appendix B

Cue Scripts for A Midsummer Night's Dream

Complete Text for the Keeper of the Book

A Midsummer Night's Dream (3.2) (adapted from First Folio, 1623, with variant spelling regularized), lines 488–603:

LYSANDER.	*Helen*, I love thee, by my life I do; I swear by that which I will lose for thee, To prove him false, that says I love thee not.
DEMETRIUS.	I say, I love thee more then he can do.
LYSANDER.	If thou say so, withdraw and prove it too.
DEMETRIUS.	Quick, come.
HERMIA.	*Lysander*, whereto tends all this?
LYSANDER.	Away, you *Ethiop*.
DEMETRIUS.	No, no, Sir, seem to break loose; Take on as you would follow, But yet come not: you are a tame man, go.
LYSANDER.	Hang off thou cat, thou burr; vile thing let loose, Or I will shake thee from me like a serpent.
HERMIA.	Why are you grown so rude? What change is this sweet Love?
LYSANDER.	Thy love? Out tawny *Tartar*, out; Out loathed medicine; O hated poison hence.
HERMIA.	Do you not jest?
HELENA.	Yes sooth, and so do you.

LYSANDER.	*Demetrius*: I will keep my word with thee.
DEMETRIUS.	I would I had your bond: for I perceive A weak bond holds you; I'll not trust your word.
LYSANDER.	What, should I hurt her, strike her, kill her dead? Although I hate her, I'll not harm her so.
HERMIA.	What, can you do me greater harm then hate? Hate me, wherefore? O me, what news my Love? Am not I *Hermia*? Are not you *Lysander*? I am as fair now, as I was ere while. Since night you lov'd me; yet since night you left me. Why then you left me (O the gods forbid) In earnest, shall I say?
LYSANDER.	Ay, by my life; And never did desire to see thee more. Therefore be out of hope, of question, of doubt; Be certain, nothing truer: 'tis no jest, That I do hate thee, and love *Helena*.
HERMIA.	O me, you juggler, you canker-blossom, You thief of love; What, have you come by night, And stoln my love's heart from him?
HELENA.	Fine i'faith: Have you no modesty, no maiden shame, No touch of bashfulness? What, will you tear Impatient answers from my gentle tongue? Fie, fie, you counterfeit, you puppet, you.
HERMIA.	Puppet? Why so? Aye, that way goes the game. Now I perceive that she hath made compare Between our statures, she hath urg'd her height, And with her personage, her tall personage, Her height (forsooth) she hath prevail'd with him. And are you grown so high in his esteem, Because I am so dwarfish, and so low? How low am I, thou painted Maypole? Speak, How low am I? I am not yet so low, But that my nails can reach unto thine eyes.
HELENA.	I pray you though you mock me, gentlemen, Let her not hurt me; I was never curst:

	I have no gift at all in shrewishness;
	I am a right maid for my cowardice;
	Let her not strike me: you perhaps may think,
	Because she is something lower then myself,
	That I can match her.

HERMIA.   Lower? hark again.

HELENA.   Good *Hermia*, do not be so bitter with me,
I evermore did love you *Hermia*,
Did ever keep your counsels, never wronged you,
Save that in love unto *Demetrius*,
I told him of your stealth unto this wood.
He followed you, for love I followed him,
But he hath chid me hence, and threatened me
To strike me, spurn me, nay to kill me too;
And now, so you will let me quiet go,
To *Athens* will I bear my folly back,
And follow you no further. Let me go.
You see how simple, and how fond I am.

HERMIA.   Why get you gone: who ist that hinders you?

HELENA.   A foolish heart, that I leave here behind.

HERMIA.   What, with *Lysander*?

HELENA.   With *Demetrius*.

LYSANDER.   Be not afraid, she shall not harm thee *Helena*.

DEMETRIUS.   No sir, she shall not, though you take her part.

HELENA.   O when she's angry, she is keen and shrewd,
She was a vixen when she went to school,
And though she be but little, she is fierce.

HERMIA.   Little again? Nothing but low and little?
Why will you suffer her to flout me thus?
Let me come to her.

LYSANDER.   Get you gone you dwarf,
You *minimus*, of hindering knot-grass made,
You bead, you acorn.

DEMETRIUS.   You are too officious,
In her behalf that scorns your services.
Let her alone, speak not of *Helena*,

| | Take not her part. For if thou dost intend
Never so little show of love to her,
Thou shalt abide it. |
|---|---|

LYSANDER. Now she holds me not,
Now follow if thou dar'st, to try whose right,
Of thine or mine is most in *Helena*.

DEMETRIUS. Follow? Nay, I'll go with thee cheek by jowl.
Exit Lysander and Demetrius.

HERMIA. You Mistress, all this coil is long of you.
Nay, go not back.

HELENA.   I will not trust you I,
Nor longer stay in your curst company.
Your hands then mine, are quicker for a fray,
My legs are longer through to run away.
Exit Hermia and Helena.

Cue Script: Helena (*MND* 3.2)

_____ **Do you not jest?**
Yes sooth, and so do you.

_____ **heart from him?**
Fine i'faith:
Have you no modesty, no maiden shame,
No touch of bashfulness? What, will you tear
Impatient answers from my gentle tongue?
Fie, fie, you counterfeit, you puppet you.

_____ **unto thine eyes.**
I pray you though you mock me, gentlemen,
Let her not hurt me; I was never curst:
I have no gift at all in shrewishness;
I am a right maid for my cowardice;
Let her not strike me: you perhaps may think,
Because she is something lower then myself,
That I can match her.

_____ **Lower? hark again.**
Good *Hermia*, do not be so bitter with me,
I evermore did love you *Hermia*,
Did ever keep your counsels, never wronged you,
Save that in love unto *Demetrius*,
I told him of your stealth unto this wood.
He followed you, for love I followed him,
But he hath chid me hence, and threatened me
To strike me, spurn me, nay to kill me too;
And now, so you will let me quiet go,
To Athens will I bear my folly back,
And follow you no further. Let me go.
You see how simple, and how fond I am.

_____ **that hinders you?**
A foolish heart that I leave here behind.

_____ **What, with *Lysander*?**

With *Demetrius*.

_____ **you take her part.**

O when she's angry, she is keen and shrewd,
She was a vixen when she went to school,
And though she be but little, she is fierce.

_____ **Nay, go not back.**

I will not trust you I,
Nor longer stay in your curst company.
Your hands then mine, are quicker for a fray,
My legs are longer though to run away.
Exit.

Cue Script: Hermia (*MND* 3.2)

_____ **Quick, come.**
Lysander, whereto tends all this?

_____ **like a serpent.**
Why are you grown so rude?
What change is this sweet Love?

_____ **hated poison hence.**
Do you not jest?

_____ **harm her so.**
What, can you do me greater harm then hate?
Hate me, wherefore? O me, what news my Love?
Am not I *Hermia*? Are not you *Lysander*?
I am as fair now, as I was erewhile.
Since night you lov'd me; yet since night you left me.
Why then you left me (O the gods forbid)
In earnest, shall I say?

_____ **and love *Helena*.**
O me, you juggler, you canker-blossom,
You thief of love; What, have you come by night,
And stoln my love's heart from him?

_____ **you puppet, you.**
Puppet? Why so? Aye, that way goes the game.
Now I perceive that she hath made compare
Between our statures, she hath urg'd her height,
And with her personage, her tall personage,
Her height (forsooth) she hath prevail'd with him.
And are you grown so high in his esteem,
Because I am so dwarfish, and so low?
How low am I, thou painted Maypole? Speak,
How low am I? I am not yet so low,
But that my nails can reach unto thine eyes.

_____ **can match her.**

Lower? hark again.

_____ **how fond I am.**

Why get you gone: who ist that hinders you?

_____ **leave here behind.**

What, with *Lysander*?

_____ **she is fierce.**

Little again? Nothing but low and little?
Why will you suffer her to flout me thus?
Let me come to her.

_____ **cheek by jowl.**

Exit Lysander and Demetrius.

You Mistress, all this coil is long of you.
Nay, go not back.
Exit.

Cue Script: Lysander (*MND* 3.2)

First Line of Scene Cutting

Helen, I love thee, by my life I do;
I swear by that which I will lose for thee,
To prove him false, that says I love thee not.

_____ **then he can do.**

If thou say so, withdraw and prove it too.

_____ **tends all this?**

Away, you Ethiop.

_____ **a tame man, go.**

Hang off thou cat, thou burr; vile thing let loose,
Or I will shake thee from me like a serpent.

_____ **is this sweet Love?**

Thy Love? Out tawny Tartar, out;
Out loathed medicine; O hated poison hence.

_____ **and so do you.**

Demetrius: I will keep my word with thee.

_____ **trust your word.**

What, should I hurt her, strike her, kill her dead?
Although I hate her, I'll not harm her so.

_____ **shall I say?**

Ay, by my life;
And never did desire to see thee more.
Therefore be out of hope, of question, of doubt;
Be certain, nothing truer: 'tis no jest,
That I do hate thee, and love Helena.

_____ **With Demetrius.**

Be not afraid, she shall not harm thee Helena.

_____ **Let me come to her.**

Get you gone you dwarf,

You minimus, of hindering knot-grass made,
You bead, you acorn.

_____ **Thou shalt abide it.**

Now she holds me not,
Now follow if thou dar'st, to try whose right,
Of thine or mine is most in Helena.

_____ **cheek by jowl.**

Exit.

Cue Script: Demetrius (*MND* 3.2)

_____ **I love thee not.**
I say, I love thee more then he can do.

_____ **and prove it too.**
Quick, come.

_____ **Away, you Ethiop.**
No, no, Sir, seem to break loose;
Take on as you would follow,
But yet come not: you are a tame man, go.

_____ **my word with thee.**
I would I had your bond: for I perceive
A weak bond holds you; I'll not trust your word.

_____ **not harm thee** *Helena*.
No sir, she shall not, though you take her part.

_____ **You bead, you acorn.**
You are too officious,
In her behalf that scorns your services.
Let her alone, speak not of *Helena*,
Take not her part. For if thou dost intend
Never so little show of love to her,
Thou shalt abide it.

_____ **is most in** *Helena*.
Follow? Nay, I'll go with thee cheek by jowl.
Exit.

Appendix C

Capstone Analysis Activity

Analyzing, Physicalizing, and Understanding a Soliloquy

Textual Exploration through Application of the Folio Technique

PURPOSE OF THE EXERCISE
Students who have previous Folio technique training can review, apply, and practice the language, verse, and rhetorical clues outlined in Chapters 4 to 6 in a comprehensive analysis of a single speech.

MATERIALS NEEDED
Copies of the clue cards from Chapters 4, 5, and 6 and Hamlet's speech.

OBJECTIVES
Students will:

- identify and analyze Folio technique clues (outlined in Chapters 4–6) found in Hamlet's speech (1.2)
- apply pertinent Folio technique clues
- score Hamlet's speech (reproduced below) using the appropriate symbols

Hamlet (1.2)

HAMLET.   Oh that this too too solid Flesh, would melt,
           Thaw, and resolve itself into a Dew:
           Or that the Everlasting had not fixed
           His Cannon 'gainst Self-slaughter. O God, O God!
           How weary, stale, flat, and unprofitable   5

Seems to me all the uses of this world?
Fie on't? Oh fie, fie, 'tis an unweeded Garden
That grows to Seed: Things rank, and gross in Nature
Possess it merely. That it should come to this:
But two months dead: Nay, not so much; not two,   10
So excellent a King, that was to this
Hyperion to a Satyr: so loving to my Mother,
That he might not beteem the winds of heaven
Visit her face too roughly. Heaven and Earth
Must I remember: why she would hang on him,   15
As if increase of Appetite had grown
By what is fed on; and yet within a month?
Let me not think on't: Frailty, thy name is woman.

Textual Exploration through Application of the Folio Technique

1. Begin again by defining words and/or phrases that are unfamiliar to your students. This could even be the assigned homework the night before you begin work on this scene. Use the online source Shakespeare's Words (www.shakespeareswords.com) to complete this work. Some words and/or phrases to look up might include:

   - resolve
   - Cannon
   - weary
   - unprofitable
   - uses
   - Fie
   - rank
   - merely
   - *Hyperion*
   - Satyr
   - beteem
   - Frailty.

2. Use the "Magic" Index Card exercise—allowing the students to speak the text aloud.

3. Use the "Sharing the Text, Sharing the Dish Towel" exercises. This will physically enhance the emotional stakes in this piece.

4. Locate and score the Ecphonesis O's found in the piece:
   - His Cannon 'gainst Self-slaughter. Ⓞ God, Ⓞ God!
   - There are times when Hamlet indeed says "Oh" and there are times when he needs an Ecphonesis O.
   - Why does Hamlet need this sound—rather than a word? What does this reveal about his inner state of mind?

5. Locate and score the capitalized words that should not be capitalized if we were editing for modern rules of grammar.
   - Flesh, Dew, Cannon, etc.
   - Why does Hamlet need these capitalized words in order to effect change in the audience?

6. Locate the full thoughts (periods, exclamation points, and question marks anywhere in the text) and underline them. Then utilize the "'Ups and Downs' of Shakespeare" exercise to physically discover the full thoughts Hamlet uses here.

   How weary, stale, flat, and unprofitable
   Seems to me all the <u>uses of this world?</u>
   <u>Fie on't?</u> Oh fie, fie, 'tis an unweeded Garden
   That grows to Seed: Things rank, and gross in Nature
   <u>Possess it merely.</u>

7. Score the full thoughts by placing an "**F**" when you find a period, exclamation point, or question mark *at the end* of the verse line.

   How weary, stale, flat, and unprofitable
   Seems to me all the uses of this world? **F**

8. Score the mid-stops in the piece by placing an "**M**" when you find a period, exclamation point, or question mark *in the middle* of the verse line.

         M
   Fie on't? Oh fie, fie, 'tis an unweeded Garden
   That grows to Seed: Things rank, and gross in Nature
                M
   Possess it merely. That it should come to this:

As you will notice, this piece is filled with mid-stop punctuation. Ask your students:

- Why do you think that Shakespeare has given Hamlet so many mid-stops in the piece?
- What does this reveal about his emotional state at this point?
- Why does he need so many mid-stops to effect change through this direct address to the audience?
- What does mid-stop punctuation do to Hamlet's pace of speaking—why is this pace needed to effect change in the audience?

Teacher Note

Once you receive input from your students, gear the discussion toward the structure of the language and how this reveals character and intent. Through mid-stops, it seems as though the structure Shakespeare provides here supports Hamlet's obsession with the thought of "How can this be?" Hamlet tries to forget the images and thoughts coming into his mind, but he can't. They keep coming back and back again into his mind—he is obsessed with this horrific situation. Mid-stop punctuation seems to support the idea of this obsession. Hamlet is so distraught that he feels he needs to clarify what the word *Uncle* means, "married with mine Uncle / My Father's Brother:" This situation is simply unbelievable to him..

9. Find the monosyllabic words and phrases. Look at the very first line of the soliloquy:

    Oh that this too too solid Flesh, would melt,

    - He begins this piece with a monosyllabic line. Why? Why is Shakespeare slowing him down here right at the beginning of the speech?
    - Why does Hamlet *need* monosyllabic words right away to effect change in the audience?

10. Repetition is another key rhetorical device that Hamlet employs. Locate and score the repetition in the piece.
    - What does this reveal about Hamlet's current emotional state of mind?
    - Why would he keep repeating words and phrases like "But two months dead," "Nay, not so much; not two," "A little Month," "Within a Month?," etc. to convince the audience of his side of the argument?

11. Next, locate and score Hamlet's use of antithesis in the piece.

    Make sure to note antithesis in ideas such as:
    - "solid Flesh" with "melt, thaw, and resolve itself into a Dew:"
    - "So excellent a King (Hamlet's father)" with "was to this (his uncle)"
    - "*Hyperion*" with "Satyr."

    Again, why does Hamlet need to use these striking contrasts and how will this help him win his persuasive argument with the audience? Perhaps discussion can center on the fact that Hamlet is arguing what is moral versus what is immoral, what is right versus what is wrong, what is attractive versus what is disgusting, etc.

    Teacher Note

    "The Pizza Toss" exercise from Chapter 6 would work well here as needed.

    - What effect does it have on the audience when he utilizes these specific terrible images?

12. Hamlet also uses listing structure throughout his soliloquy.
    - Locate and score the item or idea Hamlet uses through his listing structure.
        - Melt, Thaw, and resolve
        - Weary, stale, flat, and unprofitable
    - How does using this type of listing structure help Hamlet win his audience over to his side?

From Analysis to Performance

"Words, words, words" (*Ham.* 2.2). It's all about the words. As John Barton says in *Playing Shakespeare*, "It seems to me that the most important

Teacher Note

The "Stepping It Up with Shakespeare's Lists and Repetition" exercise applies to the analysis at this point.

point is that the characters *need the language* to express their situation and their characters" (67). Now that your students have effectively analyzed and scored the piece, it is time to pull everything together by speaking the piece aloud. You should have students work in pairs or small groups to rehearse a reading of the speech before showcasing their readings for the entire group.

Appendix D

The Clash of the Film Clips: Is It Shakespeare?

See Chapter 8 for a discussion of how to use a set of clips focusing on *Romeo and Juliet* to help students explore their expectations of what experiencing a Shakespeare play involves. Below, similar approaches for *Hamlet* and *Macbeth* are suggested.

Questions for Discussion and Analysis

- How do you know if a film is based on a play by Shakespeare? What will it sound like? What will it look like in terms of costumes and sets?
- What kind of actors do you expect to perform Shakespeare?
- How much should actors and directors add to a scene from a Shakespeare play to give it a new look or sound?
- How much should a director modernize a Shakespeare play for you to consider that it is still Shakespeare?
- Why do some writers and directors make references to characters, plot devices, or lines of dialogue from Shakespeare in a film that is not based on one of his plays?

Hamlet Clips

This set focuses on Hamlet's soliloquy, "To be or not to be" (*Ham.* 3.1):

- *Hamlet* (1948), starring Laurence Olivier—typical Renaissance costumes and setting; formalistic camerawork reflects Olivier's psychological approach to depicting the Dane's internal conflict (karldallas)
- *Hamlet* (1964), starring Innokenty Smoktunovsky—acclaimed Russian-language version (Grigoryevskaya)
- *Hamlet* (1996) starring Kenneth Branagh—nineteenth-century costume design, shot at Blenheim Palace (Bonaiuti)
- *Hamlet* (2000), starring Ethan Hawke—modern-day setting; note the details emphasized in the Blockbuster store used as location (Fandango Movieclips)

while this clip offers an abridgement:

- *Shakespeare: The Animated Tales*, "Hamlet" episode (1992), featuring the voice of Alec McCowen—a voice-over narrator helps set the stage and move the plot along to accompany Shakespeare's drastically cut text (Humphrey)

and this one a parody:

- *The Last Action Hero* (1993), starring Arnold Schwarzenegger—a fanboy imagines his favorite action hero as the "melancholy Dane" while watching the Olivier film in his English classroom (holy intertextuality) (Fandango Movieclips).

Macbeth Clips

This compilation of clips posted on YouTube (Sexton) focuses on the treatment of the witches: www.youtube.com/watch?v=UWyegNZOqQE. It features the opening scene from five different film adaptations, from Polanski's (1971) to Kurzel's (2015) versions, including a modern language version adapted by Peter Moffat from the Shakespeare Retold series. You also should seek out Orson Welles's *Macbeth* (1948) to examine his treatment of the witches, which you could play before you start the YouTube compilation. You can find that clip on the Turner Classic Movies website (www.tcm.com).

For a modern take on the witches, *Men of Respect* (1991) sets *Macbeth* in the world of organized crime in the present day. It does not retain Shakespeare's language, but it does rely on the tragedy's narrative arc and characterization. It incorporates the supernatural element in the form of a clairvoyant the Macbeth figure encounters. Look for the film on DVD, online, or streaming to capture the clip. It is rated R.

For a comedic adaptation of the Scottish play, check out *Scotland, PA* (2001), which sets the tragedy in the cutthroat world of the fast-food industry in small-town Pennsylvania the 1970s. Also rated R.

Appendix E

Building Your "Bard Bookshelf"

Here following is a list of ten resources that you should consider for your classroom/professional bookshelf, organized according to the chapter of the present book in which each was referenced. All are available in print editions, and the URL is noted for one with online access. For further details, see the full listings in the references section.

- Chapter 1—*Frames of Mind: The Theory of Multiple Intelligences* by Howard Gardner
- Chapter 2—*The Making of Shakespeare's First Folio* by Emma Smith
- Chapter 3—*The Second City Guide to Improv in the Classroom: Using Improvisation to Teach Skills and Improve Learning in Content Areas* by Katherine McKnight and Mary Scruggs
- Chapter 3—*Improvisation for the Theater: A Handbook of Teaching and Directing Techniques* by Viola Spolin
- Chapters 4 to 6—*Thinking Shakespeare: A Working Guide for Actors, Directors, Students . . . and Anyone Else Interested in the Bard* (Revised Edition) by Barry Edelstein
- Chapters 4 to 6—*Shakespeare A to Z: The Essential Reference to His Plays, His Poems, His Life and Times, and More* by Charles Boyce
- Chapters 4 to 6—*Shakespeare's Words: A Glossary and Language Companion* by David Crystal and Ben Crystal
- Chapter 7—*Creative Shakespeare: The Globe Education Guide to Practical Shakespeare* by Fiona Banks
- Chapter 7—*Secrets of Acting Shakespeare: The Original Approach* by Patrick Tucker
- Chapter 8—*Reading Shakespeare Film First* by Mary Ellen Dakin

References

Arias, Jennifer. "Questions about Teaching Shakespeare." Received by Mary T. Christel, 22 Apr. 2018.

Artese, Charlotte, editor. *Shakespeare and the Folktale: An Anthology of Stories*. Princeton UP, 2019.

Atwood, Margaret. *Hag-Seed: The Tempest Retold*. Hogarth, 2016.

Balakir, Dziyana. "Questions about Shakespeare Experiences." Received by Mary T. Christel, 24 Apr. 2018.

Banks, Fiona. *Creative Shakespeare: The Globe Education Guide to Practical Shakespeare*. Bloomsbury, 2014.

Barton, John. *Playing Shakespeare*. Methuen, 1997.

Basil, John, with Stephanie Gunning. *Will Power: How to Act Shakespeare in 21 Days*. Applause Theatre & Cinema Books, 2006.

Berry, Cicely. *The Actor and the Text*. New and rev. ed., Applause Books, 1992.

Bertacchi, Jennifer. "Questions about Teaching Shakespeare" and "Follow-up on Questions." Received by Mary T. Christel, 30 March, 7 Apr. 2018.

Billington, Michael. Review of *Dunsinane*. *The Guardian*, 17 Feb. 2010, www.theguardian.com/stage/2010/feb/17/dunsinane-review. Accessed 20 July 2018.

Boal, Augusto. *Games for Actors and Non-Actors*. 2nd ed., translated by Adrian Jackson, Routledge, 2002.

Bonaiuti, Carlo. "To Be or Not to Be – Kenneth Branagh HD (*Hamlet*)." Clip from *Hamlet*, directed by Kenneth Branagh, Castle Rock Entertainment, 1996. *YouTube*, 8 Sept. 2013, www.youtube.com/watch?v=SjuZq-8PUw0.

Boyce, Charles. *Shakespeare A to Z: The Essential Reference to His Plays, His Poems, His Life and Times, and More*. Edited by David Allen White, Facts on File, 1991.

Brown, Laura L. "Questions about Shakespeare and Technology." Received by Mary T. Christel, 13 July 2017.

Bryksenkova, Yelena, and William Shakespeare. *Romeo and Juliet*. Rock Point, 2015. Classics Unfolded.

Burrows, Cynthia. "Integrating Theater Games in ELA Classrooms." Received by Mary T. Christel, 28 June 2018.

———. "Transferring Drama Techniques to ELA Curricula." Received by Mary T. Christel, 24 Apr. 2018.

Cadeño, Laci. "*Macbeth*: Thug Notes Summary and Analysis." *TEDEd*, ed.ted.com/on/et0ddHix. Accessed 20 July 2018.

Callow, Simon. "Shakespeare's Childhood and Education." *British Library*, 15 Mar. 2016, www.bl.uk/shakespeare/articles/shakespeares-childhood-and-education. Accessed 20 July 2018.

Carbone, Courtney, and William Shakespeare. *Macbeth #killingit*. Random House, 2016. OMG Shakespeare.

———. *Srsly Hamlet*. Random House, 2015. OMG Shakespeare.

Chute, Marchette. *Shakespeare of London*. Penguin Books, 1991.

Connell, J. Diane. "Connell Multiple Intelligence Questionnaire." *Brain-Based Strategies to Reach Every Learner*, Scholastic, 2005, teachables.scholastic.com/teachables/books/teachable-product-detail-9780439590204_001.html.

Cullen, Jacquie. "Questions about Teaching Shakespeare." Received by Mary T. Christel, 5 Apr. 2018.

Crystal, David, and Ben Crystal. "Glossary." *Shakespeare's Words*, 23 Apr. 2018, www.shakespeareswords.com/Public/Glossary.aspx.

———. *Shakespeare's Words: A Glossary and Language Companion*. Penguin, 2002.

Dakin, Mary Ellen. *Reading Shakespeare Film First*. National Council of Teachers of English, 2012.

Dickson, Andrew. *Worlds Elsewhere: Journeys Around Shakespeare's Globe*. Random House, 2015.

Discovering Hamlet. Directed by Mark Olshaker, performances by Kenneth Branagh, Derek Jacobi, Larry Klein, and Patrick Stewart. Unicorn Projects/PBS Video, 1990.

Doescher, Ian. *MacTrump*. Quirk Books, 2019.

———. *William Shakespeare's Get Thee . . . Back to the Future!* Quirk Books, 2019.

———. *William Shakespeare's Much Ado About Mean Girls*. Quirk Books, 2019.

———. *William Shakespeare's Star Wars: Verily, a New Hope*. Quirk Books, 2013.

Duggan, Gerry, and Ian Doescher. *Deadpool: World's Greatest, vol. 7—Deadpool Does Shakespeare*. Illustrated by Bruno Oliveira, edited by Jeff Youngquist, Marvel Universe, 2017.

Edelstein, Barry. *Thinking Shakespeare: A Working Guide for Actors, Directors, and Students . . . and Anyone Else Interested in the Bard*. Revised ed., Theatre Communications Group, 2018.

EdPro Development. "Student Multiple Intelligence Survey." 10 Feb. 2012, edprodevelopment.com/wp-content/uploads/Student-MI-Survey.doc.

Fandango Movieclips. "*Hamlet* (6/11) Movie Clip – To Be or Not To Be." Clip from *Hamlet*, directed by Michael Almereyda, Miramax Films, 2000. *YouTube*, 16 Jan. 2015, www.youtube.com/watch?v=1Up-oGfiosE. Accessed 30 Apr. 2019.

———. "To Be or Not To Be." Clip of *The Last Action Hero—Hamlet* Parody Scene," directed by John McTiernan, Columbia Pictures, 1992. *YouTube*, 20 Jan. 2017, www.youtube.com/watch?v=9Eont_yEGZs. Accessed 30 Apr. 2019.

Freeman, Neil, editor. *The Applause First Folio of Shakespeare: In Modern Type*. Applause Theatre & Cinema Books, 2002.

Gardner, Howard. *Frames of Mind: The Theory of Multiple Intelligences*. 3rd ed., Basic Books, 2011.

Gilakjani, Abbas Pourhosein. "The Significant Role of Multimedia in Motivating EFL Learners' Interest in English Language Learning." *I. J. Modern Education and Computer Science*, vol. 4, 2012, pp. 57–66, www.mecs-press.net/ijmecs/ijmecs-v4-n4/IJMECS-V4-N4-8.pdf. Accessed 20 July 2018.

Göndöcs, Rita. "Questions about Teaching Shakespeare." Received by Mary T. Christel, 2 July 2018.

Green, John. "On Cuties and Cooties." *YouTube*, 28 Feb. 2012, www.youtube.com/watch?v=FcifZrZ_yE4. Accessed 20 July 2018.

Greg, Walter Wilson. *The Shakespeare First Folio: Its Bibliographical and Textual History*. Clarendon Press, 1955.

Grigoryevskaya, Olga. "To Be or Not to Be." Clip from *Hamlet*, directed by Grigori Kozintsev, Lenfilm, 1964. *YouTube*, 27 Oct. 2014, www.youtube.com/watch?v=biB5Q0PoQVk&fbclid=IwAR1MwfYbP5i7R8L82kPEc7Vd7PZfKpOX1k7aQIz85c80ttt5rV1MnWZtu8U. Accessed 30 Apr. 2019.

Harper College News Bureau. "Graduates Celebrate at Harper College's 50th Commencement Ceremony." *Harper College*, 19 May 2018, www.harpercollege.edu/about/news/archives/2018/posts/051918.php. Accessed 20 July 2018.

Heckel-Oliver, Christine. "Questions about Teaching Shakespeare." Received by Mary T. Christel, 15 Mar. 2018.

Heller, Stephen. "Questions about Teaching Shakespeare." Received by Mary T. Christel, 16 Apr. 2018.

Heron, John, and Peter Reason. "The Practice of Co-Operative Inquiry: Research 'with' Rather Than 'on' People." *Handbook of Action Research: Participative Inquiry and Practice*, edited by Peter Reason and Hilary Bradbury, SAGE, 2001, pp. 179–88.

Holtham, J. "Do We Even Need to Say This? Yes, Shakespeare Belongs on the Curriculum." *American Theatre*, 15 June 2015, www.americantheatre.org/2015/06/15/do-we-even-need-to-say-this-yes-shakespeare-belongs-on-the-curriculum/. Accessed 20 July 2018.

Hudson, Hailey. "Every Writer Should Do Blackout Poetry . . . Here's Why." *Craft Your Content*, 15 Oct. 2018, www.craftyourcontent.com/blackout-poetry/. Accessed 30 Apr. 2019.

Humphrey, Hubert. "To Be or Not To Be." Introduction to *Shakespeare: The Animated Tales—Hamlet*, directed by Natalya Orlova and Dave Edwards, Christmas Films, 1992. *YouTube*, 8 Sept. 2016, www.youtube.com/watch?v=OtNMjZoZNbM. Accessed 30 Apr. 2019.

Isherwood, Charles. "What Makes a Great Shakespearean? Mark Rylance and Other Standouts Share Secrets of the Trade." *New York Times*, 14 Nov. 2013, www.nytimes.com/2013/11/17/theater/mark-rylance-and-other-shakespeareans-at-work.html. Accessed 20 July 2018.

Johnston, Noel. "Questions about Teaching Shakespeare." Received by Mary T. Christel, 22 Apr. 2018.

Jones, Chris. "In 'Dunsinane' David Greig Offers a Timely Play—Set in the 11th Century." *Los Angeles Times*, 27 Mar. 2015, www.latimes.com/entertainment/arts/la-et-cm-ca-dunsinane-20150329-story.html. Accessed 20 July 2018.

karldallas. "Olivier's *Hamlet* film (1948): To Be or Not to Be Soliloquy." Clip from *Hamlet*, directed by Laurence Olivier, Two Cities, 1948. *YouTube*, 26 Jan. 2010, www.youtube.com/watch?v=5ks-NbCHUns.

Keenan, Hailey. "Questions about Teaching Shakespeare." Received by Mary T. Christel, 24 Apr. 2018.

Kennedy, John F. "Inaugural Address, 20 Jan. 1961." *John F. Kennedy Presidential Library and Museum*, www.jfklibrary.org/learn/about-jfk/historic-speeches/inaugural-address.

Lyons, Marti. *Romeo and Juliet* Rehearsal Session and Talk Back/Teacher Workshop. Chicago Shakespeare Theater, 2 Feb. 2017. Personal notes.

Manno, Michelle, and Eric Kallenborn. "The Art of Creating Classics: An Interview with Gareth Hinds." *Teach.com*, 28 Aug. 2014, teach.com/blog/gareth-hinds-interview/.

Marche, Stephen. *How Shakespeare Changed Everything*. Harper, 2011.

McCreery, Conor, and Anthony Del Col. *Kill Shakespeare: A Sea of Troubles*. Illustrated by Andy Belanger, Vol. 1, IDW Publishing, 2010.

McDuffie, Kate. "Questions about Teaching Shakespeare." Received by Mary T. Christel, 29 Apr. 2018.

McKenzie, Walter. "Multiple Intelligences Survey." *The One and Only Surfaquarium*, 1999, surfaquarium.com/MI/inventory.htm.

McKinney, Mary Jane. "Plain English: How Yoda Helps Students Master Shakespeare." *Prestwick Café*, 14 Dec. 2009, prestwickhouse.blogspot.com/2009/12/plain-english-how-yoda-helps-students.html. Accessed 20 July 2018.

McKnight, Katherine S., and Mary Scruggs. *The Second City Guide to Improv in the Classroom: Using Improvisation to Teach Skills and Improve Learning in Content Areas*. Jossey-Bass, 2008.

Midsummer in Newtown. Directed by Lloyd Kramer. Vulcan Productions, 2016.

Moston, Doug, editor. *Mr. William Shakespeare's Comedies, Histories & Tragedies: A Facsimile of the First Folio, 1623*. Routledge, 1998.

My Juliet: Romeo and Juliet *for a New Generation with Baz Luhrmann.* Directed by Michael Waldman, performances by Paterson Joseph and Baz Luhrmann. PBS Video, 2006.

National Council of Teachers of English. "Informal Classroom Drama." National Council of Teachers of English, 31 July 1982, www.ncte.org/positions/statements/informalclassdrama. Accessed 20 July 2018.

Ney, Charles. *Directing Shakespeare in America: Current Practices.* Bloomsbury Arden Shakespeare, 2016.

North, Ryan, and William Shakespeare. *Romeo and/or Juliet: A Chooseable-Path Adventure.* Riverhead Books, 2016.

———. *To Be or Not to Be: A Chooseable-Path Adventure.* Breadpig, 2013.

Noskin, David. "Questions about Teaching Shakespeare." Received by Mary T. Christel, 18 June 2018.

Onuscheck, Mark. "Questions about Teaching Shakespeare." Received by Mary T. Christel, 16 July 2018.

Partridge, Eric. *Shakespeare's Bawdy: A Literary and Psychological Essay and a Comprehensive Glossary.* Routledge and Keegan Paul, 1955.

Perry, Katy. "Hot n Cold." *One of the Boys,* Capitol, 2008.

Playing Shakespeare. Directed by John Carlaw, performances by John Barton, Patrick Stewart, Ian McKellen, Judi Dench, Ben Kingsley, David Suchet, Peggy Ashcroft, and Lisa Harrow. Acorn Media, 2009.

Powell, Mark. "Kill Bill: Why We Must Take Shakespeare Out of the Classroom." *The Guardian,* 17 Mar. 2014, www.theguardian.com/culture-professionals-network/culture-professionals-blog/2014/mar/17/kill-bill-shakespeare-classroom-theatre. Accessed 20 July 2018.

Rodberg, Simon. "Cutting Antony's Speeches." Edited by Greta Brasgalla and Corinne Viglietta, Folger Shakespeare Library Education Department, 26 July 2015, www.folger.edu/cutting-antonys-speeches.

Rollins, Cindy. "Teaching Shakespeare to Children." Circe Institute, 23 Sept. 2011, www.circeinstitute.org/2011/09/teaching-shakespeare-to-children. Accessed 20 July 2018.

Romeo Is Bleeding. Directed by Jason Zeldes. Circadian Pictures, 2015.

Rowling, J. K. *Harry Potter and the Chamber of Secrets.* Bloomsbury, 2014.

Russo, Maria. "Sketching Shakespeare: 'Macbeth' Adapted by Gareth Hinds." *New York Times,* Feb. 18, 2015, www.nytimes.com/2015/02/18/books/review/macbeth-adapted-by-gareth-hinds.html.

Russo, Robin. "Questions about Teaching Shakespeare." Received by Kevin Long, 20 Apr. 2018.

Rwanda and Juliet. Directed by Ben Proudfoot. Breakwater Studios, 2016.

Schmidt, Alexander. *Shakespeare Lexicon: A Complete Dictionary of All the English Words, Phrases and Constructions in the Works of the Poet.* Dover, 1971. 2 vols.

Sexton, Jacquie. "*Macbeth*. Compare and Contrast: Opening scenes from Five Adaptations." Directed by Roman Polanski (1971), Mark Brozel (2005), Geoffrey Wright (2006), Rupert Goold (2010), and Justin Kurzel (2015), *YouTube*, 25 Apr. 2016, www.youtube.com/watch?v=UWyegNZOqQE. Accessed 30 Apr. 2019.

Shakespeare behind Bars. Directed by Hank Rogerson. Shout Factory, 2006.

Shakespeare High. Directed by Alex Rotaru, performances by Richard Dreyfuss, Val Kilmer, and Kevin Spacey. Cinema Guild, 2011.

Shakespeare, William. *All's Well That Ends Well*. Edited by Andrew Griffin and Helen Ostovich, modern ed., *Internet Shakespeare Editions*, U of Victoria, internetshakespeare.uvic.ca/doc/AWW_M. Accessed 28 Apr. 2019.

———. *As You Like It*. Edited by David Bevington, Folio 1 ed., *Internet Shakespeare Editions*, U of Victoria, internetshakespeare.uvic.ca/doc/AYL_F1. Accessed 28 Apr. 2019.

———. *The First Folio of Shakespeare: Based on the Folios in the Folger Shakespeare Library Collection*. Edited by Charlton Hinman, 2nd ed., Norton, 1996.

———. *Globe Education Shorter Shakespeare: A Midsummer Night's Dream*. Edited by Jane Sheldon, Hodder Education, 2017.

———. *Hamlet*. Edited by David Bevington, Folio 1 ed., *Internet Shakespeare Editions*, U of Victoria, internetshakespeare.uvic.ca/doc/Ham_F1. Accessed 28 Apr. 2019.

———. *Henry V*. Edited by James D. Mardock, Folio 1 ed., *Internet Shakespeare Editions*, U of Victoria, internetshakespeare.uvic.ca/doc/H5_F1. Accessed 28 Apr. 2019.

———. *King Henry V*. Edited by T. W. Craik, Bloomsbury Arden Shakespeare, 2013. Arden Shakespeare Third Series.

———. *King Lear*. Edited by Michael Best, Folio 1 ed., *Internet Shakespeare Editions*, U of Victoria, internetshakespeare.uvic.ca/doc/Lr_F1. Accessed 28 Apr. 2019.

———. *King Lear*. Edited by Michael Best, Quarto 1 ed., *Internet Shakespeare Editions*, U of Victoria, internetshakespeare.uvic.ca/doc/Lr_Q1. Accessed 28 Apr. 2019.

———. *Macbeth*. Edited by Linzy Brady and David James, Cambridge UP, 3rd ed., 2014. Cambridge School Shakespeare.

———. *Macbeth*. Edited by Anthony Dawson, Folio 1 ed., *Internet Shakespeare Editions*, U of Victoria, internetshakespeare.uvic.ca/doc/Mac_F1. Accessed 28 Apr. 2019.

———. *Macbeth*. Edited by Anthony Dawson, modern ed., *Internet Shakespeare Editions*, U of Victoria, internetshakespeare.uvic.ca/doc/Mac_M. Accessed 28 Apr. 2019.

———. *The Merchant of Venice*. Edited by Barbara A. Mowat and Paul Werstine, *Folger Digital Texts*, Folger Shakespeare Library, www.folgerdigitaltexts.org/html/MV. Accessed 28 Apr. 2019.

———. *The Merchant of Venice*. Edited by Janelle Jenstad, Folio 1 ed., *Internet Shakespeare Editions*, U of Victoria, internetshakespeare.uvic.ca/doc/MV_F1. Accessed 28 Apr. 2019.

———. *A Midsummer Night's Dream*. Edited by Sukanta Chaudhuri, Bloomsbury Arden Shakespeare, 2017. Arden Shakespeare Third Series.

———. *A Midsummer Night's Dream*. Edited by Suzanne Westfall, Folio 1 ed., *Internet Shakespeare Editions*, U of Victoria, internetshakespeare.uvic.ca/doc/MND_F1. Accessed 28 Apr. 2019.

———. *Richard II*. Edited by Catherine Lisak, modern ed., *Internet Shakespeare Editions*, U of Victoria, internetshakespeare.uvic.ca/doc/R2_M. Accessed 28 Apr. 2019.

———. *Richard the Third*. Edited by Adrian Kiernander, Folio 1 ed., *Internet Shakespeare Editions*, U of Victoria, internetshakespeare.uvic.ca/doc/R3_F1. Accessed 28 Apr. 2019.

———. *Romeo and Juliet*. Edited by Roger Apfelbaum, Folio 1 ed., *Internet Shakespeare Editions*, U of Victoria, internetshakespeare.uvic.ca/doc/Rom_F1. Accessed 28 Apr. 2019.

———. *Romeo and Juliet*. Edited by Robert Smith and Rex Gibson, 4th ed., Cambridge UP, 2014. Cambridge School Shakespeare.

———. *The Sonnets*. Edited by Michael Best and Ian Lancashire, modern ed., *Internet Shakespeare Editions*, U of Victoria, internetshakespeare.uvic.ca/doc/Son_M. Accessed 28 Apr. 2019.

———. *Timon of Athens*. Edited by Jesús Tronch Pérez, Folio 1 ed., *Internet Shakespeare Editions*, U of Victoria, internetshakespeare.uvic.ca/Library/Texts/Tim. Accessed 24 July 2019.

———. *Twelfth Night*. Edited by David Carnegie and Mark Houlahan, Folio 1 ed., *Internet Shakespeare Editions*, U of Victoria, internetshakespeare.uvic.ca/doc/TN_F1. Accessed 28 Apr. 2019.

Shakespeare's Globe. "*Romeo and Juliet*: Rhyming Text." *Shakespeare's Globe*, Globe Education, 2014, 2013.playingshakespeare.org/rhyming-text.html. Accessed 20 July 2018.

Skinner, Edith. *Speak with Distinction: The Classic Skinner Method to Speech on Stage*. Revised with new material by Timothy Monich and Lilene Mansell, 2nd ed., Applause Theatre & Cinema Books, 2000.

Smith, Emma. *The Making of Shakespeare's First Folio*. Bodleian Library, 2015.

———. *Shakespeare's First Folio: Four Centuries of an Iconic Book*. Oxford University Press, 2016.

Sokol, Abby. "Questions about Teaching Shakespeare." Received by Mary T. Christel, 24 Apr. 2018.

Spangler, Susan. "Speaking My Mind: Stop Reading Shakespeare!" *English Journal*, vol. 99, no. 1, 2009, pp. 130–32.

Spolin, Viola. *Improvisation for the Theater: A Handbook of Teaching and Directing Techniques*. 3rd ed., Northwestern University Press, 1999.

Still Dreaming. Directed by Hank Rogerson and Jilann Spitzmiller, performances by Mayleen Adams, Gloria Albee, and Noah Brody. Film Rise, 2014.

Thompson, Ayanna, and Laura Turchi. *Teaching Shakespeare with Purpose: A Student-Centred Approach*. Bloomsbury Arden Shakespeare, 2016.

Thornburg, Laura. "Questions about Shakespeare Experiences." Received by Mary T. Christel, 6 May 2018.

Tovani, Cris. *I Read It, but I Don't Get It: Comprehension Strategies for Adolescent Readers*. Stenhouse, 2000.

Trees, Andrew. "'Romeo and Juliet' Has Led Us Astray." *Los Angeles Times*, 14 Feb. 2010, www.latimes.com/archives/la-xpm-2010-feb-14-la-oe-trees14-2010feb.

Tucker, Patrick. *Secrets of Acting Shakespeare: The Original Approach*. Routledge, 2002.

———. *Shakespeare Cue Script Scenes for the Classroom: General Selection*. London Academy of Music and Dramatic Art, 1998.

Turner Classic Movies (TCM). "Opening, Bubble Bubble." From *Macbeth*, directed by Orson Welles, Republic Pictures, 1948. *YouTube*, www.tcm.com/mediaroom/video/245406/Macbeth-Movie-Clip-Opening-Bubble-Bubble.html. Accessed 30 Apr. 2019.

Underwood, Emily. "Why Teenagers Are So Impulsive." *Science*, 11 Nov. 2013, www.sciencemag.org/news/2013/11/why-teenagers-are-so-impulsive.

Virginia Department of Education. "Learning Styles, Multiple Intelligences, and Differentiated Instruction." *CTE Resource Center*, Henrico County Public Schools, http://www.cteresource.org/featured/differentiated_instruction.html.

Walter, Claire. "Teaching Shakespeare." Received by Mary T. Christel, 22 June 2018.

Watts, Graham. *Shakespeare's Authentic Performance Texts: The Case for Staging from the First Folio*. McFarland, 2015.

White, Genevieve. "We Shouldn't Teach Shakespeare to Learners of English: False." British Council, 6 Mar. 2014, www.britishcouncil.org/voices-magazine/we-shouldnt-teach-shakespeare-to-english-learners-false. Accessed 20 July 2018.

Wing-bo Tso, Anna. "Teaching Shakespeare to Young ESL Learners in Hong Kong." *Journal of Pedagogical Development*, vol. 6, no. 2, 2016, journals.beds.ac.uk/ojs/index.php/jpd/article/view/316/497.

Wright, Brett, and William Shakespeare. *A Midsummer Night #nofilter*. Random House, 2016. OMG Shakespeare.

———. *Yolo Juliet*. Random House, 2015. OMG Shakespeare.

Index

Note: Activities are formatted in title case.

abridgements
    animated to preview a play, 152–54
    building your own, 156–65
    narrative to preview a play, 152–54
    professional printings, 154–55
    reading-viewing approach, 165–68
    right size, 174
    using, reasons for, 151–52
active approaches, rational for, 43–45. *See also* bell ringer exercises; movement exercises
active participants, creating, 43
activities, hands-on, 23
The Actor and the Text (Berry), 124
actor punctuation, 91
Adverbly Done (improv), 58
alexandrine, 103
alliteration, 120–22
Ambrose Video, 153
anaclasis, 124
anastrophe, 124
The Animated Shakespeare. See Shakespeare: The Animated Tales (HBO)
anticipation, building
    integration of creative drama for, 3
    using multiple intelligences theory, 3–4
anticipation activities
    formative, 5
    summative, 5
anticipatory exercises
    Blackout Poetry from Blank Verse, 8–9, 9*f*
    Creating a Play's Playlist, 12–13
    Learning the Conventions of a Graphic Text, 35–36
    Picture Walk, 35–36, 35*f*
    Picturing the Line, 13
    A Play in Pieces, 6, 7*f*
    Shakespeare's Sonnet Scrambled, 6, 7*f*
    Text Detective Teams, 14–15, 15*f*
    Tracking Language Motifs, 14
    World of the Play in Images, 4–5
anticipatory strategies
    variation as, 5
    Words of the Play and Pictures, 5
antimetabole, 124–25
antithesis, 123–24, 149*f*
antithesis exercise, 129–32
Applying Language Clues First, 92–94
apps
    Folger Luminary Shakespeare (app), 37
    Shakespeare (app), 37
    Shakespeare in Bits, 38–41, 39*f*, 40*f*
    Shakespeare Pro (app), 37, 73
Arden Shakespeare (series), 27–28
Arden Shakespeare (Third Series), 41
Arden Shakespeare Third Series (Craik, ed.), 122
Arias, Jennifer, 12, 29, 157
Artese, Charlotte, 17, 186
assessment
    literary analysis essay, 194–95
    paraphrasing, 192–93
    performing, 194
    producing, 193–94

assonance, 120–22
audiences, Elizabethan, 114

Balakir, Dziyana, 40, 84, 137
Banks, Fiona, 165, 172
Bantam Classic (series), 27
Barnet, Sylvan, 27
Barron's Shakespeare Made Easy (series), 29–30
Barton, John, 124, 191, 197, 217
Basil, John, 179
The Beard of Avon (Freed), 184
Beautiful Stories from Shakespeare (Nesbit), 153
bell ringer activities
    advanced, 56–63
    audience approval norms, 57
    goal of integrating, 63
    introducing, 45
    objectives, 57
    purpose of, 43–45
    time for, 45
bell ringer exercises
    Adverbly Done (improv), 58
    Diving into the Fishbowl of Life, 57
    introducing, 45
    Loosen Up Those Lips! 46–47
    Oh! Why? Sorry! (improv), 60–63
    Shakespeare's Charades (improv), 59–60
    Tackling Tougher Tongue Twisters, 47–48
    Warming Up the Voice, Warming Up for the Bard, 48–49, 50*f*
Berry, Cicely, 124
Bertacchi, Jennifer, 16, 18, 44, 60, 80, 85, 101, 131, 178
Bevington, David, 27
"big but" words, 16–18, 149*f*
Blackout Poetry from Blank Verse, 6, 8–9, 9*f*
Boal, Augusto, 63
Bodleian First Folio (website), 24
The Book of Will (Gunderson), 184
Boyce, Charles, 73, 80, 124
Branagh, Kenneth, 152, 191
breathing, 142, 143
Breathing Life into Ecphonesis O with an Added Oscar Moment, 85–87
Buckley, Kate, 197
Burrows, Cynthia, 3, 49, 63, 99, 118, 138

Caesar, Julius, 5
Cain, Bill, 184
Callow, Simon, 113
Caxton, Henry, 21
Césaire, Aimé, 184
characters
    cogitating, 113, 134
    normal heartbeat of, 102–6
    poetic humanness of, 113
Chicago Shakespeare Theater's teacher handbooks (seasons 2013–2019) (website), 166
Clark, Donté, 190
The Clash of the Film Clips: Is It Shakespeare?, 180–81
classical comics, 32–33
Classics Unfolded, 186
classroom drama, integrating informal, 43
classrooms, bringing the bard to elementary school, 15–17
clue cards, 89, 111–12, 149–50
Coleman, David, 198
collaborative activities
    text detectives, 13–15
    verse nurses, 13–14
colons, 137, 143–44, 150*f*
comic books, 5, 32–33
commas, 134–36, 142, 149–50*f*
Companion Documentaries: Performing Shakespeare in Schools, in Prison, in Nursing Homes, on the Stage, 189–90
companion novels and plays, pairing Shakespeare with
    Classics Unfolded, 186
    companion novels, 219–20
    contemporary plays, 183–85
    Deadpool Does Shakespeare, 185
    Hogarth Shakespeare Series, 182–83
    Kill Shakespeare (McCreery & Del Col), 185–86
    OMG Shakespeare (series), 186
    Shakespeare and the Folktale: An

Anthology of Stories, 186–87
To Be or Not to Be and *Romeo and/or Juliet* (North), 186
William Shakespeare's Much Ado about Mean Girls, William Shakespeare's Get Thee . . . Back to the Future, MacTrump (Doescher), 185
World's Elsewhere: Journeys around Shakespeare's Globe, 187
YA fiction, 182
Condell, Henry, 21
Connell Multiple Intelligence Questionnaire (website), 2
consonance, 120–22
contemporary plays, 183–86
Craik, T. W., 122
Creating a Play's Playlist, 12–13
Creative Shakespeare: The Globe Education Guide to Practical Shakespeare (Banks), 165, 172
Cry of Players (Gibson), 184
Crystal, Ben, 73
Crystal, David, 73
cue scripts, 65, 168–74
cue scripts activity, 172–74
Cullen, Jacquie, 38–39
"Cutting Antony's Speeches" lesson plan (Rodberg), 165

Deadpool Does Shakespeare, 185
Del Col, Anthony, 185–86
Dialogue: "Shakespeare's First Folio" (Idaho Public Television), 23
Dickson, Andrew, 186–87
diction, exercises to physicalize, 127–29
digital Shakespeare, full text
  Folger Luminary Shakespeare, 37
  Heuristic Shakespeare, 37
  OpenSource Shakespeare, 37
  PlayShakespeare.com, 37
  Shakespeare, ShakespearePro, 37
  Shakespeare in Bits, 38–41, 39f, 40f
Discovering Hamlet, 191
Diving into the Fishbowl of Life, 57
DIY First Folio (Folger Shakespeare Library), 23
documentaries, pairing Shakespeare with, 191

Doescher, Ian, 185
dramaturg, 4

Ecphonesis O, 75–76, 85–87, 89f
Edelstein, Barry, 72, 81, 116, 138
ELA curricula
  "Informal Classroom Drama" (NCTE), 3
  integration of creative drama, 3
ELLs, bringing the bard to, 15–17
end-of-verse lines, 138–40
engagement
  Diving into the Fishbowl of Life, 57
  learning about the First Folio, 22–24
  plays as anchor text supplement, 176
  using multiple intelligences theory, 2–3
enjambing, 138, 144–45, 150f
Equivocation (Cain), 184
exclamation point verse clue, 97–98
experiential knowing, 18

fairy tales, Shakespeare's stories as, 15–16, 17
The Fault in Our Stars (Green), 178
feminine line, 103
film clips to illustrate plays, 180–81
First Folio of 1623. *See also* digital Shakespeare, full text
  celebrating the, 20–21
  compositors, 21
  editing the, 23
  engaging students in learning about, 22–24
  facsimile versions online, 24
  graphic novels and texts compared, 30, 32, 34–36
  impact of textual variants in early modern print editions, 24–25
  importance of, 21–22
  language elasticity, 21–22
  online options, 24
  print editions compared, 37–41, 39f, 40f
  Text Detectives activity, 25, 25–26f
The Fishbowl of Life (activity), 57
Folger, Emily Jordan, 27

Folger, Henry Clay, 27
Folger Luminary Shakespeare (app), 37
Folger Shakespeare (series), 27
Folger Shakespeare Library (website), 24
Folger Shakespeare Library Education Department (website), 165
Folio language clues
    activating the text using, 80–88
    Ecphonesis O, 75–76, 89*f*
    internal capitalization, 76–77, 79, 87–88, 89*f*
    key words and meanings, 74–75, 89*f*
    prereading exercise, 77–80
    sentence structure, 79–80
    textual differences compared, 79–80, 79*f*
Folio language clues, exercises
    Breathing Life into Ecphonesis O with an Added Oscar Moment, 85–87
    Getting Comfortable with Weird Pronouns, 82–85
    Magic Index Card, 81–82
Folio technique
    background, 65, 197
    clue cards and scripts, 65, 89, 111–12, 149–50
    integrating into plays taught, 178–79
    language decoding strategies, 66
    magic Mamet moment, 139
    overview, 66
    prereading, using, 77–80, 88
    pronoun clues, 70–72
    pronunciation, 69–70
    speeches for further study, 199–201
    text clues, 65
    textual exploration through application, 214–17
    variant/phonetic spellings, 66–69, 78
    words, and definitions, 66, 72–74
folktales, Shakespeare's stories as, 17, 186–87
formative activities
    Creating a Play's Playlist, 12–13
    Getting Graphic, 5
    Picturing the Line, 13
    Sonnet Completion Challenge, 10–11, 10*f*, 11*f*
    Text Detective Teams, 14–15, 15*f*
    Tracking Language Motifs, 14
Frames of Mind (Gardner), 2
Freed, Amy, 184
full stop verse clues, 97–98, 111*f*
full thoughts, 97, 137

Gaines, Barbara, 158, 197
Games for Actors and Non-Actors (Boal), 63
Gardner, Howard, 1, 2–3, 5, 43, 176
Getting Comfortable with Weird Pronouns, 82–85
Getting Graphic website, 35–36
Getty Images, 4
Gibson, William, 184
Gilakjani, Abbas Pourhosein, 40, 166
Göndöcs, Rita, 69, 95, 181
Google Images, 4
"Graduates Celebrate at Harper College's 50th Commencement Ceremony" (Coleman), 198
Graphic Novel Reporter, 34
graphic novels
    Gareth Hinds's adaptations, 32
    No Fear Shakespeare (series), 31–32
    Shakespeare's plays, selecting and evaluating modern editions of, activities, 30–32
    the world of the play in images, 5
graphic texts, learning the conventions of, 35–36
Green, John, 1, 19, 178
Gunderson, Lauren, 184

Hamlet
    abridgements, 152
    antithesis, 124
    colons and semicolons, 143–44
    commas, 135–36
    end-of-verse lines, 139–40
    film clips, 218–19
    inversion, 126
    prose in, 146
    textual exploration using Folio technique, 213–14
Harbage, Alfred, 27
heartbeat, speech and, 102–6

Heckel-Oliver, Christine, 5
Heller, Stephen, 17
Heminges, John, 21
Henry V
    lists, 122–23
    transitions, 117
    variant/phonetic spellings, 66–67
The Herbal Bed (Whelan), 184
Heuristic Shakespeare (app), 37
Hinds, Gareth, 32
Hinman, Charlton, 24
Hogarth Shakespeare (series), 182–83
How Shakespeare Changed Everything (Marche), 187
How to Act Shakespeare in 21 Days (Basil), 179

iambic pentameter, 97, 101–8
iambic pentameter exercise, 107–9
Iambic Pentameter Step–Heel, 107–9
"I have a dream" speech (King), 118
images, 4–5
improv exercises
    Adverbly Done, 58
    Oh! Why? Sorry!, 60–63
    Shakespeare's Charades, 59–60
Improvisation for the Theater: A Handbook of Teaching and Directing Techniques (Spolin), 63
incomplete lines, 103–4
"Informal Classroom Drama" (NCTE), 3
intelligence spectrum, 2–3
Internet Shakespeare Editions (website), 24, 78, 158
interpersonal intelligence, 2
interpersonal intelligence activities, 13–15
InThinking subject (website), 35
intonation, 134
intrapersonal intelligence, 2
inversion, 149*f*
Isherwood, Charles, 110

Jacobi, Derek, 191
Johnston, Noel, 38–41
Jonson, Ben, 21

Keenan, Hailey, 44, 109, 171, 185
keeper of the book, 172
Kill Shakespeare (McCreery), 185–86
Kill Shakespeare (McCreery & Del Col), 185–86
kinesthetic intelligence, 2, 13–15
King, Martin Luther Jr., 118
King Lear
    quarto and folio version differences, 25, 25–26*f*
    shaping and revising the First Folio, 24–26, 25–26*f*
Kleon, Austin, 8
Knight, Edward, 21
knowing, four kinds of, 18
Kulick, Brian, 151–52

language decoding strategies, 66–88
Learning the Conventions of a Graphic Text, 35–36
lines, incomplete, 103–4
linguistic intelligence, 2, 5
lists, 122–23, 149*f*
list exercise, 127–28
literary analysis essay for assessment, 194–95
literary and popular culture companions, 187
logical intelligence, 2
Loosen Up Those Lips! 46–47
Luhrmann, Baz, 190
Lyons, Marti, 156

Macbeth
    abridgements, 166–68
    film clips, 219–20
    inversion, 125
    language and punctuation clues, 92, 93*f*
    repetition in, 119, 122, 128–29
    rhymes, 109
    speeches for further study, 200–201
    from verse to prose in, 146–47
Mad Libs, 10
Magic Index Card, 30, 81–82, 93
magic Mamet moment, 139
Making Machines, 55–56

The Making of Shakespeare's First Folio (Smith), 23
manga, 33
"manga Effects" on the TVTropes (website), 34
manga glossary of terms pertaining to manga (website), 34
manga iconography (online), 34
Manga Shakespeare, 33–34, 193
Manga Shakespeare Learning (website), 33
Marche, Stephen, 187
Marking Up the Body, 52–53
masculine line, 103
McCreery, Conor, 185–86
McDuffie, Kate, 132
McKnight, Katherine S., 45, 63
media texts, pairing Shakespeare with
    companion novels, 219–20
    contemporary plays, 183–85, 219–20
    documentaries, 189–91
    film clips, 218–20
    performing, 189–90
    plays, 179–81, 218–20
    poetry, 190
    Shakespeare and the Folktale: An Anthology of Stories, 17, 186
    video, online, 191–92
    YouTube, 191–92
media texts, pairing Shakespeare with specific
    Classics Unfolded, 186
    Companion Documentaries, 189–90
    Deadpool Does Shakespeare, 185
    Discovering Hamlet, 191
    Kill Shakespeare, 185–86
    Midsummer in Newtown, 190
    My Juliet: Romeo and Juliet *for a New Generation* (Luhrmann), 190
    OMG Shakespeare (series), 186
    Playing Shakespeare (Barton), 191
    Romeo Is Bleeding (Clark), 190
    Rwanda and Juliet, 190
    Shakespeare behind Bars (Rogerson), 190
    Shakespeare High, 191
    Shakespeare Retold (BBC series), 188–89
    Shakespeare's Globe Theatre on Screen, 189
    Shakespeare Uncovered (BBC series), 188
    Still Dreaming (Rogerson), 190
    To Be or Not to Be and *Romeo and/or Juliet* (North), 186
    William Shakespeare's Much Ado about Mean Girls, William Shakespeare's Get Thee . . . Back to the Future, MacTrump, 185
    World's Elsewhere, 186
Merchant of Venice, 91f
mid-stop verse clues, 98–99, 111f
Midsummer in Newtown, 190
A Midsummer Night's Dream
    cue scripts, 170–74, 170f, 202–12
    lists, 123
    repetition of words and phrases, 119–20
    Secrets of Acting Shakespeare: The Original Approach (Tucker), 169
    transitions, 116–17
Mirror Me, 52
Modern Library (series), 27
monosyllabic words, 115–16, 149f
Moston, Doug, 114
movement exercises
    Making Machines, 55–56
    Marking Up the Body, 52–53
    Mirror Me, 52
    My Name, My Action, 53–54
    Shake Out by Eight, 50–51
    Wait for the "Yes," 54
    Walk the Space, 54–55
Mowat, Barbara A., 27
"Multiple Intelligences Survey" (McKenzie), 3
multiple intelligences theory, 1–3, 5, 43, 176
musical intelligence, 2, 11
My Juliet: Romeo and Juliet *for a New Generation* (Luhrmann), 190
"My Love Is Like to Ice" (Sonnet 30) (Spenser), 8
My Name, My Action, 53–54

Nesbit, Edith, 153

Newlin, Nick, 155
No Fear Shakespeare (series), 16, 29, 31–32
Norman, Marc, 184
North, Ryan, 186
Noskin, David, 192–93

Oh! Why? Sorry! (improv), 59–63
O'Hara, K. J., 155
OMG Shakespeare (series), 186
Onuscheck, Mark, 29, 152, 156, 176, 183
OpenSource Shakespeare, 37

parallel text, 16
paraphrasing for assessment, 192
Partridge, Eric, 73, 105
Pelican Shakespeare (series), 27
performance, exploring key scenes through, 168–74
performing
    for assessment, 194
      plays, 189–91
      soliloquies, 213–17
periods verse clue, 97–98
phrases, 149f
picture walks, 35–36, 35f
Picturing the Line, 13
platt, 171
players, students as, 43
playfulness, purposeful, 1
Playing Shakespeare (Barton), 124, 191, 197, 217
plays
    additional resources, 179
    anchor vs. supplement, 176, 177–78
    companion novels, 219–20
    companion plays, 182–85
    contemporary plays, 219–20
    essentials, previewing the, 179–81
    Folio technique, integrating the, 178–79
    media texts, pairing Shakespeare with, 179–87, 218–20
    performing, 189–91
    persuasion techniques in, 177–78
plays, selecting and evaluating modern editions of

    classical comics, 32–33
    digital option, full text, 36–37
    ebook option, 40–41
    going beyond the mass-market paperback edition, 41–42
    graphic novels, 31–32
    graphic texts in print, 30–31
    individual play apps, 37–41
    Magic Index Card activity, 30
    manga, 33–34
    parallel text, 30
    parallel texts in print, 29–30
    print options, 26–30
    side-by-side texts in print, 29–30
PlayShakespeare.com, 37
podcasts, 22–23
poetry, pairing Shakespeare with, 190
Powell, Mark, 175
practical knowing, 18
presentational knowing, 18
producing for assessment, 193–94
prompters, 172
pronouns in Folio technique
    strategic use of, 72
    thee/thou vs. *you/your*, 70–71
propositional knowing, 18
prose as rhetorical strategy, 145–48
Prose Example to Analyze, 146–48
prose exercises, 146–48
punctuation
    at end of verse lines, 150f
    indicating breathing, 92
    messy vs. clean, 91–92
punctuation verse clues, 90–92

question mark verse clue, 97–98
Quince, Peter, 168–74
quizlet (website), 35

rehearsals
    cue scripts, 65, 168–74
    limited, 168–72
repetition
    of individual sounds, 120–22, 128–29
    of words and phrases, 118–20
rhetoric, exercises to physicalize

Stepping It Up with Shakespeare's Lists and Repetition, 127–29
Tossing Pizzas Topped with Antithesis, 129–32
Working Inverted Syntax with Master Yoda and Bill the Bard, 132–33
rhetorical analysis, diction and syntax in, 114
rhetorical clues, Folio
    antithesis, 123–24, 149*f*
    "big but" words, 116–18, 149*f*
    colons, 137, 150*f*
    commas, 134–36, 149–50*f*
    end-of-verse lines, 138–40, 150*f*
    inversion, 124–27, 149*f*
    lists, 122–23, 149*f*
    monosyllabic words, 115–16
    repetition, 118–22, 150*f*
    semicolons, 137, 150*f*
    transitional words, 116–18, 149*f*
rhetorical devices, purpose of, 148
rhetorical strategies
    actor-ly, 113–14
    clue card, 149–50
    prose, 145–48
rhyming verse clues, 109–10, 112*f*
rhythm and rhythm changes, 92, 103*f*, 104
Richard II, 67–68
Richard III, 126
Rodberg, Simon, 165
Rogerson, Hank, 190
Rollins, Cindy, 152–53
Romeo and Juliet
    antithesis, 130
    Blackout Poetry from Blank Verse, 8–9, 9*f*
    comic books, 5
    commas, 135
    complementary titles, 177–78
    film adaptations, 180–81
    graphic novels, 5
    images, websites for sample, 4
    inversion, 125
    misspellings, 68–69
    playlist, 12
    prereading exercise, 77–79
    repetition of individual sounds, 121
    rhyming in, 110
    Snapping exercise, 140–43
    speeches for further study, 200
    Text Detective Teams, 14–15, 15*f*
    textual differences compared, 79*f*
Romeo Is Bleeding (Clark), 190
Royal Shakespeare Company (RSC) series), 27
Russo, Robin, 87
Rwanda and Juliet, 190

scansion, 102
Schmidt, Alexander, 73, 116
Scruggs, Mary, 63
The Second City Guide to Improv in the Classroom: Using Improvisation to Teach Skills and Improve Learning in Content Areas (McKnight & Scruggs), 63
The Secret Life of Books: "Shakespeare's First Folio" (BBC Scotland), 23
Secrets of Acting Shakespeare: The Original Approach (Tucker), 169
semicolons, 137, 143–44, 150*f*
Shake Out by Eight, 50–51
Shakespeare (app), 37
Shakespeare, reasons for reading, 1
Shakespeare, William
    additional resources, 221
    education, 113–14
    importance, 21
    legacy, 23
    reputation, 23
    teaching, xi–xv
    a teller of tales, 17
    unlocking, 18, 197
Shakespeare: The Animated Tales (HBO), 153, 188
Shakespeare and the Folktale: An Anthology of Stories (Artese), 17, 186
Shakespeare A to Z (Boyce), 73, 80, 124
Shakespeare behind Bars (Rogerson), 190
Shakespeare High, 191
Shakespeare in Bits, 38–41, 39*f*, 40*f*
Shakespeare in Love (film), 184
Shakespeare Lexicon: A Complete Dictionary of All the English Words, Phrases and Constructions in the Works of the Poet (Schmidt), 73, 116

Shakespeare Pro (app), 37, 73
The Shakespeare Quartos Archive (website), 24
Shakespeare Retold (BBC *School Radio* series), 17, 152, 188–89
Shakespeare's Authentic Performance Texts: The Case for Staging from the First Folio (Watts), 23
Shakespeare's Bawdy: A Literary and Psychological Essay and a Comprehensive Glossary (Partridge), 73, 105
Shakespeare's Charades (improv), 59–60
"Shakespeare's Childhood and Education" (Callow), 113
Shakespeare Set Free (series) (Folger), 45, 56
Shakespeare's First Folio: Four Centuries of an Iconic Book (Smith), 23
Shakespeare's Globe Theatre on Screen, 189
Shakespeare Shorts for Schools and Performance (O'Hara, ed.), 152
Shakespeare's Sonnet Scrambled, 6, 7*f*
Shakespeare's Words (website) "Glossary" (Crystal & Crystal), 73, 93, 214
Shakespeare Uncovered (BBC series), 188
Shakespeare Unlimited (podcast) (Folger Library), 22–23
shared line verse clue, 99–101, 111*f*
Sharing the Text/Dishtowel, 94–96
Shorter Shakespeare: Globe Education, 155
sides, 171
Signet Classic (series), 27
Smith, Emma, 23
Sokol, Abby, 54, 105, 165, 193
soliloquies
  analyzing, 213–17
  for further study, 199–201
  performing, 216–17
Sonnet Completion Challenge, 10–11, 10*f*, 11*f*
sounds, 149*f*
Spangler, Susan, 176
speech. *See also* rhetorical entries
  alexandrine, 103
  breathing, punctuation indicating, 92
  diction, exercises to physicalize, 127–29

  emotion correct for, 99
  ending syllables, 69, 89*f*
  exercises to physicalize, 127–29
  feminine lines, 103
  full stops, 97–98
  heartbeat and, 102–6
  iambic pentameter, 101–8
  iambic pentameter guidelines, 101–8, 111*f*
  incomplete lines, 103–4
  intonation, 134
  masculine lines, 103
  mid-stops, 98–99
  present tense, 134–35
  rhetorical analysis, diction and syntax in, 114
  rhythm and rhythm changes, 92, 103*f*, 104
spelling in Folio technique
  ending syllables, 69–70
  misspellings, 68–69
  spelling for emphasis, 67
  variant/phonetic, 66–70, 78
Spenser, Edmund, 8
Spolin, Viola, 63
Steal Like an Artist (Kleon), 8
Stepping It Up with Shakespeare's Lists and Repetition, 127–29
Still Dreaming (Rogerson), 190
Stoppard, Tom, 183, 184
storytelling, 17
"Student Multiple Intelligence Survey" (Word doc) (EdPro Development), 3
students
  transforming from passive to active, 43
  unlocking Shakespeare for, 18, 197
summative activity
  Text Detective Teams, 14–15, 15*f*
  Tracking Language Motifs, 14
  Words of the Play and Pictures, 5
Sweets, Sparky, 180
syllables, ending, 69, 89*f*
syntax, physicalizing, 127–29, 132–33

Tackling Tougher Tongue Twisters, 47–48
Tales from Shakespeare (Lamb), 153

Teaching Shakespeare with Purpose: A Student-Centered Approach (Thompson & Turchi), 28
TED-Ed Shakespeare Videos and Lesson Ideas, 180
The Tempest, repetition in, 121
textbooks, traditional, 175
text clues, 65
Text Detective activity, 25–26, 25–26*f*
text detectives, 13–14, 66
Text Detective Teams, 15*f*
thee/thou vs. *you/your*, 70–71
thinking in the moment, physicalizing
    Snapping (the Commas) with Shakespeare, 140–43
    To Enjamb or Not to Enjamb, That Is the Question, 144–45
    Walking with Shakespeare's Colons and Semicolons, 143–44
Thinking Shakespeare (Edelstein), 72, 81, 116, 138
30-Minute Shakespeare (Newlin), 152
Thompson, Ayanna, 28
Thornburg, Laura, 74, 82, 96
Thug Notes, 179–80
To Be or Not to Be and *Romeo and/or Juliet* (North), 186
To Enjamb or Not to Enjamb, That Is the Question, 144–45
Tofteland, Curt L., 190
Tossing Pizzas Topped with Antithesis, 129–32
Tovani, xii
Tracking Language Motifs, 14
transitional words, 149*f*
Trees, Andrew, 177
Tucker, Patrick, 101, 169
Turchi, Laura, 28
Twelfth Night
  antithesis, 124
  exercises to physicalize, 128
  inversion, 126–27
  speech analysis, 103*f*, 104

Une Tempête (*A Tempest*), 184

variation as anticipatory strategy, 5
verse clue exercises
  Applying Language Clues First, 92–94
  Full Thought, 97
  Iambic Pentameter Step–Heel, 107–9
  Magic Index Card, 93
  Sharing the Text/Dishtowel, 94–96
verse clues, controlling rhythm, 90
verse clues, Folio techniques for understanding
  breathing, punctuation indicating, 92
  characters, complex with complicated emotions, 90–92
  emotion, 92, 110
  exclamation points, 97–98
  full stops, 97–98, 111*f*
  full thoughts, 96, 111*f*
  iambic pentameter, 101–9, 111*f*
  meaning, 92
  mid-stops, 98–99, 111*f*
  periods, 97–98
  punctuation, 90–92
  question marks, 97–98
  rhyming, 109–10, 112*f*
  shared lines, 99–101, 111*f*
verse nurses, 13–14, 101
versification, 102, 113
video, online, 180, 191–92
visual intelligence, 2, 4–5
visual references (website), 34
vocabulary, 34
vocal exercises
  Loosen Up Those Lips!, 46–47
  Tackling Tougher Tongue Twisters, 47–48
  Warming Up the Voice, 48–50

Wait for the "Yes," 54
Walking with Shakespeare's Colons and Semicolons, 143–44
Walk the Space, 54–55
Walter, Claire, 29, 31, 34, 41, 42
Warming Up the Voice, Warming Up for the Bard, 48–49
Watts, Graham, 23, 113
Wells, Orson, 158
Werstine, Paul, 27
"What Makes a Great Shakespearean?" (Isherwood), 110

Whelan, Peter, 184
Whiteford, Caleb, 8
Wikimedia Commons, 4
William Shakespeare's Much Ado about Mean Girls, William Shakespeare's Get Thee . . . Back to the Future, MacTrump (Doescher), 185
Wing-bo Tso, Anna, 18
words, repeated, 149*f*
words and definitions in Folio technique
    Ecphonesis O, 75–76, 89*f*
    importance of, 72–73
    internal capitalization, 76–77, 79, 87–88, 89*f*
    key words and meanings, 74–75, 89*f*
Working Inverted Syntax with Master Yoda and Bill the Bard, 132–33
World's Elsewhere: Journeys around Shakespeare's Globe (Dickson), 186–87

YA fiction, 182
YouTube, 152

Zeffirelli, Franco, 155, 166

Authors

Kevin Long is an associate professor of theatre at Harper College. He was nominated for the 2015 Tony Award for Excellence in Theatre Education, received the 2018 Motorola Solutions Foundation Endowed Award for Teaching Excellence as well as the 2012 Illinois Theatre Association Award for Excellence in College Theatre Teaching, and is an associate member of the Stage Directors and Choreographers Society, a past president of the Illinois Communication and Theatre Association, and the current president of the  Illinois Theatre Association. Long has been directing and teaching acting and theater classes for more than twenty-five years. Additionally, he is a recognized expert in teaching the Folio technique and frequently presents his workshop "Shakespeare Whispers into Your Ear," which explores the language and theater of Shakespeare through the use of the First Folio. Most notably, he has taught the Folio technique for Ten Chimneys; Chicago Shakespeare Theater for many of their show-specific teacher workshops, the Bard Core teacher professional development program, and the theater's Shakespeare Slam; the Actors Training Center; the National Council of Teachers of English; and at various institutions and theaters in the tristate region. See also www.kevinlongdirector.com.

Mary T. Christel taught world literature, media and film studies, and theater at Adlai E. Stevenson High School in Lincolnshire, Illinois, from 1979 to 2012. She taught Shakespeare at the Center for Talent Development, Northwestern University, from 1998 to 2001. Drawing on her undergraduate theater training at Northwestern University, Christel has contributed chapters to *Teaching Shakespeare Today: Practical Approaches and Productive Strategies* (1993), *Teaching Shakespeare into the Twenty-First Century* (1997), and *For All Time? Critical Issues in*

Teaching Shakespeare (2002). She also coauthored *Acting It Out: Using Drama in the Classroom to Improve Student Engagement, Reading, and Critical Thinking* (2017). From 2002 to 2012, she provided teaching materials related to the Chicago Humanities Festival and, from 2004 to 2005, participated in developing lesson plans for the Theater History Initiative with the Shakespeare Theater Company in Washington, DC. Currently she is a regular contributor to online teacher resource handbooks for Chicago Shakespeare Theater  and teaching activities for TimeLine Theatre's Living History program, as well as a reviewer of prospective lesson plans for the ReadWriteThink website. When Christel is not writing about Shakespeare or theater arts, she is writing about teaching superhero narratives to complement existing ELA curricula for the Comic Connections series.

This book was typeset in TheMix and Palatino by Barbara Frazier.

Typefaces used on the cover include Chronicle Text and Galaxie Polaris.

The book was printed on 50-lb. White Offset paper by Seaway Printing.

www.ingramcontent.com/pod-product-compliance
Lightning Source LLC
Chambersburg PA
CBHW060312240426
43661CB00059B/2733